LIBRARY OF NEW TESTAMENT STUDIES

693

formerly the Journal for the Study of the New Testament Supplement series

Editor
Chris Keith

Editorial Board
Dale C. Allison, Lynn H. Cohick, Kylie Crabbe, R. Alan Culpepper,
Craig A. Evans, Jennifer Eyl, Robert Fowler, Juan Hernández Jr.,
John S. Kloppenborg, Michael Labahn, Matthew V. Novenson,
Love L. Sechrest, Robert Wall, Catrin H. Williams, Brittany E. Wilson

The Importance of Outsiders to Pauline Communities

Opinion, Reputation and Mission

Emma Louise Parker

LONDON • NEW YORK • OXFORD • NEW DELHI • SYDNEY

T&T CLARK

Bloomsbury Publishing Plc, 50 Bedford Square, London, WC1B 3DP, UK
Bloomsbury Publishing Inc, 1359 Broadway, New York, NY 10018, USA
Bloomsbury Publishing Ireland, 29 Earlsfort Terrace, Dublin 2, D02 AY28, Ireland

BLOOMSBURY, T&T CLARK and the T&T Clark logo are trademarks
of Bloomsbury Publishing Plc

First published in Great Britain 2024
Paperback edition published 2026

Copyright © Emma Louise Parker, 2024

Emma Louise Parker has asserted her right under the Copyright,
Designs and Patents Act, 1988, to be identified as Author of this work.

For legal purposes the Acknowledgements on p. xi constitute
an extension of this copyright page.

All rights reserved. No part of this publication may be: i) reproduced or transmitted in any form, electronic or mechanical, including photocopying, recording or by means of any information storage or retrieval system without prior permission in writing from the publishers; or ii) used or reproduced in any way for the training, development or operation of artificial intelligence (AI) technologies, including generative AI technologies. The rights holders expressly reserve this publication from the text and data mining exception as per Article 4(3) of the Digital Single Market Directive (EU) 2019/790.

Bloomsbury Publishing Plc does not have any control over, or responsibility for, any third-party websites referred to or in this book. All internet addresses given in this book were correct at the time of going to press. The author and publisher regret any inconvenience caused if addresses have changed or sites have ceased to exist, but can accept no responsibility for any such changes.

A catalogue record for this book is available from the Library of Congress.

ISBN: HB: 978-0-5677-1380-3
PB: 978-0-5677-1384-1
ePDF: 978-0-5677-1381-0
eBook: 978-0-5677-1383-4

Series: Library of New Testament Studies, 2513-8790, volume 693

Typeset by Integra Software Services Pvt. Ltd.

For product safety related questions contact productsafety@bloomsbury.com.

To find out more about our authors and books visit www.bloomsbury.com
and sign up for our newsletters.

I dedicate this book to my loving parents, David and Sheila Johnson.
1 Corinthians 13.7

Contents

Acknowledgements		xi
1	Introduction: Paul and the Outsiders	1
	1.1. Two Distinct Groups: Believers and Unbelievers	1
	1.2. The Concern for the Outsider	3
	1.3. The Juxtaposition	5
	1.4. Social Identity Theory	7
	1.5. SIT and New Testament Scholarship	11
	1.5.1. Wayne Meeks	11
	1.5.2. Philip Esler	12
	1.5.3. Alistair May	14
	1.5.4. David Horrell	16
	1.5.5. Summary	19
	1.6. Conclusion	21
2	The Dimension of 'All' and the Influence of 'With': 1 Thessalonians	27
	2.1. Introduction	27
	2.2. The Dimension of 'All' (3.12; 5.15)	31
	2.2.1. Love one another and all (3.12)	31
	2.2.2. Pursue the good for one another and for all (5.15)	33
	2.2.3. Work the good towards all (Galatians 6.10)	35
	2.2.4. Summary	36
	2.3. The Influence of 'With' (4.11-12)	37
	2.3.1. Walking honourably (4.12a)	38
	2.3.1a. Περιπατέω	39
	2.3.1b. Εὐσχημόνως	40
	2.3.1c. Summary of 4.12a	41
	2.3.2. The way to walk honourably	42
	2.3.2a. Living quietly and minding your own affairs	43
	2.3.2b. Work with your own hands	44
	2.3.3. Connecting verses 11 and 12	45
	2.3.3a. Reputation: drawing positive attention	45
	2.3.3b. Reputation: taking charge of visibility and interaction	47
	2.3.4. Summary	50
	2.4. Conclusion	51

3	In Pursuit of Peace and Praise: Re-Creating the Public Image in Romans 12–13	57
	3.1. Introduction	57
	3.2. Romans 12	61
	3.2.1. Introduction: inward and outward orientation	61
	3.2.2. Givers of blessing (12.14)	63
	3.2.3. Givers of good and pursuers of peace (12.17-18)	66
	3.2.4. Providing for your enemy and changing the narrative (12.20)	69
	3.2.5. Summary	72
	3.3. Romans 13	73
	3.3.1. Introduction	73
	3.3.2. Defining the outside authorities	74
	3.3.3. What the insiders think of the outsiders	76
	3.3.4. What the outsiders think of the insiders	77
	3.3.5. Summary	83
	3.4. Conclusion	84
4	That They Might Be Saved: 1 Corinthians	93
	4.1. Introduction	93
	4.2. 1 Corinthians 7.12-16	98
	4.2.1. Introduction: the marital overlap between insider and outsider	98
	4.2.2. The unbelieving spouse: the importance of their approval	99
	4.2.3. The unbelieving spouse: their sanctification and salvation	101
	4.2.4. Summary	104
	4.3. 1 Corinthians 10.23–11.1	104
	4.3.1. Introduction: the decision over food	104
	4.3.2. The importance of conscience	106
	4.3.2a. Paul's understanding of conscience	108
	4.3.2b. The meaning of conscience in 1 Corinthians 10	109
	4.3.3. The motivation: 'that they might be saved'	111
	4.3.4. Summary	115
	4.4. 1 Corinthians 14.13-25	115
	4.4.1. Introduction: worship and edification	115
	4.4.2. The unlearned and the unbeliever	116
	4.4.3. The importance of what unbelievers think	118
	4.4.4. Deepening unbelief or building up belief	119
	4.4.5. Summary	121
	4.5. Conclusion	122

5	Reputation and Relationship: 1 Timothy and Titus	131
	5.1. Introduction	131
	5.2. The Pastoral Epistles: Insiders and Outsiders	132
	5.3. The Importance of Reputation	135
	5.3.1. Overseers, slaves and women	135
	5.3.2. The underlying concern	138
	5.4. Building on Reputation: The Importance of Relationship	140
	5.4.1. Introduction: 1 Timothy 2.1-7	140
	5.4.1a. Praying for all (1 Timothy 2.1-2a)	140
	5.4.1b. In all piety and respectability	143
	5.4.1c. The Saviour God of all	146
	5.4.1d. Summary: relationships linking prayers and salvation	148
	5.4.2. Introduction: Titus 3.1-8	149
	5.4.2a. Foundations for relating to rulers and authorities	151
	5.4.2b. Foundations for relating to every outsider: a commitment to good works	152
	5.4.2c. Foundations for relating to every outsider: speech flowing from character	154
	5.4.2d. Underlying motivation	156
	5.4.2e. Summary	158
	5.5. Conclusion: Reputation and Relationship	158
6	Conclusion	165
	6.1. Introduction	165
	6.2. Overview	165
	6.3. Social Identity Theory in Dialogue with the Pauline Corpus	171
	6.4. Conclusion and Implications for the Church	172
References		175
Index of Biblical References		186

Acknowledgements

I would like to thank my PhD supervisor, Professor John Barclay, for his time kindly given and for his wisdom generously shared. He has been a constant source of encouragement. My colleagues at Cranmer Hall have also supported me in so many ways and I am grateful for their wisdom and kindness. I would also like to thank my parents for always believing in me, my husband James who has constantly encouraged me in my different vocations, and for my daughter Sophie, my hope and joy.

1

Introduction: Paul and the Outsiders

1.1 Two Distinct Groups: Believers and Unbelievers

During a heated conference discussion regarding the role of women in the church, one person audibly lamented, 'I dread to think what the rest of the world thinks about us when they see us like this.' Immediately, another voice responded with, 'It shouldn't matter what the rest of the world thinks: we should be able to make decisions about how we live our lives regardless of those outside the church. Outsiders should not influence our decision-making.' This latter response was echoed in various forms throughout the rest of the day, and seemed to reflect three assumptions: firstly, that the church does not need to heed the opinions that those outside the church have regarding the church; secondly, that those who do not belong to a particular group have no right to influence or inform the decision-making process of the other group; and thirdly, that the lives of Christians, shaped by their particular theology, are distinct from and even morally superior to those who are not Christians.

These assumptions may have understandably arisen from what Horrell describes as the 'rhetoric of distinction' (2016: 147) or what Meeks calls the 'language of separation' (1983: 94). Throughout the New Testament, detailed and polarized descriptions are used to build an understanding of the existence of two different groups in the world, which, crudely put, are those who believe in Jesus Christ as the Son of God, and those who do not.[1] This is most notably seen in the Pauline corpus, where this 'rhetoric of distinction' creates a majestic picture of the believers as those who are God's beloved (Rom. 1.7), who are saints (1 Cor. 1.2; 2 Cor. 1.1; Phil. 1.1), who are on the one hand citizens of heaven (Phil. 3.20; see also 2 Cor. 5.1) but who are also the dwelling places of God on earth (1 Cor. 3.16).[2] They are part of a new family, and as such are called 'brothers' (e.g. 1 Cor. 1.10, 26; 2.1; 2 Cor. 1.8; Gal. 1.2; 3.15; Phil. 1.12, 14; 3.1; 1 Thess. 1.4; 2.1) as children of God the Father (Gal. 1.3; Phil. 2.15), and metaphorically also children of Paul (Gal. 4.19; 1 Cor. 4.15; 1 Thess. 2.7, 11). In distinction, those who are not part of this family are usually painted in a negative and disparaging way. They are the 'unbelievers' (1 Cor. 6.6; 7.12-15; 10.27; 14.22-24; 2 Cor. 4.4; 6.14-15) who do not even know God (1 Thess. 4.5; Gal. 4.8) and as such they are not just geographically but also spiritually 'the outsiders' (οἱ ἔξω, 1 Cor. 5.12-13; 1 Thess. 4.12; also Col. 4.5).[3] They are the 'unrighteous ones' (1 Cor. 6.1, 9; see also Gal. 2.15) who share no part in God's kingdom now or in the future (1 Cor. 6.9-10).

This contrast is sharpened all the more in passages which explicitly compare and contrast the two groups of believers and unbelievers. For example, the believers in Thessalonica are described as 'sons of light and sons of the day' (υἱοὶ φωτός ἐστε καὶ υἱοὶ ἡμέρας) for they are not 'of night or of darkness' (νυκτὸς οὐδὲ σκότους), the implication being that this latter description belongs to unbelievers (1 Thess. 5.5). As such, they should act accordingly, being 'awake' and 'sober' (v. 6) unlike those of the darkness who are sleeping and drunk (v. 7). The consequence is carried through into eschatological terms, whereby believers are appointed to salvation rather than to wrath (v. 9). The point is clear: a subjective description of their contrasting identities (children of light/dark; day/night) leads to an objective description of their behaviour (awake/asleep; sober/drunk) which in turn raises an eschatological description of their status as destined for salvation or wrath.[4] In another passage where the contrast between believers and unbelievers is unflinchingly described, the contrast again begins with describing believers as children, this time using τέκνα and identifying them as children of God (Phil. 2.15). Their nature is 'without blemish', and this stands so starkly against the backdrop of those who are 'crooked' and 'perverted' that Paul describes them as shining ὡς φωστῆρες ἐν κόσμῳ ('like stars in the world', Phil. 2.15).

This rhetoric of distinction could naturally give rise to the assumption that the lives of believers are entirely unique and distinct from unbelievers. Indeed, evidence of this line of thought is found in the Pauline corpus, particularly in texts where the believers are reminded of the lives they used to have, the corollary being that unbelievers still lead these immoral lives. For example, in 1 Thess. 1.9, Paul uses the verb ἐπιστρέφω ('to turn') to describe the conversion of the believers in Thessalonica: they 'turned' from worshipping idols to the 'living and true' God (also 1 Cor. 12.2).[5] The verb ἐπιστρέφω conveys a strong image of these Thessalonians deciding to change their mind on this matter, and so Lieu describes this as 'a clear instance of crossing a boundary' (2004: 127).[6] Similarly, in reminding the believers in 1 Corinthians that the ἄδικοι are not heirs of the kingdom of God, Paul also reminds them that they too used to be as these people are now (1 Cor. 6.9-11). The turning point for these believers was that they were washed, sanctified and justified 'in the name of the Lord Jesus Christ and in the Spirit of our God' (v. 11).[7] Interestingly, whereas the use of ἐπιστρέφω conveys a sense of agency in the believers themselves crossing over the boundary, in 1 Corinthians 6 the emphasis appears to be more on God's activity in enabling the believers to transfer identity from outsider to insider, although clearly it does not negate the need for the person's own will in this process.

It becomes clear that this transferring of identities, or crossing of boundaries, needs both the will of the person making the transfer, and the power of God. For, the transfer is based not just on a decision but also on death and new life (Rom. 6.3-11; Col. 1.21-23). Paul describes baptism as an act of sharing in the death of Jesus, in order to share in his resurrection, which then allows believers to 'walk in newness of life' (Rom. 6.4). Thus, the transfer from being an outsider to an insider is no little act; it is so significant that the only way to cross the boundary is metaphorically to die and be re-born.[8] Furthermore, this description of the process of crossing the boundary between outsider and believer starts to expose the resulting qualitative and ethical transformation. The baptism candidate is now clothed in Christ (Gal. 3.27) whereby the particulars of one's prior identity regarding gender, ethnicity and social status appear to be no longer the defining elements of identity (Gal. 3.28). Rather, one's identity is now primarily defined by being in Christ.[9] Henceforth, believers are no longer 'slaves to sin' (Rom. 6.17-22; 7.5-6), disobedient to God (Rom. 11.30), or conducting their body with 'lustful passion' (1 Thess. 4.5).[10] The crossing of the boundary requires the person involved to desire to worship Jesus Christ as Lord, but it also needs the power of God to enable the transformation necessary in crossing over the boundary and in changing identities. Lieu also perceptively observes that Paul has thus constructed a boundary not only between believers and unbelievers but also between the past (pre-converted life) and the present, and that this boundary is not constructed 'by any other more specific social or cultural practices but by catalogues of vices' (2004: 130).[11]

Given that it takes a metaphorical death and re-birth to join the believing community, it would be understandable for believers to conceive that they now have no similarity with unbelievers, that there is no sharing of ideas, behaviours or values between the two groups. A short and complex passage in 2 Cor. 6.14-18 appears to reflect this view since it asks, in a series of five rhetorical questions, why a believer would have a relationship with an unbeliever when it is clear that their identities are the foil of the other.[12] As such, this passage appears to instruct believers not to have any relationship or partnership with unbelievers, although the type of relationship being referred to here is debated amongst scholars (v. 14).[13] Hence, if all of the above texts are read together in isolation from the rest of the Pauline corpus, one could justifiably come to the conclusion that there would be no need to be attentive to the presence of unbelievers nor be concerned about their opinions when making internal decisions and clarifying the shape of one's life and worship.

1.2 The Concern for the Outsider

However, upon reading the whole of the Pauline corpus it is noticeable that there is, quite surprisingly given all of the above, a significant sensitivity to the presence of outsiders and a concern for how they will experience and perceive the believers. This seems to drive some of the instructions given to the believers, which, as we will see, range from simple cautions to take thought for how outsiders might react to them, to exhortations for believers to seek a positive response from outsiders. As such, in Thessalonica although believers are encouraged to live quiet, independent lives (1 Thess. 4.11), they are to do this 'in order to walk honourably among outsiders' (ἵνα περιπατῆτε εὐσχημόνως πρὸς τοὺς ἔξω, 4.12). Moreover, rather than repaying evil for evil they should 'always seek to do good to one another and to all' (πάντοτε τὸ ἀγαθὸν διώκετε [καὶ] εἰς ἀλλήλους καὶ εἰς πάντας, 5.11).[14] Thus, as much as the Thessalonians should seek to keep themselves to themselves, an overriding exception is that they are to be intentional in doing good to outsiders, which clearly involves discerning what would be perceived and received as 'good' by outsiders.

This is also made explicit in Gal. 6.10 when Paul declares that at any opportunity 'we should work the good towards all' (ἐργαζώμεθα τὸ ἀγαθὸν πρὸς πάντας). Since he clarifies that the recipients of this work of goodness must also include the 'household of faith' (τοὺς οἰκείους τῆς πίστεως), the implication is that the command to do good 'to all' is inclusive of outsiders. Similarly, the Roman believers are urged to take thought for what is good before all people (προνοούμενοι καλὰ ἐνώπιον πάντων ἀνθρώπων), the implication being that they should also *do* that which they determine to be good (12.17). There is an expectation that the believers should be proactive in 'doing good' which should not be restricted to acts within the faith community alone. That they should be a visible, positive presence among all is further evidenced in Phil. 4.5, where the believers are urged to let their 'gentleness be known to all' (τὸ ἐπιεικὲς ὑμῶν γνωσθήτω πᾶσιν ἀνθρώποις).

Furthermore, the believers in some situations should seek to accommodate the desire of the outsider. Paul makes it clear that the decision on whether or not a marriage between a believer and an unbeliever should continue is entirely dependent upon what the unbeliever thinks (1 Cor. 7.12-16). Believers should also be aware of how an unbeliever might misinterpret their practices and so they are to make the necessary changes to guard against this, seeking rather to cause no offence (1 Cor. 10.23-33). Paul reveals how important he himself considers to be the practice of seeing life from the perspective of the other person, when he describes how he has 'become all things to all people' to 'save some' (1 Cor. 9.19-23). Clearly, these passages reveal that the believers will not be isolating themselves from the rest of society. There is a presumption that they will be seen by outsiders, and, conversely, an expectation that the believers in turn should also be aware of and show consideration towards the outsiders. They are to take thought for how outsiders might react to them, and should seek to act in ways that would be regarded as 'good' in the eyes of the outsider.

However, there are also passages in the Pauline corpus which seem to expect more of the believer, in the sense that the believer should be more proactive in proving and convincing outsiders that they are a positive, and indeed, a praiseworthy presence in wider society. The Roman believers for example are exhorted to behave in a way that would attract the attention of outsiders and win the commendation of the outgroup for their exemplary behaviour (Rom. 13.3). Achieving a positive reputation among outsiders is a thread that runs persistently throughout these letters, and this even appears to drive the instructions given to the Corinthians regarding worship (1 Cor. 14.20-25). Here, the concern is how an outsider might experience and react to finding believers using tongues in worship, and the fear is that they might conclude that the believers are 'out of their minds' (v. 23). As a result, Paul urges the believers to change their act of worship so that, instead of the unbelievers responding with shock or derision, they are rather drawn to 'bow down and worship God' (v. 25). These two passages specifically show both a concern for how outsiders view believers, and a resulting change in behaviour (or encouragement of a particular behaviour) that would generate a positive response (or at least avoid criticism) from outsiders not just to the believing community but also to God.

Two other letters within the Pauline corpus contain a plethora of verses which illustrate a significant concern for the presence and opinion of the outsider: 1 Timothy and Titus.[15] Although it is apparent that there are critical internal situations to deal with, not least with the apparently divisive work of the false teachers and the need to pay attention to the structures of the faith community, there are nevertheless many indications that a pressing concern motivating some of the parenesis is the reputation of the faith community in the eyes of the outsiders (e.g. 1 Tim. 3.7; 6.1; Tit. 2.5). All members of the faith community are urged to behave in ways that would be seen as acceptable and honourable in the eyes of the outsider, with the hope that this will in turn impact positively on how the outsider views and responds to the gospel. Furthermore, the letters suggest that beyond striving for a good reputation, the believers should also strive for good relationships with outsiders, and are therefore to pray in different ways for all people (1 Tim. 2.1-2), revealing and demonstrating that believers are a positive presence in wider society through leading lives of devotion and respectability (1 Tim. 2.3). Believers are to be obedient to the authorities, showing care and tolerance in all their conversations with everyone, and the Author twice comments on how they are not only to be ready for every good work but also to understand that the life of a believer is one that is constantly engaged in doing good works (Tit. 3.1-2, 8).

Clearly, all of these passages are embedded in longer letters to specific faith communities who are living amongst different outsiders. Although the contexts change, and therefore the quality of relationship believers have with their unbelieving neighbours will differ, there is still a constant thread throughout the Pauline corpus that calls the believers firstly to be aware of the outsiders, and secondly to be sensitive to how such outsiders might view and interpret them. This requires the believers to be considerate and thoughtful about how they might not cause offence, and how they might actively pursue ways in which they can in fact benefit outsiders and win their praise.

1.3 The Juxtaposition

From this brief survey, it is apparent that we find an interesting juxtaposition. On the one hand, Paul is committed to *describing* a sharp distinction between the believers and the unbelievers and to *explaining* this distinction by drawing on baptismal language of dying and of being re-born, and therefore of believers having a new identity in Christ and a morally transformed (and superior) life. But on the other hand, Trebilco is correct in pointing out that whilst we have a 'clear demarcation of the Christ-believing group and the use of strongly excluding outsider designations' there is nevertheless no 'vilification or social distance' (2017: 112). It can be seen from the passages in Section 1.2 that there is a recommendation and an assumption that believers will not only be visible to outsiders but will associate with them to different degrees and in different contexts. Furthermore, rather than dismissing the outsiders, believers are to take account of their opinions. Despite the fact that the outsiders do not know God (1 Thess. 4.5; Gal. 4.8), there is a recognition that what outsiders think about the believers' lifestyle and presence in the wider community is not to be overlooked or ignored, and may even in fact drive or shape how the believers should conduct their lives and their worship.[16] Finally, it appears that underpinning all of these passages is the belief that there is in fact a shared agreement or an overlap area between believer and unbeliever on what is considered to be good and honourable.[17] There is not only an appeal to the believers to recognize the existence of this overlap but also a charge to reveal this, by their behaviour and lifestyle, to outsiders. Therefore, whilst some passages describe the believers and outsiders as belonging to two distinct (and seemingly incompatible) groups, others reveal more of a complex picture where the two distinct groups share some values, where the believers are to take thought for what outsiders think, and consequently, should be prepared to allow this to influence their relationships, worship and practice.

However, it is apparent that the concern for what outsiders think has not been a major focus in scholarship, and studies of Paul or his ethics 'have largely neglected the theme of views of outsiders' (Horrell 2016: 271). Unnik wrote a short essay in 1964 in which he traces and highlights the concern for the reaction of unbelievers through early Christian teaching, and he explores some possible motivations for this concern (namely, guarding against God's name or word being blasphemed, creating peace in the community and enabling mission). He argues that this concern for the reaction of outsiders was a 'tradition' that was handed down, and thus it found its way into some of Paul's letters. As such there grew a respect among early believers for the fact that 'daß Leben und Lehre beurteilt wurden von den Nicht-Christen' ('life and doctrine were judged by non-Christians', 1980: 321). The brevity of this essay, however, means that there is lacking within it a depth of engagement with the Pauline corpus so that the reader is left looking at an array of pertinent teaching in the NT and early Christian writing but with little critical exploration to make sense of it or understand its significance. Similarly, although Furnish in a chapter entitled 'Inside Looking Out' (2002: 104–24) highlights passages in which Paul appears to notice outsiders, he restricts his study firstly to 1 Thessalonians and 1 Corinthians and secondly to how Paul views outsiders. He also simply notes the obvious findings without giving thought to any underlying motivations (although he quickly dismisses any evangelistic or missionary ones) and admits that his 'summary observations' are not conclusions but 'may provide guidance for further research' (2002: 123). In 2014, Jacobus Kok et al. published a collection of essays under the title *Sensitivity towards Outsiders,* but the essays on the Pauline corpus are more concerned with boundaries and ethics, rather than exploring the regard for the opinion of outsiders or the impact of the believer upon the unbeliever (and vice versa).

Finally, David Horrell (2016) offers a fresh and thorough insight into Paul's ethics by combining his study with questions of group dynamics, boundaries, and key differences and similarities within the faith community, and also with regard to the unbelievers. His penultimate chapter explores the intersection between Pauline ethics and the outsider (2016: 271–99). After investigating a possible assumption within the Pauline corpus of 'universal ethics' (Rom. 1–2; 13.1-7), he then identifies three passages that reveal a concern for how outsiders might react to Christians: 1 Thess. 4.11-12, 1 Cor. 10.32 and 14.22-25. Whilst he concludes that the motivation for this concern is largely negative (regarding the need to avoid criticism), Horrell then highlights other passages which convey a more 'positive exhortation to ethical action' which is primarily for the benefit of the outsiders (2016: 288). These centre on the commands to 'do good to all' which presuppose a common acceptance of what is good and evil. However, like the above studies, this chapter is also brief, and Horrell limits his research to the undisputed letters. Furthermore, although he highlights the common ground that seems to exist between the two distinct groups, he does not appear to probe it further to ascertain if it is present merely as an assumption within Paul's world view, or if, for Paul, it has meaning and function in itself for the Pauline communities.

Therefore, the aim of this book will be to provide a thorough textual exploration of the instructions given to believers within the Pauline corpus that appear to be motivated by a sensitivity to the presence of outsiders and a concern for what they think, but it will also ask what might be motivating this concern for the outsider, and therefore seek to determine the importance of the outsider to the Pauline communities. Are the outsiders more of an 'afterthought' in some of the Pauline parenesis, or do they hold more of a key position in determining the identity of Pauline communities? It will therefore assess the importance of the outsider in the formation, maintenance, and growth of the faith community. To help with this exploration, it would be useful to have a greater understanding of groups, boundaries and relating across these boundaries. Social science can shed light upon this, particularly social identity theory and how this has been used recently in New Testament scholarship.

1.4 Social Identity Theory

Before social identity theory (SIT) became known as such, the anthropologist Fredrik Barth (1969) highlighted the need for difference between groups for social boundaries to exist. He wrote that 'ethnic groups only persist as significant units if they imply marked difference in behaviour, i.e. persisting cultural differences' (1969: 15–16). Some of these key differences are described as 'overt signals or signs' (e.g. language and dress), whereas others are 'basic value orientations' (1969: 14). However, despite this, he also recognized that in maintaining this difference and in preserving boundaries, a complete prevention of social interaction between groups is not necessary. He noted that 'boundaries persist despite a flow of personnel across them' (1969: 9) and that when social interaction does occur between two different social groups, the differences that help maintain the boundaries are rather 'reduced' for 'interaction both requires and generates a congruence of codes and values—in other words, a similarity or community of culture' (1969: 15).

He developed this theory by stating that there must be agreed 'prescriptions' between the two social groups which govern situations of contact, but that this agreement on 'codes and values need not extend beyond that which is relevant to the social situations in which they interact' (1969: 16).[18] There will also be 'proscriptions' which prevent social interaction or the agreement of codes and values in other areas.[19] Even with these proscriptions, though, Barth suggests that for boundaries to exist amidst close 'inter-ethnic contact' there must still be stability with regard to the cultural differences of each group (1969: 19). Thus, whilst Barth recognizes that there will be interaction between two different social groups, and that this interaction is made possible by the recognition of a common sharing of codes and values between the two groups, nevertheless the existence and maintenance of the social boundary is wholly dependent on the social group being confident and coherent in the ways in which it is different from the other group. Thus, *difference* between groups is more important than similarity.

This importance of difference became a key feature in SIT, which was developed during the 1970s from some initial experiments of intergroup behaviour by Henri Tajfel and his colleagues (Tajfel 1970; Tajfel et al. 1971).[20] In the first of these experiments, participants were randomly placed into two groups and were asked to make decisions about rewarding other pairs of participants with money; the recipients of the money were anonymous, except for their group membership. The results showed that 'categorisation leads to in-group favouritism and discrimination against the outgroup' for the participants were more likely to favour ingroup members, and they strived to compete with outgroup members to stress difference between the two groups (Tajfel and Turner 1979: 39). There was no existing hostility between the two groups, nor were there any other reasons provided which would have given a motivation for the discrimination. This suggests that simply the perception of belonging to a distinct group is enough to 'trigger intergroup discrimination favoring the in-group' or 'the mere awareness of the presence of an out-group is sufficient to provoke intergroup competitive or discriminatory responses on the part of the in-group' (Tajfel and Turner 1979: 38). For competition or conflict to arise, there does not need to be 'incompatible group interests' or a clash in ideologies, beliefs, interests, behaviour or ritual, for example, but simply a cognitive understanding of social categorization: that there exists a boundary creating two (or more) separate groups.

Thus, Tajfel and Turner argued that a group is firstly a collection of individuals who 'perceive themselves to be members of the same social category': this is called the cognitive component of group membership (1979: 40).[21] Bar-Tal later developed the function of the cognitive component, for although he agrees with Tajfel's findings that the fundamental group belief of belonging to a group is sufficient to trigger ingroup favouritism and outgroup discrimination, he argues that beyond the experiments and in the reality of everyday situations, further central group beliefs are needed to provide the defining characteristics and rationale for the existence of the group, but also to describe the feelings, thoughts and actions of group members (1998: 93–113). These group beliefs include norms, values, goals and ideology (1998: 95–101), and they not only define group boundaries and provide the basis for categorizing individuals as group members (or not), but they also unify ingroup members (1998: 94–5) and 'supply the basis for cementing social identity' (1998: 110). Thus, he writes that 'beyond the simple self-definition "We are a group", these beliefs provide the group's credo' (1998: 102).

Alongside the cognitive component, Tajfel and Turner also identified an emotional component whereby membership may be accompanied by certain attitudes and dispositions towards ingroup and outgroup members, such as love, hate, respect and reviling. Finally, they described an evaluative component whereby the group compares and contrasts itself with other groups, particularly choosing aspects of their group identity which would result in a positive comparison for the ingroup (Tajfel 1978: 63; Tajfel and Turner 1979: 40; Tajfel 1981: 229, 255). It is this evaluative component that appears to be the major focus of SIT. Being able to positively evaluate one's group against another group is important for the social identity and self-esteem of individual members, and therefore there is a pressure to emphasize difference, for the 'aim of differentiation is to maintain or achieve superiority over an out-group on some dimensions' (Tajfel and Turner 1979: 41). In the situation when a positive evaluation of the ingroup is not achieved, then an ingroup member might choose to leave the group (if possible) and join another group which would provide a more positive identity (Tajfel 1981: 256). Other options include what has come to be known as 'social creativity', which may involve reinterpretation of negative characteristics so that they become positive, or the creation of new characteristics which again would have a positively valued distinctiveness from the superior group (explored at some length in Hinkle et al. 1998: 166–79). Another option is to change the outgroup with which the comparisons are made so that the new outgroup holds the inferior status (Tajfel and Turner 1979: 43).[22]

However, what is often lost in highlighting the fact that competition, comparison and thus difference is important, is the obvious point that some comparisons will happen on a dimension which both groups value similarly. In this case, both groups will 'attempt to differentiate themselves from each other towards the same positively valued pole' (Turner 1978: 105). Although Turner recognizes this, he proceeds to focus upon the competition and effort towards differentiation between groups rather than explore this dimension of similarity, and how it is this area of similarity or agreement that sets up the opportunity for competition and evaluation. When the importance of similarity does become a focus in SIT, it is rather regarding the need for the ingroup to reduce differentiation and increase similarity *within* the ingroup (Deschamps and Doise 1978: 141–58). This involves referring to, and emphasizing, 'group beliefs' (Bar-Tal 1998) or 'norms' which include 'rules for how group members should behave and thus are the basis for mutual expectations among the group members' (Brown 2000: 56). These norms or beliefs identify, clarify and shape acceptable and unacceptable behaviour for ingroup members, and ensuring that all members adhere to these norms is important in group cohesion and unity. In maintaining group boundaries, a strong similarity within the ingroup appears to be just as important as having a strong difference with the outgroup.

This factor of similarity within the ingroup, however, gives rise to stereotypes, which are generalizations about members of a group and are largely negative for members of outgroups, and positive for the ingroup (see Hogg and Abrams 1988: 64–91; Brown 2000: 290–306). However, what is interesting for this book is that Bar-Tal notes (albeit very briefly) that since group beliefs provide information about that group to another group, then 'group beliefs may determine the attitudes and behaviours of an outgroup towards the group' (Bar-Tal 1998: 111). Thus, it is not only a stereotype that is created by a group's beliefs or norms, but he implies that there is a deeper, internal response in members of the outgroup upon realizing the beliefs and norms of the ingroup. He continues, 'This information enables acquaintanceship with the group and in turn influences the type of intergroup relations that may develop' (1998: 111). In other words, the group beliefs of one group will naturally elicit a response in the onlooker (the outsider) towards the ingroup, which might be demonstrated in a particular behaviour or action of the outsider (e.g. affirmation or conflict) but which will almost certainly involve a particular attitude or opinion (positive or negative). This relationship between group beliefs in the ingroup and the attitude of the outgroup towards the ingroup is certainly assumed in the Pauline corpus. However, although Bar-Tal shows a brief recognition of outgroup attitudes towards the ingroup and how this may impact upon intergroup relations, he does not pursue this further.

Over time, SIT became a catalyst in stimulating further ideas and theories which encompassed other aspects of group phenomena (such as reward allocations and linguistic behaviour) and explored other dimensions of intergroup relations and group processes.[23] Most research, however, has focused on ingroup bias, comparison and, consequently, the emphasis upon differentiation. Even when it is recognized that there may be a cross-over or overlap of membership between groups, so that a member of one group may also be a member of several other groups, the focus has been on the impact upon social identity rather than upon the prevalence of shared values and its impact on intergroup relations (Crisp and Hewstone 2000). There have also been attempts to find out how to reduce ingroup bias and intergroup conflict, most notably by Gaertner et al., in the 'common ingroup identity model', whereby the boundary is redrawn so that the two groups essentially become one, and own together superordinate goals; no longer is there language of 'us' and 'them' but rather 'we' (Gaertner et al. 2000). In other words, there is an attempt at 'redrawing the group boundaries so that those who were once classified as outgroupers can be regarded as fellow ingroupers within a larger superordinate category' (Capozza and Brown 2000: xiv). This recategorization 'shapes relationships, social perceptions, group attitudes and the treatment of others' so as to 'initiate more harmonious interpersonal and intergroup relations' (Gaertner et al. 2000: 148).[24]

Even in this brief overview of SIT, it is evident that the emphasis is largely upon the importance of difference between groups. Barth's original thesis, in which he raised an awareness of the necessity for 'a congruence of codes and values' between groups for interaction (1969: 15), does not appear to have been developed by the original or later proponents of SIT to a great extent, and thus the importance of similarity between groups is not fully explored. Nevertheless, Turner does at least recognize the presence and importance of similarity between groups in order for groups to compare themselves with others (1978: 105; also Lieu 2004: 100), and Bar-Tal's assertion that the beliefs or norms of an ingroup will determine how an outgroup reacts to it (1998: 111), does coincide with the earlier findings of passages in the Pauline corpus that feature a concern over the interaction between the believers and unbelievers. For, in discovering and outlining the juxtaposition (1.3) it was found that there is an acknowledgement in some passages of this 'congruence of codes and values' between believer and unbeliever, a sensitivity to how the ingroup is seen by the outgroup, and consequently, how the outgroup reacts in attitude (opinion) and behaviour towards the ingroup. Before this is explored, we will briefly survey how SIT has been used in New Testament scholarship.[25]

1.5 SIT and New Testament Scholarship

1.5.1 Wayne Meeks

Wayne Meeks argued in *First Urban Christians* (1983) that to understand the New Testament (NT) and early Christianity, it is important to explore the social world of the first Christians in the first century (1983: 2). Thus, in chapter 3 he looks at the formation of the church community and its boundaries using a social-historical lens. He recognizes that the first Pauline communities 'enjoyed an unusual degree of intimacy, high levels of interaction among members, and a very strong sense of internal cohesion and of distinction both from outsiders and from "the world"' (1983: 74). Although he writes that his task is more historical than sociological (1983: 74), he nevertheless employs language and concepts associated with SIT in exploring the Pauline correspondence (1983: 85).

By tracing some of the descriptive language in the Pauline corpus, he illustrates how the language of belonging functions to draw the boundary between *them* and *us* and aids the process of resocialization whereby individuals who once belonged to the outside group are stripped of their old identity and are given a new one (1983: 85–96). He highlights the unparalleled frequency of familial language in the Pauline corpus in which believers are described as 'children of God' and the affectionate language used to describe Paul's concern for believers (e.g. 1 Thess. 2.7) which builds intimacy and personal ties between Paul and the communities (1983: 85–7). He explores how the distinctive beliefs held by the believers reinforced their ingroup coherence and their difference from outsiders (1983: 91–4) and how the 'language of separation' (by which he refers to how outgroup members are described) led believers to assume that there is 'a qualitative difference between outsiders and insiders' (1983: 95).

However, Meeks also proposes that a boundary can be modified to sharpen the distinction between groups or to do the opposite, depending upon how insiders and outsiders interpret this boundary, and thus influencing the level of interaction across it. For example, there is a 'lowering' of a boundary by the 'strong' in 1 Corinthians 8, who, because they believe eating idol meat does not threaten their faith (v. 4), 'adopt a weak-boundary position' for they should be able to share meals with outsiders. The 'weak' believers, however, perceive that idolatry is 'real and dangerous' and so they adopt a strong-boundary position to distinguish between idolaters (outsiders) and worshippers of the one true God (1983: 97–8). Meeks also shows awareness of how outsiders may influence the nature of the boundary for he argues that if the lowering of the boundary is interpreted by outsiders as an acceptance of idolatry, then it is prohibited (1983: 98, 100).[26]

Furthermore, Meeks refers to 'gates' in the boundaries (1983: 105–7) which firstly make it possible for believers to carry on with their daily lives; their difference does not mean a withdrawal from the world.[27] Paul did not tolerate this interaction as 'inevitable' but 'positively encouraged it' and showed how believers need not fear contamination (1983: 105). Meeks continues to note that mission is a reason to 'encourage openness toward the world' (1983: 105) and thus gates secondly allow for believers to declare the gospel to all people. He concludes this section, noting that one of the characteristics of the Pauline church was 'the vigor of its missionary drive, which saw in the outsider a potential insider' (1983: 107). He finds in this 'missionary drive' the reason for the 'tension' in needing to 'promote a strong internal cohesion' and 'clear boundaries', separating believers from unbelievers, and 'the intention to continue normal and generally acceptable interactions with outsiders' (1983: 107).

Meeks briefly turns to highlight the passages that show a recognition that 'the ordering of the internal life of the sect takes place not in complete isolation, but with an eye toward how outsiders will perceive the Christians' (e.g. 1 Thess. 4.11-12; 1 Cor. 14.23; 10.32-33; 9.19-23; Romans 13). He also points to those texts that encourage behaviour which complies not just with the will of God but with 'standards that the outsiders recognize as good' especially to the hierarchically ordered household, fundamental to Greco-Roman society (Col. 3.18–4.1; Eph. 5.21–6.9).[28] Meeks argues that the motivation behind such texts is defensive, for they serve 'as a defense against the typical objection which Greco-Roman writers urged against novel cults: that they corrupt households and hence threaten the basis of the whole social fabric' (1983: 106). Although Meeks does acknowledge the influence of outsiders on the ingroup, Meeks mainly focuses upon the *difference* between believers and outsiders and the importance of internal coherence. When Meeks observes the overlap of boundaries between insiders and outsiders and a concern for how the latter views the former, the attention given to this is minimal.

1.5.2 Philip Esler

Like Meeks, Esler also argues that to understand Paul's theology in a particular letter, there must firstly be a recognition that this theology 'was developed in a particular *social* context', and secondly, a desire to understand this context (1998: 39). As such, he frequently uses SIT throughout his commentaries. In his commentary on Galatians, Esler focuses almost entirely upon the evaluative component of group membership for it becomes clear that Paul is concerned to persuade his readers that they have a better positive identity if they remain members of the ingroup rather than of the negatively evaluated outgroups (1998: 42–3). From the beginning of the letter to the Galatian church, there is an air of deep frustration in Paul's words to the congregation, for the believers are being persuaded to turn from the true gospel of Christ and are listening to those who are perverting it (1.6-7). Thus, Paul describes his divine commission to proclaim to the believers the true gospel of Christ (Gal. 1.1, 6, 11-12) in comparison to those who are perverting the gospel and who have no divine commission (1.6-7; Esler 1998: 120). Esler notes that in Galatians 3 (vv. 2, 5) Paul attempts to generate a positive social identity for his congregation by reminding his readers that 'the Spirit and associated miraculous phenomena arrived among them from proclamation of the faith, not through works of the (Mosaic) law' (1998: 52). This evaluative component is also clearly seen in chapter 5, when the negative works of the flesh are attributed to the identity of the outgroup, whereas the fruits of the Spirit belong to the identity of the ingroup (vv. 16-25; 1998: 228–9).

Barth's work is also significant to Esler, and he uses it to understand the potential risks Paul saw in the boundaries between the believers, the Israelites and the Gentiles. Esler argues that the 'boundaries were at risk of exhibiting permeability of an illicit type (as far as Paul was concerned) if the proscriptions necessary for the congregations of Christ-followers to continue as distinctive groups broke down' (1998: 91). According to Paul, believers did not need to be circumcised (e.g. Gal. 5.2-6); this was a fixed belief that belonged to the true gospel and it maintained the distinctiveness of the ingroup from the Israelite outgroup. It was therefore, in Barth's terms, a proscription, an area of belief or practice that could not be compromised or a boundary that could not be lowered to facilitate intergroup relations. Esler hence finds that the very nature of the context behind the letter to the Galatians means that when it is viewed through the lens of SIT, the distinctiveness of the ingroup assumes central importance, and any overlap found between groups is not a positive aspect but is seen as presenting a risk to the existence of the ingroup.[29] Esler's focus and aim in this commentary is upon how Paul is forging and strengthening a distinctive identity for the believers, which is separate from the identity of the Israelite and Gentile outgroups.

However, in his commentary on Romans, Esler identifies that, because the issues in this letter are very different (namely that Paul is concerned with how to hold together and reduce tension within the ingroup), then the focus is less upon the boundary between ingroup and outgroup(s) and more upon the ingroup itself (see 2003: 25). Accordingly, throughout his commentary on Romans he mainly draws upon the idea of recategorization, or the 'common ingroup identity model' which, as we have seen in Section 1.4, is concerned with redrawing boundaries so that an outgroup becomes part of the ingroup to reduce intergroup conflict. Esler takes this theory and applies it not to intergroup conflict but to intragroup conflict, namely, the tensions between Gentile and Israelite believers (2003: 30). As such, he strives to show how, rather than trying to erase all the differences in ethnic identities within the ingroup, Paul attempts to bring about reconciliation by highlighting the common identity that members of the ingroup now share together (2003: 133, 143).

For example, Esler points to Rom. 1.16, where Paul categorizes ingroup members as those who have faith (and therefore salvation) and shows that this ingroup consists of two subgroups, Judeans and Greeks (2003: 140). Esler proposes that this common ingroup identity is developed further in chapter 4, where Paul explains that Abraham is the prototype for both the Judean and non-Judean believer (4.11-12). Esler argues that Paul 'has recategorized the two subgroups of the Christ-movement in Rome into an ingroup identity that is unified by virtue of their sharing exactly the same relationship with Abraham' (2003: 190). The olive tree metaphor later in chapter 11 also offers 'a textualized image of the recategorization of two subgroups in which Paul is engaged throughout Romans'; however, 'that Israelites and non-Israelites form one social category in Christ in no way means that the differences between these subgroups have been erased, or that one is not superior to the other' (2003: 305).

Esler also refers to Dovidio, Validzic and Gaertner (1998: 117) who propose that for recategorization to be successful, both groups need to have an equal status (but on different dimensions, otherwise competition would create division once again) which engenders respect and value among members and provides a reason for members of one subgroup to believe that the other subgroup will bring a positive contribution to the ingroup (Esler 2003: 144). For Esler, Rom. 1.18–3.20 is a good example of this, for Paul shows how prior to their recategorization as believers, both Judeans and Greeks are 'equal in respect of their subjection to the power of sin but they are different in the way they have reached that result—Judeans under the law of Moses and Greeks in the absence of that law' (2003: 144). However, although this 'equality' does not produce respect or show how the presence of one group might benefit the other, it nevertheless reduces any feelings of ethnic superiority over the other and thereby lays foundations for building up a common ingroup identity (2003: 145–54).

When looking at other chapters within Romans, Esler returns to some of the more traditional core insights of SIT. For example, turning to Romans 12–13, he argues that ἀγάπη takes prominence here and that it provides the faith community with an important 'norm' or 'identity-descriptor' (2003: 322). He suggests that the 'thirty unadorned assertions' in Rom. 12.9-21 function to 'portray the meaning of ἀγάπη' (2003: 322) and that this norm of ἀγάπη is to characterize and drive the believers' interactions with each other (he leaves open the possibility that the persecutors mentioned in v. 14 could be fellow believers; 2003: 324, 329) and with all people. However, what is striking is that when Esler turns to Romans 13, although he acknowledges that the first seven verses refer to outsiders (including 'Roman political authorities'), he offers a very brief exegesis which focuses only on two difficult features (concerning the meaning of the 'sword' and paying taxes, Rom. 13.6; 2003: 331–2). There is therefore no deep engagement with how believers should interact with outsiders and no application of SIT to understand this or how Paul is providing a new way for believers to perceive the identity of the outgroup (specifically the authorities as divinely ordained, Rom. 13.1-2). Furthermore, there is no observation of Paul's concern for the positive opinion of the outsider and how this should therefore shape the ingroup's norms.

Nevertheless, Esler's work with SIT and its developments have resulted in a rich and at times unique interpretation of Galatians and Romans, not just for individual verses but for the letters as a whole – their purpose, function and drive. The content and purpose of these two Pauline letters naturally means that Esler's focus is largely upon ingroup phenomena and the importance of difference between ingroup and outgroup. However, it is noticeable that when opportunity does arise for Esler to apply the insights of SIT to the interaction between believer and outsider, he fails to grasp this; like Meeks, his attention is firmly on the ingroup.

1.5.3 Alistair May

In *The Body for the Lord: Sex and Identity in 1 Corinthians 5-7*, May studies 'the part played by sexual ethics in the formation of Christian identity' which involves exploring sex, boundaries and behaviour (2004: 2). He draws from SIT to explore the sexual ethics of believers: how these might be distinct from those of outsiders and therefore helpful in creating difference between the two groups.[30] May begins his study with reference to Barth and a proposal that 'cultural overlap' (2004: 17) between believers and their Greco-Roman or Jewish neighbours does not necessarily dissolve a sense of belonging, distinction or 'a breakdown in the group boundary' (2004: 19). He even admits that 'if we were to seek for a "unique culture" among Paul and his converts, we may encounter some difficulties', since Paul's sexual ethic overlaps with that found in Judaism and Greco-Roman values (2004: 21). This gives no reason for worry, May insists, for groups can persist despite having overlaps (2004: 21), and even poses the possibility that (in the terminology of Barth) prescriptions are more important than the proscriptions when looking at intergroup activity (2004: 22). This might lead us to expect that May will present a slight turning point in NT scholarship using SIT by exploring this area of overlap and its function in creating social identity and guiding intergroup relations, rather than simply looking at difference. However, as we will see later in this section, the opposite turns out to be the case, for the thrust of his study is that in 1 Corinthians, Paul's great concern is to identify and strengthen the great dichotomy between believer and outsider, and where an overlap in ethics exists its significance lies in the potential for creating a positive stereotype for the ingroup, rather than in enhancing intergroup relations.

May uses the ideas of SIT to note that Paul begins the letter in chapters 1–4 by creating a strong sense of belonging and distinction, by building up stereotypes of the believers and the outsiders, and a positive social identity for believers, the superior ingroup (2004: 49–51). May proposes that this should increase the cognitive, evaluative and emotional components of group belonging: 'Believers will increasingly be aware of their new social identity in Christ, evaluating it positively, and investing emotionally in it', as well as group cohesion and conformity (2004: 52; see also 52–4, 57). Accordingly, this would also create a negative evaluation of the outside world and a negative attitude towards outsiders (2004: 52) and would 'encourage disengagement from them' (2004: 57). May suggests that a similar strategy is used by Paul in chapters 5–7, where a great distinction is drawn between the believer and the outsider, the ἅγιοι and the ἄδικοι (1 Cor. 6.9-11), and where the ethical and eschatological boundaries between the two are strengthened (2004: 87). Members of the outgroup are categorized by their eschatological fate and their vices (2004: 55), and as such, 'the outgroup is stereotypically polluted' (2004: 56). He concludes:

> Ethics, and sexual ethics in particular, are just as much the boundary as faith, or justification. They define both insider and outsider. Πόρνοι is what the Christians were (6.11), πορνεία is the defining trait of the unbelievers around them (5.9-10) and the abstention from πορνεία is thus to be the visible difference between the community and the outside.
>
> (2004: 57)

Having made this great dichotomy, Paul then turns in horror to the fact that there is an anomaly: he is forced to make a negative intergroup comparison, for a member of the ingroup has acted in a sexually immoral way that is not even condoned or heard of in the outgroup (5.1).[31] May writes that in doing such, Paul 'undermines the group's positive self-evaluation', and that this undermining is made all the worse because the previous four chapters have outlined how immoral and foolish the outgroup are (2004: 63). However, May states that this is not a 'comment on pagan morals' but rather it is simply serving as a rhetorical comparison (2004: 63). He later adds: 'The fact that the Christian sexual ethic shares its condemnation of incest with the outside world matters little' (2004: 80), for May sees that Paul's concern is primarily about the risk that the immoral offence endangers the dichotomy Paul set up earlier with the positive stereotype for believers and the negative one for unbelievers, and also that it endangers the reputation of the church (2004: 80). This concern for preserving and strengthening the dichotomy is seen in Paul's solution, for he instructs the congregation to cast out the immoral brother and any other immoral believers. May concludes: 'For Paul's ethical dualism, it is impossible to contemplate the holy people having πορνεία in them' (2004: 67).

What is particularly interesting for our study is not only May's initial proposal that there appears to be some common ground regarding sexual ethics for both ingroup and outgroup, but also that he concludes that this 'lack of difference is not what is significant' (2004: 262). Rather, the significant finding for May is that Paul nevertheless is still able to maintain, promote and strengthen the great dichotomy between believer and unbeliever, namely that 'all outside the church are stereotypically denoted by vice, and particularly by sexual vice' (2004: 262). In May's reading of Paul, what is essential is the difference that results from comparing two groups regarding an area of shared ethics or values (the evaluative component) which gives rise to a positive or negative stereotype. Thus, the overlap area is important not because of the opportunity it might give for interaction between groups, but for the opportunity it gives to compare the groups and provide the ingroup with a more positive identity than the outgroup. This in turn strengthens the difference between the groups and gives the ingroup internal cohesion and confidence.

This is undoubtedly true and clearly reflects the mood of these passages. However, because May has chosen to use SIT to look at these passages where Paul is largely concerned about internal issues, then to some extent there is no surprise that May's finding of the overlap area leads him to conclude that the importance of such is related to a concern for the insider, rather than a concern for the outsider. However, when he turns to Paul's instructions in 1 Corinthians 7 to believers married to unbelievers (where there is an explicit concern for the outsider), there is neither an appeal to SIT to shed any light on these verses, nor any recognition of the significant weight Paul gives to the opinion of the outsider in discerning whether or not a believer should remain in this marriage (2004: 225–30). Rather, May uses this passage as another opportunity to emphasize 'the strength of the categorical distinction between believers and unbelievers' (2004: 230).

1.5.4 David Horrell

In *Solidarity and Difference: A Contemporary Reading of Paul's Ethics* (first edition 2005), Horrell offers a fresh approach to exploring Pauline ethics by seeking to determine the 'key moral values' whilst asking how these are connected to group dynamics such as social identity, boundaries, difference, and interaction with outsiders (2016: 2). He is concerned to place Paul's ethics within a framework that takes seriously the importance of communities, and as such provides a study that gives an insight into the complex interaction between ethics and the forming and maintenance of groups, which also includes a consideration of the outgroup. The title of the book, *Solidarity and Difference*, is inspired by the work of Daniel Boyarin, who asks, based on his reading of Gal. 3.28-29, if differences of gender and ethnicity are valuable in themselves to Paul, or if they are 'obstacles' in his vision for a 'new humanity of no difference' (Boyarin 1994: 3, 5). Clearly, some differences cannot be erased, but Boyarin proposes that, in the striving for 'human one-ness' (1994: 6), the differences are simply tolerated, which then means that they would become, as Horrell remarks, 'a matter of *in*difference, which in fact undercuts the integrity of such differences' (2016: 47). As such, Horrell is intrigued as to how 'human communities' can be conceived of 'as places of solidarity and difference' (2016: 48) and this forms the basis for some of his subsequent chapters in looking at Pauline ethics in the faith community and beyond.

Thus, in chapter 4, 'The Construction of Community: Corporate Solidarity in Christ', although Horrell does not refer directly to SIT he nevertheless uses the insight of groups needing 'norms' in order to engender and maintain ingroup coherence, or, 'solidarity' (2016: 109–45).[32] He argues that 'the first and most fundamental moral value, a metanorm, in Pauline ethics is that of corporate solidarity, a form of human solidarity with egalitarian impulses' (2016: 109), and Paul seeks to 'restore and strengthen it in the face of conflict and division' (2016: 110; see also 127–33).[33] He demonstrates how Paul seeks to generate this 'corporate solidarity' through his teaching on baptism (Rom. 6.1-14; 1 Cor. 12.12-13; Gal. 3.26-29) where, for Paul, 'baptism constructs a new form of human solidarity which transcends the lines of previous distinctions' (2016: 116) and the Lord's supper (1 Cor. 10.16-17; 11.17-34) which 'is meant to confirm and consolidate that solidarity, demonstrating through the concrete sharing of a meal that many have become one body in Christ' (2016: 120). This is, for Horrell, the key to corporate solidarity: that because the death and resurrection of Jesus Christ is central to both of these rituals then the believers' solidarity is about being united with Christ – they have 'solidarity in Christ' (2016: 121).

Horrell shows how Paul's frequently used title ἀδελφοί for the believers enhances this solidarity (2016: 121–6) but also that this solidarity of being one body shapes how believers are to relate with one another (the 'emotional' component in SIT), specifically through the 'reversing of existing hierarchies' and in 'the appeal for an equality of regard and care among all members of the body' (1 Cor. 12.25; 2016: 143). Horrell notices that there will nevertheless be some tension between the old life and the new life, since he argues that the solidarity the believers find of being incorporated into Christ does not necessarily transform 'all aspects of social location and interaction' (2016: 144).

Therefore, having set out his proposal for Paul's vision for solidarity, he then turns to discover how this *solidarity* in Christ provides the *difference* needed for the boundary to exist between believers and unbelievers. It is chapter 5, 'Purity, Boundaries and Identity: The Rhetoric of Distinction' (2016: 147–82) that also features most of Horrell's work with SIT. Here, Horrell firstly traces the language that Paul uses to contrast the identity of the believers with that of unbelievers (2016: 148–52), and how, using the insights from SIT, this can be understood as Paul's attempt to 'reinforce a strong sense of positive group identity' and a strong boundary between believers and unbelievers (2016: 153).[34] The work of Fredrik Barth (1969) regarding boundary-maintenance and the prescriptions or proscriptions that govern interaction across boundaries leads Horrell to search for the essential distinctive aspects of the believer's social identity in Pauline thought. He does so by exploring Paul's responses to issues of sexual immorality and idolatry in 1 Corinthians 5–7 (2016: 156–66). He concludes that the key distinctiveness of believers is found in the 'ideas and practices associated with the body and its union with Christ' (2016: 167). In other words, the key 'metanorm' of corporate solidarity (being in Christ) also distinguishes believers from outsiders since it guides and determines their practice. For, it is their union in Christ that must be protected against 'competing unions', and as such, a place of proscription for interaction across the boundary would be any behaviour defined as being idolatrous or sexually immoral (2016: 169).[35]

However, because Horrell argues that the key distinguishing mark between believer and outsider is to do with the believer's union in Christ, then this means that their difference does not necessarily depend upon their ethical norms – and in fact, that there is an element of overlap or similarity with outsiders regarding ethics. Like Meeks and May, Horrell also finds that 'when it comes to sexual morality ... it becomes evident that Paul shares a good deal in common, not only with Jewish ethics, but also with Greco-Roman moral philosophy' (2016: 171). Regarding 1 Cor. 5.1-13, whilst it is not Paul's primary aim to reveal 'that his ethical judgments cohere with those of their wider society', it is surely significant that Paul's judgement to cast the offender out of the church (the only place in Paul's letters where this is advocated) 'represents a point of moral agreement, shared "common ground," between him and his contemporaries outside the church' (2016: 175), for nowhere in the passage does Paul attempt to explain why this particular sexual relationship is immoral. Horrell highlights the fact that Paul's instructions are 'entirely premised on the assumption that the man *is* a πόρνος, because of his conduct in this matter. In other words, Paul simply assumes and accepts the general ethical norm—that a sexual relationship with one's stepmother is unacceptable—and proceeds to argue on this basis' (2016: 123, 126).

As such, for Horrell, 1 Corinthians 5 explicitly illustrates how believers can paradoxically share ethical norms with outsiders but also have 'a sense of distinct (and morally superior) identity' (2016: 175). He argues that this tension can only be resolved 'if we perceive Paul's claim to be *not* so much that Christians live by *distinctive* ethical standards but rather that they live up to, and beyond, the ethical standards that others share but do not follow' (2016: 178). Horrell recognizes that these shared ethical norms are in fact essential for allowing a positive identity to be created, as they provide the comparative basis for defining and developing group identity (2016: 178, 180; see Turner 1978: 105). Like Meeks, Horrell therefore highlights the finding that Paul is concerned to distinguish the believers from the unbelievers, but this happens not because believers have a radically different stance on sexual ethics, but because both groups are located on the same moral scale and believers are found (or should be found) to be dominating the higher end of the morality scale than the outsiders. In fact, a claim to superior group identity 'is, at least in part, *dependent* on shared ethical values' (2016: 182). For Horrell, the nature of the *solidarity* of the faith community drives the believers' *difference* from outsiders, and their *difference* is therefore not threatened by the *similarity* in ethical norms between the two groups. It is the metanorm of being incorporated into Christ that provides the believers with corporate solidarity and with the boundary of difference.

Whilst Horrell appreciates the significance of the outgroup in strengthening the positive identity of the ingroup, he continues to explore the relationship between Paul's ethics and the outgroup in chapter 8, 'Ethics and Outsiders'. However, what is interesting for this book is that, unlike when Horrell explored the areas of difference and similarity between insider and outsider in chapter 5 (but with the focus on the ingroup), when he turns to develop the theme of intergroup similarity and how the believers should view and respond to outsiders (with the focus more on the outgroup), he does not seem to draw from the ideas or language of SIT. This has been a recurring theme among our NT scholars in Sections 1.51, 1.5.2, 1.5.3, that when they have noticed the focus on the outgroup (and Horrell does this more than Meeks, Esler, and May), there has been little attempt to correlate this with SIT. This raises an important question regarding the nature of SIT and its application in the Pauline corpus. Because of its bias towards difference and ingroup-focus, does this render SIT unhelpful when focusing more on the outgroup and how this impacts upon the ingroup? Or have those who have employed SIT (whether as a sociologist or NT scholar) limited its use to difference and ingroup-focus and thus failed to develop its potential to help understand to a deeper degree the importance of the outgroup for the formation, maintenance and development of the ingroup?

1.5.5 Summary

The use of SIT in the work of Meeks, Esler, May and Horrell to interpret and understand Paul's teaching has provided a rich and detailed study on how Paul forms and strengthens the boundary between believer and unbeliever. These scholars have used different dimensions of SIT (or at least, its language and concepts) as a framework to identify the importance of the ingroup having a positive social identity, and how Paul manages to achieve this, often in situations of crisis and conflict. This has meant that there has also been an emphasis on the evaluative component of group membership, but also therefore a recognition of an area of overlap between groups (or, in Esler's work on Romans, between subgroups within the ingroup). However, because of the nature of the Pauline passages that were explored using the lens of SIT, where most were concerned with internal conflict or misbehaviour, the significance of this area of overlap is ironically solely rooted in enabling the *difference* of the ingroup to be strengthened by re-establishing the expectation for believers to have a morally superior identity. The importance of the creation of a positive identity has been the thrust of most of these passages or letters, so that where there has been a glance to the outsider, the focus has nevertheless been upon the insider. As such, these scholars have focused upon the dimensions of SIT that emphasize difference and the importance of ingroup identity and cohesion. The concern has been for the insider, not for the outsider.

The use of SIT in NT scholarship has of course continued, although there is an increasing use of other approaches or insights into social identity alongside the use of SIT, or even instead of using SIT. For example, Tucker (2010) uses SIT to explore how Paul forms the social identity of the believers in Corinth, looking specifically at 1 Corinthians 1–4, a passage in which there are many signs of opposition and conflicts at play within the community.[36] But he notes that whilst SIT provides a useful framework for his study of 1 Corinthians 1–4, there are gaps in this theory, and concludes that: 'an eclectic integration of the work of other scholars would provide the necessary resources to assess the way Paul was seeking to form the social identity of the Corinthian Christ-followers in 1 Corinthians 1–4' (2010: 60). He therefore draws from a further seven scholars with their own insights into social identity.[37] A few years later Tucker, together with Baker, compiled a collection of twenty-one essays written by NT scholars using social identity to explore different aspects of the formation and maintenance of the early Christian community, as seen through the different gospels and letters of the NT (2014). Not every essay specifically draws from SIT, but those that do offer new ways of understanding significant themes and how challenges were negotiated in the creation of these early Christian communities.[38]

It appears that whilst SIT is still considered to provide a refreshing and important lens with which to understand community formation in the Pauline corpus, it is clear that it is nevertheless underdeveloped in some areas of social identity.[39] Therefore, when looking at how it has been used by the above NT scholars, perhaps the weakness lies in SIT itself and not just in the use of it by NT scholars. It is possible that NT scholars have not been able to make much use of SIT in considering other Pauline material (such as that which we will explore in this book), because SIT itself does not fully explore how group identity is formed through positive interaction with the opinions of outsiders, and because of its emphasis on the importance of difference between groups.

However, another sociologist, Richard Jenkins, in writing on identity by bringing together insights from sociology, anthropology and social psychology, argues that there is always an 'internal–external dialectic' in the formation of the definition of an identity, so that it is a combination of internal self-definition but also external definition by others (2008: 40, 42). He uses 'identity' in a looser sense than that which has been defined here as social identity using SIT, so that it is about 'a process of "being" or "becoming"' (2008: 17), but his proposition is nevertheless interesting for this book and our consideration of SIT and its use within NT scholarship. For he argues that 'what people think about us is no less significant than what we think about ourselves', and that there is an ongoing interplay between self-image and public-image (2008: 42). However, because he is not working specifically within SIT, he does not link this insight to how this impacts upon, what he terms, the 'content' or 'cultural stuff' of the ingroup, or how it gives a fresh view of the function of intergroup similarity (2008: 44). In other words, he observes what I have highlighted as important in the Pauline corpus – that what others think about the believing community is important – but he does not go on to delineate explicitly *how* or *why* this then might be allowed to form or perhaps create fluidity within what SIT terms as the ingroup's norms, or the importance of similarity or contact points between the groups. He also recognizes that what others think is significant: 'Others don't just perceive our identity, they actively constitute it. And they do so not only in terms of naming or categorising, but in terms of how they respond to or treat us. In the dialectic of individual identification the external moment can be enormously consequential' (2008: 96).[40] He later describes these 'consequences' in terms of whether the ingroup receives 'resources or penalties' from the outgroup, depending upon how they identify the ingroup, or what they think of them (2008: 198–9).

Additionally, Tucker, whilst exploring 1 Corinthians 1–4 using different theories on social identity (including Jenkins), also writes, 'Identities are not simply asserted. They are negotiated within the context of communal life and in the interaction between the way one views oneself and the way one is viewed within the community' (2010: 207). Hence, both Tucker (from a NT perspective) and Jenkins (from an anthropological, sociological and psychological perspective) appear to be tantalizingly close to what this Introduction has begun to uncover in the thought of Paul and the Author, but this insight has not yet been applied thoroughly to the passages in which the outsiders are clearly in the forefront of Paul and the Author's mind. This is what this book hopes to address. Jenkins' insights from a broader social-scientific base do therefore suggest that there is the possibility of developing SIT so that it includes and recognizes the importance of the outsider in forming and maintaining the social identity of the ingroup. This book will therefore use the insights of SIT to explore those passages within the Pauline corpus that show a sensitivity to the outsider, by highlighting the concepts of difference and similarity and group norms, but it will also endeavour to develop SIT so that it can be used to reveal the importance of what others think in the forming of the cognitive and emotional components, as well as the group norms, of the social identity of the ingroup.

1.6 Conclusion

The beginning of this chapter highlighted the finding that within the Pauline corpus there are passages that are concerned with defining the difference between the believer and the outsider, either through using 'rhetoric of distinction' (Horrell 2016: 147) to describe the identities of believer and unbeliever in polar terms, or by reminding believers of their former (pre-converted) identity. The strong language that is used to describe the process of crossing over the boundary between unbeliever and believer, which involves not only the desire of the person to do so but also the transforming power of God, also conveys a sense that because believers are 'new creations' (2 Cor. 5.17), distinct from unbelievers on so many dimensions (e.g. spiritual, ethical, eschatological), then interaction between these two groups must not only be impossible but futile. However, adjacent to these very passages are those that contradict this logical presumption. For, throughout the Pauline corpus there is an assumption and a recommendation for believers to be visible to unbelievers and to interact with unbelievers, all the while showing a sensitivity to how they might be seen and how they might be experienced. Furthermore, there is an expectation for believers to be concerned about and take heed of the opinion of outsiders, and even be prepared to moderate or change some aspects of their practice and behaviour.

This suggests that for Paul and the Author, important in boundary maintenance and in the understanding of group identity and purpose, is the attitude, opinion and reaction of the outgroup to the ingroup. Whereas SIT (and therefore NT scholarship using SIT) has largely emphasized the importance of difference and internal cohesion in the maintenance of the group boundary and ingroup norms, this book will explore the importance of outsider opinion in such, and will ask if the recognition of an overlap area functions solely to provide the ingroup with a more positive stereotype for its own sake (e.g. for internal confidence) or whether there are other underlying motivations.

Therefore, the aim of this book will be to provide a thorough textual exploration of the instructions given to believers within the Pauline corpus that appear to be motivated by a sensitivity to the presence of outsiders and a concern for what they think, but it will also ask what might be motivating this concern for the outsider, and therefore seek to determine the importance of the outsider to the social identity of the Pauline communities.

Hence, in the following study, I will first turn in Chapter 2 to Paul's teaching in 1 Thessalonians which urges the believers to love all (3.12), to behave honourably among outsiders (4.11-12) and to do good to all (5.12). In Chapter 3 I will explore the instructions in Romans for believers to take a specific stance towards their particular outsiders, roughly summarized as them responding to evil with what is considered as good in the eyes of all, and for them to pursue approval from the governing authorities, letting the command to love guide their interactions with all (12.14-21; 13.1-10). Chapter 4 will trace the teaching in 1 Corinthians concerning believers being married to unbelievers, sharing meals with unbelievers, and worshipping with unbelievers in their presence (7.12-16; 10.23-33; 14.13-25). Finally, Chapter 5 will consider the teachings given in 1 Timothy and Titus for their congregations, focusing first on those that reveal a concern for the reputation of the church (e.g. 1 Tim. 3.7; 6.1; Tit. 2.5) and then on the call for believers to pray for outsiders and to demonstrate in their interactions with outsiders the same mercy and goodness they received from God before their conversion (1 Tim. 2.1-7; Tit. 3.1-8).

At the beginning of each chapter I will use the learnings from SIT to trace how Paul defines the identities of the believers and unbelievers, before taking a closer look at the passages that highlight the importance of the outsider in forming (or enhancing) the group beliefs, norms and practices of the believer. In so doing, I will also seek to determine whether these passages give any glimpses as to what the underlying motivation(s) might be for the concern about what others think, and if the role of SIT is limited to discussing difference and ingroup cohesion, or if there is the possibility of developing its theory to incorporate the importance of the outsider (specifically, what the outsider thinks of the insider) in the formation, maintenance and growth of the ingroup identity.

Notes

1 In the first century those who did not believe in Jesus Christ were often nevertheless still 'believers' and participants of other religions; however, for clarity and simplicity in this book I will reserve the term 'believer' to identify those who believed in Jesus Christ, and use 'unbeliever' for those who did not join this movement to become disciples of Christ. This also follows the convention in 1 and 2 Corinthians for naming those who were not members of Christ as οἱ ἄπιστοι (1 Cor. 6.6; 7.12, 13, 14 (twice), 15; 10.27; 14.22-24 (four occurrences); 2 Cor. 4.4; 6.14, 15. See also 2 Thess. 2.12; 1 Tim. 5.8; Tit. 1.15).

2 For the purpose of this book I will be following the near-universal consensus of contemporary New Testament scholarship that the undisputed epistles include

3   Throughout this book I will use the term 'outsider' to refer specifically to unbelievers.
4   See also 1 Cor. 1.18, where the cross is described as 'foolishness to those who are perishing' in distinction to it becoming the 'power of God' for those who are 'being saved'.
5   However, Paul in frustration asks the believers in Galatia how they are now turning (ἐπιστρέφω) once again to empty religion (Gal. 4.9).
6   Kok and Roth, however, believe that this is too simplistic. They briefly refer to 'Dialogical Self Theory' in arguing that many new converts to Christianity would still have held onto some old identities. Rather than completely turning away from their old lives, they would have 'experienced the dialogical tension of being' and they refer to an example of a Christian wife who is still married to a pagan man (2014: 6–7). However, the image of turning away from the practices and behaviour of the 'old life' is very different from turning away completely from old acquaintances and relationships (as Paul notes in 1 Corinthians 7) and in fact Paul charges them not to sever these relationships with unbelievers (see 1 Cor. 5.10), whilst still expecting them to turn away from behaviour that is not fitting for a follower of Christ.
7   Paul here is most likely referring to their baptism, which was an act of initiation that symbolized this crossing over a boundary (see also Lieu 2004: 136) and which came as a response to a confession of Jesus Christ as Lord (e.g. Acts 8.12).
8   In Eph. 2.1-10 and Col. 2.13-14 the imagery is changed slightly so that believers are described as being already dead in their pre-converted identity, so that the crossing of the boundary from unbeliever to believer is when God made them alive.
9   Boyarin asks if this 'baptismal declaration' in Gal. 3.28-29 means that differences are eradicated in 'the new humanity of no difference' (1994: 5). However, it will become clear in this book that although the believers are united by a primary identity of being 'in Christ', their differences are still important and shape to some degree how they are expected to live among each other.
10 However, although Paul often describes the believers as having been morally transformed, he also issues imperatives which suggest that they are still acting as if they had not undergone this transformation (e.g. Gal. 5.13-15). Bultmann first thoroughly explored this paradoxical relationship between indicative and imperative in Paul (1924) which is summarized succinctly in Horrell (2016: 11–13), who also offers a resolution (2016: 102–3).
11 Peerbolte also comments that Paul often 'fences off the past' by creating a boundary between the past and the present, and specifically points to 1 Thess. 1.9-10 (2014: 213).
12 It is notable, however, that this pattern of thinking in 2 Cor. 6.14-18 is not repeated elsewhere in the Pauline corpus, that its authenticity is questioned and there is no clear consensus among scholars as to Paul's influence over this passage. For example, Furnish suggests that it is non-Pauline but that Paul himself incorporated it into the letter (1984: 383), Martin concludes that 'in all probability Paul had some control over this passage' (1986: 193), and Harris, that it was written by Paul at an earlier time but is now inserted by Paul into his letter (2005: 14–25). Some, however, are adamant that it is Pauline (e.g. Seifrid 2014: 287; Murphy-O'Connor 1991: 68).
13 Whilst some commentators believe that this instruction might be warning against marriage between the believer and unbeliever (e.g. Meeks 1983: 227, footnote 13),

Rabens argues persuasively that Paul is not restricting every kind of relationship and contact that might occur between the believer and unbeliever, but that he is encouraging 'a selective demarcation from idolatrous people outside the church – the believers are to avoid covenant-forming relationships with them' (2014: 307). Rabens also develops his theory by arguing that Paul is also referring to 'idolatrous' people *inside* the church.

14   See also Col. 4.5,'Ἐν σοφίᾳ περιπατεῖτε πρὸς τοὺς ἔξω τὸν καιρὸν ἐξαγοραζόμενοι.
15   Scholars argue over the authenticity of these letters (see Chapter 5) but for simplicity I will refer to the author(s) of the Pastoral Epistles (PE) as 'the Author'.
16   This is in direct contrast to the comments overheard at the diocesan debate referred to in Section 1.1.
17   See also 1 Cor. 5.1 (we shall explore this in more detail later) and 1 Tim. 5.8.
18   This concords with the 'overlap area' between believers and unbelievers noticed in some of the passages explored in Sections 1.2 and 1.3.
19   See also Lieu who writes, 'In practice, boundaries are "permeable" – boundaries permit, and indeed encourage, interaction, while providing rules for it; they are not merely defensive but also allow for trade' (2004: 100). Wolter also comments on the impact that 'inclusive' and 'exclusive' boundaries or acts have on the identity of the group (2009: 129).
20   For details of other experiments, see Tajfel 1981: 268–73.
21   Later, Turner developed this aspect and formed the 'self-categorisation theory' where he explored how a person understands their personal individual identity and their social identity, and how these two interact (1987: 42–67).
22   The relationship between a positive social identity and discrimination of the outgroup (or favouritism of the ingroup) has sometimes been debated and amended. For example, Páez et al. (1998) argue for a more complex understanding of how ingroups may both view outgroup members and compare themselves with outgroups: they found that high-status groups will be more likely to show favouritism towards ingroup members than low-status groups, who will in turn show favouritism towards outgroup members whilst nevertheless viewing themselves as superior with regard to some specific values (1998: 211–29).
23   Capozza and Brown provide a useful overview of the developments and reactions to SIT in the first twenty years after it was published (2000: vii–xv).
24   It appears that this theory might gain support in Eph. 2.11-22, where the author describes how God has made the two groups of Jew and Gentile into one (especially v. 14).
25   It should be noted, however, that the following survey consists of brief summaries of the salient points for this current exploration, and therefore cannot do justice to the depth or detail of work by each scholar.
26   Meeks concludes that the emphasis in Paul's teaching in 1 Cor. 8-10 is 'upon internal cohesion' (1983: 100). This might be true, but he seems to overlook Paul's concern for the outsider in 1 Cor. 10.27-33 and focuses his own work almost entirely on the ingroup.
27   In discussing boundaries, Meeks's argument often resonates with that of Fredrik Barth's (1969) particularly around how groups can still interact across boundaries.
28   Meeks also notes that 'the sexual purity for which the Pauline Christians strive in an impure world is defined mostly in terms of values that are widely affirmed by the larger society' (1983: 101).

29 In a short essay that draws upon some aspects of SIT to analyse Galatians, Punt also highlights the fact that although the letter 'shows as awareness of the existence of outsiders, the letter's concern nevertheless is unambiguously about insiders' (2014: 242).

30 His interaction with SIT, however, is to a much lesser degree than that in Esler's work, and he only uses SIT in his exploration of 1 Corinthians 1–4 and 5–6, although he continues some basic language of boundary into his study of 1 Corinthians 7. We will mainly focus on his use of SIT when looking at 1 Cor. 5.

31 There is difficulty in translating this verse since there it lacks a verb, and so commentators have tended to supply one: Barrett (1968: 121) writes that 'such fornication as is not practised even among the Gentiles'; Hays (1997: 81) writes that even Gentiles would find this 'reprehensible', and Garland (2003: 155) that 'it is not even tolerated among the Gentiles'. Clearly this behaviour would have occurred, but Paul is using a rhetorical device to shame the believers into realizing that they are acting far below what is commonly held as acceptable behaviour.

32 Horrell defines his use of 'solidarity' to mean 'a sense of corporate bound-togetherness' (2016: 4).

33 For Horrell, a 'metanorm' is that 'which determines the moral framework within which other norms, values and customs can be articulated and practised' (2016: 109 footnote 2). In chapter 7, Horrell also identifies another 'metanorm' as 'other-regard', which is 'shaped and inspired by the example of Christ' for it means that one believer should be ready to forgo their freedom if this would be harmful to another person (2016: 219). This metanorm is important for Horrell because he concludes that, contrary to Boyarin, 'diversity and difference are sustained and protected' precisely because of Paul's call for believers to imitate Christ and practise 'other-regard' which 'sustains rather than erases this diversity' (2016: 304). The call for solidarity and imitating Christ is not a call to sameness but to behave in a Christ-like manner that allows for and enables difference within the body.

34 In an earlier chapter, however, Horrell also helpfully proposes that SIT can help to resolve the apparent 'paradoxical nature of the Pauline indicative-imperative formulations' (see Section 1.1) whereby the indicatives are understood to be 'identity-descriptors and group norms which need to be constantly affirmed' (2016: 103).

35 However, this also means that there is no need, as Barth suggested, for 'a stance of social isolation in all aspects of social life' (2016: 168). As such, Horrell briefly highlights passages where this social interaction with outsiders is recognized and encouraged (e.g. 1 Cor. 5.9-10; 7.12-16; 10.25-28; 2016: 168–9).

36 Tucker concludes that these internal problems are symptoms of the fact that in the believers' holding together of their different social identities (specifically of their 'in Christ' identity and their Roman identity) there can occur conflict on points of ethos, particularly around 'the social implications of the gospel' (2010: 270). Paul therefore needs to show the believers how their 'in Christ' identity should hold a primary position over and above any other social identities (see, e.g. 2010: 41).

37 Jenkins 2008; Bar-Tal 1990, 2000; Halbwachs 1992; Lawler 2008; Stryker and Burke 2000; Stets and Carter 2006; Kiecolt 1994.

38 For example, Barentsen (chapter 21) looks at stereotyping and leadership in 1 Timothy, and Tucker (chapter 22) explores how, for Paul, existing social identities (and here in particular, that of being a slave) continue but as subgroups within the superordinate identity of being 'in the Lord' (Phlm. 16c). Muir argues that SIT

helps the reader to understand the emphasis on community-building in Hebrews in the face of persecution, as well as the importance of group maintenance, competition and comparison when looking at intergroup relations (chapter 23), and Still and Webb propose that SIT can 'serve as a useful tool in studying' how Christian identity was formed in the early church, and make particular use of the cognitive, evaluative and emotional components in SIT when looking at that community formation in 1 Peter (ch. 25).

39 For this book, this point of underdevelopment is concerned with how SIT views the function and importance of intergroup similarity and of the very existence of the outgroup for the social identity of the ingroup.

40 At this point he goes on to explore 'labelling' and the sociology of deviance (Jenkins 2008: 96–9).

2

The Dimension of 'All' and the Influence of 'With': 1 Thessalonians

2.1 Introduction

Throughout Paul's earliest letter we constantly find evidence of his affection, concern and love for the Thessalonian believers, alongside a fairly negative and unpromising portrayal of the unbelievers. Members of the ingroup are the 'believing ones' (τοῖς πιστεύουσιν, 1 Thess. 2.10, 13) who have been chosen by God and who are beloved by God (1.4), and who have turned away from lifeless idols (1.9). Paul uses ἀδελφός to address or refer to the congregation eighteen times during the letter (1.4; 2.1, 9, 14, 17; 3.7; 4.1, 6, twice in 4.10, 13; 5.1, 4, 12, 14, 25, 26, 27), but he also describes his role as being more like a parent. Thus, Paul writes that he, Timothy, and Silvanus have been like 'a nurse tenderly caring for her own children' (2.7b), and also like 'a father with his children' in desiring for the believers' behaviour to match that of their new membership (2.11). Paul's hope is that they can live up to that which is required or expected of their membership of God's 'own kingdom and glory' (2.12). Furthermore, Paul reminds the believers that it is God himself who has invited them to be an 'insider', for God is the one identified here as 'the one calling' (τοῦ καλοῦντος, 2.12) people to join this group. Paul highlights that the owner and originator of the ingroup is God, but also that this ingroup is not just a localized faith community group, but part of a larger, cosmic and divine kingdom.

The impact of this short verse in 2.12 would not have been insignificant: Paul is raising the believer's own opinion of their social identity because their membership is based not simply on the fact that they personally joined this ingroup, but on the fact that God had a significant part to play in their membership. Describing God as choosing (1.4) and calling them into his kingdom (2.12) attributes divine desire and approval to the moment they stepped over the boundary to become a believer. Their transition from being an outsider to an insider is personal and special, and the picture conveyed by this description of God calling is one that would imbue into the believer a positive social identity. Clearly, however, Paul understands his and his colleagues' own part in enabling the formation of this community and he describes the Thessalonian believers as their 'crown of boasting before our Lord Jesus at his coming' (2.19).[1]

In contrast, Paul paints a negative picture of those who are found outside this believing community, who are, in general, the unbelieving public. Some who belong to the outgroup are those who are creating opposition and conflict (2.2, 14). Outgroup members are also on occasion simply referred to as 'the rest' (οἱ λοιποί, 4.13; 5.6) who are physically and spiritually 'outsiders' (οἱ ἔξω 4.12). Such people are those who have no hope (4.13), who fall asleep (5.6) and who will therefore be surprised when the Lord returns (5.4). Hence, they are the children of the night and of darkness (5.5), who sleep and get drunk (5.7) and who are destined for wrath (5.9).[2] Those who do not know God allow their 'lustful passion' to control their bodies (4.5). Paul builds up a picture of the unbeliever by creating various impersonal names for outgroup members (e.g. 'the rest', 'the outsider', 'children of the night') and by ascribing to them behaviour that is deemed immoral and inappropriate. This rhetoric of distinction functions to create a strong metaphorical boundary between the believer and the unbeliever.

However, Paul's focus in this letter is upon the believers, and especially upon their visible expression of faith. Paul describes the great agony and distress that he, Silvanus, and Timothy experienced when they were separated from the Thessalonian believers, and in a slightly strange reversal of the parent–child metaphor used earlier (2.7b, 11), writes that this experience of separation meant that they themselves became like orphans, and Paul emphasizes that he especially never gave up the desire to see them face to face (2.17-18). It becomes clear that this anxiety over their separation is mostly an anxiety about the health and strength of the Thessalonians' faith, and this is the reason Paul sent Timothy to them (εἰς τὸ στηρίξαι ὑμᾶς καὶ παρακαλέσαι ὑπὲρ τῆς πίστεως ὑμῶν, 3.2). Paul is worried about the impact opposition might be having upon their faith (3.3), and Timothy is charged with finding out about their faith for he was afraid that ὁ πειράζων had caused them to turn away from it, causing Paul to lament that their labour would then have been in vain (3.5). As it is, he already believes that their faith is somehow not quite complete (3.10). Unsurprisingly then, encouragement is a thread that runs through the letter, and Paul understands that it is not just his role but the role of each member of the ingroup to encourage and support each member in their faith (παρακαλέω 2.12; 3.2; 4.18; 5.11, 14). Indeed, there is not even a hint of rebuke in the letter (cf. 1 Cor. 1.10-17), nor does Paul devote space to correcting their understanding of the gospel he had previously taught them (cf. Gal. 1.6-9). It is rather a letter of encouragement, of 'positive reinforcement' (Barclay 1992: 51).

Perhaps this is not surprising, as persecution, opposition or suffering is mentioned on many occasions and this forms the backdrop to the whole letter. For example, Paul praises the believers for the joy with which they 'received the word' despite it being ἐν θλίψει πολλῇ (1.6) and ἐν πολλῷ ἀγῶνι (2.2, cf. v. 14), and he is concerned that he should provide enough encouragement so as to prevent their faith from being shaken ἐν ταῖς θλίψεσιν ταύταις (3.3) even though they were warned that this would happen (3.4). Furthermore, Paul instructs the believers not to repay anyone κακὸν ἀντὶ κακοῦ (5.15). There is clearly a significant degree of social conflict in Thessalonica between believers and outsiders. Although the letter lacks any specific description of the nature of this opposition and any specific cause, it is known that as these faith communities grew they attracted a degree of attention and suspicion since believers refused to partake in various social expectations, including the worship of other gods (see also 1 Pet. 4.4). In some areas this suspicion resulted in slander and in other places it resulted in threatening behaviour, arrest and, as history shows us, torture and death.[3] It might be that the Thessalonians were actually 'too good' at turning *en masse* completely away from idols (1.9) and that this sent shock-waves throughout Thessalonica, which was a religiously pluralistic city.[4] Of course, in turning away from these gods the believer was turning towards Jesus Christ and the proclamation that Jesus was Lord and King. This in turn threatened the political stability of the community, for peace and freedom depended upon all citizens displaying loyalty to the emperor.[5] It certainly seems, however, that the Thessalonian believers had not wavered in their belief in Jesus as Lord nor had they been persuaded to turn back to idols since Paul commends them for their faith and their perseverance in proclaiming ὁ λόγος τοῦ κυρίου (1.7-8).

Another factor that might have increased friction between believer and unbeliever was the apparent emphasis in Paul's teaching on the imminent return of Jesus Christ as Lord and Judge. For, as Still asserts, this teaching 'may well have given rise to the charge that the Christians were setting up Jesus as a rival to Caesar' (1999: 77). This emphasis runs throughout the letter itself so that in every single chapter there is an eschatological reference: Paul writes that Jesus will rescue the believers from the coming wrath (1.10), that the Thessalonians are the 'crown of boasting' belonging to Paul, Silvanus, and Timothy before Jesus at his coming (2.19), and Paul prays that the believers would be found blameless at the coming of Christ (3.19; 5.23). They are not to grieve or to worry about other believers who have died before the coming of Christ for they will also be raised up alongside those who are alive (4.13-18), and they are reminded of their difference from outsiders for they are destined for salvation and hope, rather than for grief and wrath (4.13; 5.2-10). Hence, Paul's anxiety concerning the resilience of the Thessalonians' faith in the face of persecution is also driven by a strong belief that Christ's coming is imminent; he is therefore concerned for the believers to be found faithful and blameless for 'the moment of their vindication was near' (Barclay 1992: 51). Without further evidence in the letter itself, we can only (but safely) suggest that the hostility was arising because in this place 'it was perceived to be politically provocative to believe that a new age had dawned outside of the jurisdiction of the civic cult', and also 'that a new savior was present' (Jewett 1986: 132).

Given the opposition that the ingroup appears to be facing from those outside, it is understandable that Paul not only encourages the believers a great deal but also praises them. Using insights from SIT, we can see that this letter would create a positive ingroup identity, persuading ingroup members that, despite their suffering, they still have a better social identity by belonging to this group rather than any other. Thus, as we have seen, he compares them favourably on moral grounds to the outsiders (4.5), but he also compares them favourably to other believing groups in different locations, writing that the Thessalonian believers became τύπον πᾶσιν τοῖς πιστεύουσιν ἐν τῇ Μακεδονίᾳ καὶ ἐν τῇ Ἀχαΐᾳ (1.7). In so doing, a superior identity is created for the Thessalonian believers not only in relation to their immediate context of unbelieving outsiders but also in relation to their wider context of other believing neighbours. Paul is emphasizing their difference in positive terms, and thus raising the self-esteem and importance of members of the ingroup, which is arguably even more important when the ingroup is facing persecution or opposition from outside. The emphasis on the coming of Christ is also functioning to remind the believers of another positive reason to belong to this group rather than any other, for they are destined for safety and salvation.

In the previous chapter we saw that Tajfel and Turner identified three important components of social identity: cognitive, evaluative and emotional (1979: 40). It could be understood that Paul's rhetoric of distinction as explored above enables the ingroup to have a secure cognitive understanding of their own social identity and group membership. Indeed, the cognitive *and* evaluative components of the Thessalonians' social identity is strongly and persuasively constructed within Paul's letter and helps to reinforce a strong boundary between believer and unbeliever specifically by highlighting the difference between the two groups. The third component refers to how membership of a group may be accompanied by certain attitudes and dispositions towards ingroup and outgroup members (Tajfel and Turner 1979: 40; Tajfel 1978: 63; Tajfel 1981: 229, 255). We are led to believe that members of the congregation in Thessalonica looked kindly upon Paul and his companions (3.6), and they are instructed twice to increase in their love for each other (3.12 and 4.10) and τὸ μὴ ὑπερβαίνειν καὶ πλεονεκτεῖν ἐν τῷ πράγματι τὸν ἀδελφὸν αὐτοῦ (4.6), which, given the use of πλεονεξία in 2.5, Witherington argues means that they should not 'act covetously toward the brother' (2006a: 117; see also Best 1972: 166). Again, in a command that uses ἀγάπη, the believers are urged to respect those members who labour among them and who lead them, and to do so 'most exceedingly in love' (καὶ ἡγεῖσθαι αὐτοὺς ὑπερεκπερισσοῦ ἐν ἀγάπῃ, 5.12-13). And the call to find peace among themselves is appealing to a certain attitude of maturity and wisdom that should be upheld among members (5.13). Finally, there is an expectation that believers should each be responsible for caring for and urging along those in their congregation who are struggling in any way (5.14).

There is nothing too surprising here with regard to how believers should view and respond to each other. However, when we turn to assess how the Thessalonian believers are to view outsiders, we do find an interesting occurrence. For, on the one hand, Barclay is surely correct in writing that the apocalyptic language used in the letter 'injects a strong dose of hostility into their attitudes towards others', for outsiders 'are viewed as actual or potential aggressors' and the 'whole of life is a battle-field' (1992: 55). However, on the other hand we discover that in those instructions that provide group norms, the believers are instructed to love one another and *all* (3.12), to walk honourably *with outsiders* (4.11-12), and to seek to do good to *all* rather than repay evil for evil (5.15). These instructions are specifically focused on how the ingroup member should behave towards the outsider, and they also therefore dictate the attitude with which the ingroup member should view the outsider. Thus, in turning back to the main questions of this study, we find that these verses reveal a sensitivity to the presence of outsiders; the rest of this chapter will therefore explore these three instructions in more detail, examining any concern for what these outsiders might think of the insiders, and asking what might be motivating this concern for the outsider. This chapter will thus seek to determine the importance of the outsider in the social identity of the Thessalonian faith community.

2.2 The Dimension of 'All' (3.12; 5.15)

Twice in this letter, whilst Paul is focused upon writing seemingly uncomplicated instructions to the faith community, he then suddenly clarifies that the behaviour he is endorsing is not just to determine ingroup relationships but also to shape relations with outsiders. In 3.12 and 5.15 Paul issues commands whereby the believers are to love one another and 'all' and to pursue whatever is good for one another and 'all'. Rather than the addition of καὶ εἰς πάντας in 3.12 and 5.15 being simply to emphasize that *all* without exception within the ingroup should be the recipients of love and acts of goodness from their fellow believers, Paul appears to widen the focus to include those found outside the faith community, who may even have a high degree of contempt for the insider.

2.2.1 Love one another and all (3.12)

At the end of chapter 3 we find what is sometimes referred to as a 'wish-prayer', where Paul firstly emphasizes his hope and prayer that God would enable him and his colleagues to visit the Thessalonian believers (v. 11), secondly that the believers would be able to increase and abound in love εἰς ἀλλήλους καὶ εἰς πάντας (v. 12), and thirdly that their hearts would be found blameless when Christ returns (v. 13).[6] All three aspects of this prayer are found as concerns throughout the rest of the letter. The first part of this prayer captures the relationship that Paul and his colleagues have with the Thessalonian believers and their desire to be reunited (e.g. 2.17-18; 3.1-3, 6). The final part of the prayer reflects a significant concern for the quality of faith and holiness that is found in the believers (e.g. 2.12; 3.1-3, 5, 10; 4.1-7), and Paul ends the letter once again hoping that their spirit, soul, and body may be kept blameless until the coming of Christ (5.23). The second part of the prayer in 3.12, where Paul uses two synonymous verbs (πλεονάσαι καὶ περισσεύσαι) to express and emphasize the magnitude with which he hopes their love could grow, also draws attention to an important motif in the letter, that of ἀγάπη. For, the Thessalonian believers are not only described as beloved by God (ἀδελφοὶ ἠγαπημένοι ὑπὸ [τοῦ] θεοῦ, 1.4) and beloved to Paul and the other apostles (διότι ἀγαπητοὶ ἡμῖν ἐγενήθητε, 2.8), but they also have a reputation for their 'work of faith and labour of love' (ὑμῶν τοῦ ἔργου τῆς πίστεως καὶ τοῦ κόπου τῆς ἀγάπης, 1.3) which causes Paul, Silvanus and Timothy to give thanks for them in their prayers (1.2). Additionally, despite their suffering, Timothy can report back to Paul about the 'good news' of their faith and love (3.6). In chapter 4 Paul writes concerning ὁ φιλαδελφία and remarks that he need not write anything more on this for firstly they were taught by God to love one another (ἀλλήλους, 4.9) and secondly that they already do this 'to all the brothers in the whole of Macedonia' (εἰς πάντας τοὺς ἀδελφοὺς [τοὺς] ἐν ὅλῃ τῇ Μακεδονίᾳ, 4.10). Nevertheless, Paul does in fact continue to write more about love for he encourages them to 'abound more' in love for one another (4.10, using the same verb here for 'abound', πλεονάζω as in 3.12), and in chapter 5 reminds the believers that they have clothed themselves with a 'breastplate of faith and love' (θώρακα πίστεως καὶ ἀγάπης, 5.8) and that they should 'respect' those in leadership with a great love (5.13).

From these references it is clear that faith and love are linked together and that they should characterize the ingroup, whereby believers should let faith and love direct their actions towards one another and shape their attitude to others. Paul does not indicate what he means by their 'work of love' (κόπος τῆς ἀγάπης, 1.3) and whether or not this impacts upon their relationships with outsiders, but the other references are largely concerned with how the believers should relate to other believers and how they should increase and challenge themselves to love one another even more (4.10; 5.13). The command to love in this letter largely has an inward frame of reference. The one exception to this is found in the instruction to love 'one another and all' in 3.12, which, as the fifth of these nine references to love, finds itself nestled in the middle (1.3, 4; 2.8; 3.6, 12; 4.9, 10; 5.8, 13). This love-command is unusual because of the addition of καὶ εἰς πάντας. As such, whilst Fee acknowledges that in 1 Thess. 3.12 Paul might mean that their love could 'also embrace their enemies', he sees that καὶ εἰς πάντας is an ambiguous 'add-on' and should not be pressed or given too much weight, for v. 13 brings the focus of love back onto 'internal relationships' (2009: 132).[7] Malherbe argues that although Paul is referring to unbelievers in 1 Thess. 3.12, this only means those unbelievers who happen to be present in the 'Christian assemblies' rather than all those who are outside the faith community (2000: 213).[8]

In contrast, many other scholars argue that, despite the suffering of the believers for their faith, Paul insists that they should not live apart from outsiders but rather include outsiders in their offering of love, driven by their faith.[9] Although both Holtz and Wanamaker are keen not to ignore the importance of the command to love one another since this new community of converts was 'heterogeneous' (Holtz 1986: 144), consisting of people from 'varying social and economic strata within the communion' (Wanamaker 1990: 142–3), they both note that the addition of καὶ εἰς πάντας is a desire for this command to trespass the boundary and include outsiders.[10] Furnish argues that 'all' refers not to 'the whole of humankind' but to local unbelievers 'with whom the Thessalonian believers are in daily and continuing contact' (2002: 109). However, as Horrell notes, this is 'an unnecessary and vacuous distinction' (2016: 289); the importance of Paul including 'and all' is rooted in the fact that he commands believers to love the 'other', the 'outsider'. In addition, the very fact that Paul has often referred to the Thessalonians' suffering and persecution in the letter even before this instruction in 3.12 means that it would not be unusual for him to suddenly refer to those outside the faith community (e.g. 1.6; 2.14; 3.1-5).

Furthermore, this additional dimension of 'all' appears to come with divine blessing. Although verse 12 indicates Paul's own hope and prayer for the believers to 'increase and abound in love for one another and for all', it also carries with it a presumption that this is something that would not only come with divine approval, but would also be caused by divine power. He writes, 'and may the Lord cause you to increase and abound in love' (ὑμᾶς δὲ ὁ κύριος πλεονάσαι καὶ περισσεύσαι τῇ ἀγάπῃ εἰς ἀλλήλους καὶ εἰς πάντας, v. 12). Even if part of the motivation behind loving all is for the believers to be found blameless and holy at the parousia (v. 13), it still nevertheless indicates that *God* thinks it is important how believers respond to unbelievers, and here, with reference to love, that they should treat them indiscriminately in the same way that they would view and treat fellow believers.[11] Paul seems to understand that God imbues value on outsiders by desiring for them to draw the attention of and be the objects of the believers' love. The mere presence of outsiders, and the value God gives to them signals in turn their importance in the formation and understanding of the social identity of believers – in other words, in how the believers understand their identity and reason for existence (the cognitive component), and in how they understand they are to view not only fellow insiders but also outsiders (their emotional component). And, if the believers' love for outsiders does result in keeping their hearts blameless or in establishing their hearts as such, then this also reveals the important place that outsiders have in enabling insiders to achieve their group goals, and perhaps even more significantly, how they are to be found, and judged, in the parousia.

2.2.2 Pursue the good for one another and for all (5.15)

Returning to the addition of 'and to all', there is further evidence in the letter itself (and in the wider Pauline corpus) that this addition is intended to apply an outward focus to the love-command. For, in chapter 5 there is another verse that attracts our attention: ὁρᾶτε μή τις κακὸν ἀντὶ κακοῦ τινι ἀποδῷ, ἀλλὰ πάντοτε τὸ ἀγαθὸν διώκετε [καὶ] εἰς ἀλλήλους καὶ εἰς πάντας (5.15). Thus, after urging believers not to render to anyone evil for evil, we find the same phrase applied to the action of pursuing good works, that these should be 'for one another and for all'.[12] This instruction is similarly found in the middle of a passage which is focused upon the believers' internal relationships: in verses 12-14 believers are told how to respond to different members of the ingroup, and in verses 16-22 instructions are given as to how the believers should form their own character and spirituality. Thus, given the internal focus of the passage anyway, if the instruction to persevere in doing good was intended to be only for the benefit of insiders, then there would be no need for καὶ εἰς πάντας. But the addition of this phrase indicates that believers should also pursue doing good towards those outside the faith community.[13] Thus, Wanamaker argues that here Paul 'demands an unqualified concern on the part of all his readers for the well-being of both those within and outside the community' (1990: 199). Moreover, Paul gives the command in such a way that implies that this is a community responsibility to 'see to it' (ὁρᾶτε) that *no one* retaliates with evil, but that *everyone* should pursue what is good for *all*. The use of ὁρᾶτε both signals the community responsibility for the following command and emphasizes the importance of the command. Similarly, the use of the verb διώκω to describe how believers are to pursue 'the good' for all people also emphasizes this importance.[14] This verb carries with it a sense that the believers must continually seek to do good to all people, rather than it being something that is 'done at one's convenience' (Fee 2009: 212), and this is also emphasized with Paul's use of πάντοτε.

There is some discussion as to what 'pursuing the good' means and several scholars argue that Paul is using τὸ ἀγαθόν to refer to acts of love. Morris for example argues that this instruction must 'refer to acts of love in the face of hostility rather than to ethical goodness in general' (1991: 171) and Best that it is neither referring to 'a moral idea' nor is it originating from 'an ethical system' but rather the command to do good comes 'from God himself, who loves and demands love' (1972: 234; also Neil 1950: 126). The 'good' which Paul refers to is therefore 'expressed in loving activity' (Best 1972: 234). So too, Holtz sees that although Paul does not specify what doing good looks like, nevertheless this instruction: 'calls for all action to be constantly and entirely directed towards the formation of love' ('Und sie ruft dazu, alles Handeln beständig und ganz auf die Gestaltwerdung der Liebe gerichtet sein zu lassen', 1986: 256). Furnish points to 1 Cor. 14.1 where Paul instructs the believers to 'pursue love' (Διώκετε τὴν ἀγάπην) and also to Rom. 12.9-21 where 'good' and 'love' are used interchangeably (2002: 110), and concludes that doing good means 'acting with love' (2002: 111). However, this is unpersuasive as an argument as Paul often uses the verb διώκω with reference to pursuing many different things (righteousness in Rom. 9.30, 31; hospitality in Rom. 12.13; peace in Rom. 14.19), and the use of ἀγάπη and ἀγαθόν in the same passage is not necessarily an indication that they are synonymous. In contrast, Malherbe argues that, considering that the immediate context of the passage is about issues of pastoral care, then 'the good in mind is that which is achieved through pastoral care' and hence that it is about acting in a way that would be beneficial to outsiders, rather than causing injury or harm (2000: 322).

There is no doubt that one cannot separate love from goodness; however, since Paul has already commanded the believers to love the outsider (3.12), the use of τὸ ἀγαθόν in 5.15 suggests that he is advocating a nuanced way of behaving towards outsiders. Thus, rather than love (3.12) and good (5.15) being used interchangeably, Paul is deliberately using τὸ ἀγαθόν to give a slightly more focused example of how they are to behave towards outsiders, and of course it is an action that is presented as the opposite of the evil that they themselves may receive. In this case then, doing good would mean that the believers should focus on actions for and towards outsiders that would seek to bless them and edify them, rather than evil which seeks to destroy and humiliate. Secondly, given that in 4.12 he encourages the believers to consider how outsiders might view them (as we shall explore below), it would follow that in 5.15 he is asking the believers to consider what is good in the eyes of outsiders, or what actions they would receive as being good in the sense of being beneficial to them. The believers are to recognize a shared sense of what is good, and to let this shape their behaviour towards outsiders. Hence, Malherbe's interpretation above would seem to be the most persuasive. Thus, pursuing the good means that the believers must constantly seek ways in which they can act and show goodness to one another and the outsider, and in a way that is beneficial rather than harmful to the recipient.

Therefore, although scholars differ in their exact understanding of what is envisaged by 'doing' or 'working' good, they are generally united in their understanding that here, Paul is signalling that the believers should be concerned not just with their inner community but also with those outside it.[15] Betz sees this as an extension of God's redemptive character displayed for all of humanity: 'If God's redemption in Christ is universal, the Christian community is obliged to disregard all ethnic, national, cultural, social, sexual, and even religious distinctions within the human community' (1979: 311). Ngewa adds a nuance that is neither implicit nor explicit in the text, for he comments that although there should be no partiality in how believers behave, believers are called first to 'meet the needs among ourselves' and then believers can 'move out to help all others as we have resources' (2010: 163). However, Paul is not signalling that believers should give what is left to outsiders; rather, he sees believers as having enough of an ability and capacity to do what is good for all people, which undeniably includes the inner community, but which does not see the outsiders as beneficiaries of only the scraps of good works.

2.2.3 Work the good towards all (Galatians 6.10)

Thus, returning to Paul's addition of 'all' to these two commands of love and of doing good, it is perhaps also helpful to note that we find a very similar phrase in Galatians: ἄρα οὖν ὡς καιρὸν ἔχομεν, ἐργαζώμεθα τὸ ἀγαθὸν πρὸς πάντας, μάλιστα δὲ πρὸς τοὺς οἰκείους τῆς πίστεως (6.10). This verse is equally nestled in a passage that is broadly about discipleship and specifically about letting the Spirit of God rule over the flesh of the believer so that the way in which they can live is full of good fruit and good work. Paul urges his Galatian readers to persevere in doing what is right and in 'sowing to the Spirit' (6.8), and thereby they should use every opportunity to work what is good 'towards all people and especially the household of faith' (6.10). Here it can clearly be seen, because of the clarification of the phrase τοὺς οἰκείους τῆς πίστεως, that when Paul uses πάντας he means all people including those outside the household of faith. Martyn notes that Paul is reminding his readers that 'God is summoning his new creation onto the world scene by calling into existence the church that exists for the sake of "all"' (1997: 554; also Meiser 2007: 306–8), and Dunn that 'Paul did not seek to encourage his churches to turn in upon themselves or to hide away from the world' (1993: 332). Thus, when we look at all three verses (Gal. 6.10; 1 Thess. 3.12 and 5.15), we see that there is a command (to love or to do good), an identification of the recipients, followed by a further clarification. In 1 Thess. 3.12 and 5.15 the first identification is simply pointing to the community of faith with the use of εἰς ἀλλήλους and then follows the clarification: καὶ εἰς πάντας. In Gal. 6.10 the order of identification is reversed so that the first identification is πρὸς πάντας followed by the more specific τοὺς οἰκείους τῆς πίστεως.

However, a few scholars when commenting on Gal. 6.10 appear to be reticent about putting too much emphasis upon Paul's use of πᾶς and thus largely dismiss it as insignificant and are unwilling to engage with its meaning, impact and motivation. Thus, whilst Matera, Keener and Esler acknowledge that the command to do good in Gal. 6.10 is directed to all people, they nevertheless only focus on the latter part of the verse, writing that 'the members of the Church have a special claim upon their charity' (Matera 1992: 223), that the 'first priority' of the believers was to attend to the 'needs of their spiritual household' (Keener 2018: 278) and that 'it is hard to know how much emphasis Paul placed on this obligation [to do good to all] given his preoccupation with life inside the communities and the heavily negative stereotypes he applies to those outside' (Esler 1998: 233). Perhaps this reticence is to do with what Esler rightly highlights, that Paul elsewhere and in these letters seems to create a rhetorical divide between believer and unbeliever. However, as we noted in Chapter 1, this is not the whole picture, for throughout the Pauline corpus there is a notable collection of verses which specifically turn the attention of the believer to the outsider, signalling the importance of their presence and opinion.

There are also other verses that echo 1 Thess. 3.12; 5.15 and Gal. 6.10. For example, in Rom. 12.17 (which we shall look at in detail in Chapter 3) Paul urges the believers to 'take thought for what is good in the sight of all' (ἐνώπιον πάντων ἀνθρώπων). However, this instruction is followed with a reassurance that God will avenge (vv. 19-20) and so the good acts of the believers are done in the knowledge that 'God's wrath will exact retribution in the judgment so that it is unnecessary for Christians to avenge themselves in the here and now' (Wanamaker 1990: 199).[16] Rather, in 1 Thess. 5.15 Paul shows an 'unqualified concern … for the well-being of both those within and outside the community without offering either negative or positive motivation' (1990: 199). Additionally, in Phil. 4.5 Paul writes: 'let your gentleness be known to all people' (πᾶσιν ἀνθρώποις). Many scholars agree that here the frame of reference for πᾶσιν ἀνθρώποις is universal and hence includes outsiders; it may especially mean those who are hostile (Marshall 1991: 112; Osiek 2000: 115–116) and therefore that Paul is advocating for the believers to focus not on their own unjust suffering, but upon 'a fundamental element of Christian behaviour: preferring others above themselves' (Silva 2005: 194). It can be seen then that the case for understanding καὶ εἰς πάντας in 1 Thess. 3.12 and 5.15 as referring to outsiders is supported by similar verses found throughout the Pauline corpus, which are also largely found in letters where there is also a backdrop of persecution.

2.2.4 Summary

Paul signals early on in 1 Thess. 3.12 that a norm that should characterize every believer is that they should endeavour to apply the dimension of 'all' to some of their actions, namely in their abundant offering of love (3.12) and in their pursuit of doing what is good (5.15). The boundary between believer and unbeliever is still firmly in place, but the boundary is not a wall without gates; and one of these gates is constituted by 'love' and the other by 'good acts'. Paul urges the believers to deepen their love and care for each other, but in so doing, apply as much commitment to demonstrating their love and care for the outsider. However, this does not come from Paul alone, but appears to have divine approval and causation: it is the Lord who can make believers abound in love for all, including outsiders, and Paul prays that this would be so in Thessalonica. This would have had a powerful impact on the believers' understanding of their relationship with outsiders, for despite the conflict they are to show a concern for the outsider and are not simply to love the outsider but are to seek to 'increase and abound in love' for them, just in the same way that Paul and the other apostles 'abound in love' for the Thessalonian believers (3.12b). Nor are they simply to 'do good' to others but are to see this as a way of life that they need to pursue and prioritize as an identity marker of a believer. These two verses reveal the importance of the outsider on how the insider understands their own social identity. They reveal how the outsider contributes to the insiders' understanding of how God views all people, regardless of group identity, and therefore on how they are to shape their norms, attitudes and even beliefs. I have also argued that the quality of the believer's heart as seen at the parousia is in some way dependent upon how they treat the unbeliever (3.12-13); in other words, the unbeliever holds an important role *now* in how the believer will ultimately be seen by God at the coming of Christ.

Thus, whereas SIT, built on the experiments by Tajfel and his colleagues (1970: 96–102), proposes that a person's understanding of belonging to one group will lead them to treat outgroup members in a very different way as to how they would treat ingroup members (and perhaps with a bias to discriminate against outgroup members and to favour ingroup members), Paul is adamant that whereas the outsiders in Thessalonica may treat believers with negative discrimination, believers are to treat outsiders with love and goodness in the same way that they would treat insiders. Although Paul builds up a negative stereotype of the unbelievers and categorizes them as those who are far from God, this should not shape how the believers are to behave (negatively) among them and towards them. In fact, by placing the expectation for believers to love outsiders within a 'wish-prayer', Paul is signalling that this action is related to an important group belief, for this action is also understood by Paul to be authorized by and enabled by God. Hence, although Bar-Tal is surely correct that 'group beliefs may determine the attitudes and behaviours of an outgroup towards the group' (1998: 111), we see here that group beliefs also determine the attitudes and behaviours of an ingroup towards the outgroup. Moreover, this consistent and intentional show of love and of good to the outsider would have the potential to have a positive impact on how the outsider views the insider, perhaps even to change how the outsider stereotypes the believers, although this is not articulated by Paul here. Nevertheless, these two verses in 3.12 and 5.15 reveal a sensitivity towards the outsider and a concern for their presence, with an implicit concern for what they think. Later in the letter, however, we do find a verse that explicitly exposes a concern for how outsiders view and experience insiders, and it is to this verse that we shall now turn.

2.3 The Influence of 'With' (4.11-12)

1 Thessalonians 4 begins with Paul urging his readers to remember and put into action the instructions they had previously taught the Thessalonian believers, specifically how δεῖ ὑμᾶς περιπατεῖν καὶ ἀρέσκειν θεῷ (4.1). The following verses continue with Paul reminding them what instructions (group norms) they had already given to the believers, and they function to provide specific details on *how* they should live and please God (vv. 2-12). The first collection of group norms is around what it means for the believers to live in holiness (vv. 2-8), and the second collection begins with inward-looking instructions but finishes with a clear focus on the outsider (vv. 9-12). Thus, in the same way that the believers are encouraged to walk in God's way and please God more and more (περισσεύητε μᾶλλον, 4.1b), they are also reminded that the love they have for one another (ἡ φιλαδελφία, 4.9) should abound more and more (περισσεύειν μᾶλλον, 4.10b). However, Paul then also urges them to 'aspire to live quietly' (φιλοτιμεῖσθαι ἡσυχάζειν), to 'mind their own affairs' (πράσσειν τὰ ἴδια), and thirdly to 'work with their own hands' (ἐργάζεσθαι ταῖς [ἰδίαις] χερσὶν ὑμῶν, v. 11). But it seems that the reason for this is: ἵνα περιπατῆτε εὐσχημόνως πρὸς τοὺς ἔξω

καὶ μηδενὸς χρείαν ἔχητε (v. 12), which gives a textual link back to 4.1, when Paul calls the believers to 'to live and please God' (περιπατεῖν καὶ ἀρέσκειν θεῷ). The use of περιπατέω with regard to how believers should live with reference to God and with reference to outsiders subtly suggests that these two ways of living are not entirely distinct, so that how the believer is to live 'properly' among outsiders is also how the believer is to 'please' God.

From a brief overview of this passage, it becomes apparent that throughout this section there are some repetitions and themes. Firstly, Paul refers several times to the fact that the following teaching has already been given to the believers (4.1, 2, 6, 9, 11), and secondly that the purpose of reminding them of this teaching is so that they are even more able to walk or live according to God's ways and please him (4.1) and that they can live 'decently' among outsiders and 'be dependent on no one' (4.12).[17] Thirdly, the image of 'walking' is used to describe how they should behave and live with reference to God (v. 1) but also with reference to the outsiders (τοὺς ἔξω, v. 12), and fourthly, the theme of holiness or decency pervades the passage, again with reference to God and to the outsider. As such, the believers are to control their bodies ἐν ἁγιασμῷ καὶ τιμῇ (v. 4, which is in contrast to the inability of the Gentiles to do so, v. 5), they are called by God not to live in impurity but ἐν ἁγιασμῷ (v. 7), and finally they are to walk in a manner that is decent and respectable (εὐσχημόνως, v. 12) towards outsiders.

It is verse 12 that firstly demands our attention. For not only does Paul specifically refer here to 'the outsiders' (τοὺς ἔξω, 4.12), but he also reveals a concern for how the believers are to behave among these outsiders. Although some commentators debate which of the previous instructions are linked to the ability to live decently among outsiders (we shall return to this in Section 2.3.3), it is apparent that at least some of them are intended to enable the believers to live among their outsiders in a way that is perceived as decent or honourable. Thus, just as Paul intends for the believers to live in a way that would be pleasing to God, he also intends for them to live in a way that would be seen as being honourable to the outsiders. He stops short of saying that the believers should 'please' the outsiders, but the thrust of the instruction is clear – the believers are to take thought for how the outsiders are to perceive, receive and think of the believers in their relations with them. We shall turn first to examine verse 12a, specifically looking at what Paul might mean by using the adverb εὐσχημόνως and the verb περιπατέω in describing the relationship between the believer and the unbeliever; this will then provide a framework within which it is easier to see how the preceding instructions are connected to a concern for and sensitivity towards the outsider.

2.3.1 Walking honourably (4.12a)

Paul hopes that the believers will recognize the presence and the importance of outsiders in how they shape their lives, for they are to make sure that they can 'walk' with outsiders in a way that is honourable or decent (ἵνα περιπατῆτε εὐσχημόνως πρὸς τοὺς ἔξω, 4.12a). The verb περιπατέω is used by Paul earlier in the letter in 2.12 and twice in 4.1. In these verses it is always used to describe how the believers should behave with and relate to God. Thus, he reminds the believers of how, when he and the other apostles were with them, they were like a father with his children (2.11) in urging and desiring for them 'to walk worthily of God' (περιπατεῖν ὑμᾶς ἀξίως τοῦ θεοῦ, 2.12). Again, in 4.1 he reminds them of this previous instruction, this time with the addition of his desire for them to please God: περιπατεῖν καὶ ἀρέσκειν θεῷ, together with a swift confirmation that they are indeed walking with God (καθὼς καὶ περιπατεῖτε), and a final plea for them to do so more and more. It is not difficult to pick up here a sense of anxiety and urgency in the voice of Paul; he is both convinced of and convincing about the need for the believers to be found living in a way that is appropriate and fitting for the one who is a child of God, that they should not become lacklustre in this or even satisfied with their progress but that they should strive to do so more and more. This image of 'walking' also conveys the sense that the one walking is not doing so alone, but in reference to and in sight of the other – in this case, God. Their style of walking (in other words, their style of living) is not done so in isolation but in companionship with other believers *and* with God, and it is *God* who determines the direction of walking.

Just a few verses later, however, we now find the expectation that the Thessalonian believers should also strive to live in a certain way precisely so that they 'walk honourably with outsiders' (4.12a).[18] In the same way that the commands to love all (3.12) and to do good to all (5.15) appear to be abrupt insertions into passages that are largely about internal relations and expectations of the believer, here we also find this goal on how to 'walk' with outsiders abruptly inserted into a passage that appears to be largely about how to walk according to the ways of God, and using a word that is previously only used to describe the relationship between the Thessalonian believers and God. Paul however gives very little detail to what this means for the believer or the outsider, so that it reads as if it should be self-explanatory, or at the very least that the reader should find this goal unsurprising rather than unusual. It will therefore be helpful to look to the rest of the Pauline corpus to discover firstly how the image of 'walk' is used, and secondly to the description that this should be done 'honourably'.

2.3.1a Περιπατέω

Paul uses περιπατέω generally to describe the two ways in which one can choose to live: according to the flesh (and so this describes the believers' past behaviour, but also that they can revert back to this lifestyle), or according to the Spirit (e.g. Rom. 6.4; 8.4; 14.15; Gal. 5.16; Phil. 3.17, 18; 2 Cor. 3.3; 4.2; 10.2, 3; 12.18; also Eph. 2.2, 10; 4.1, 17; 5.2, 8, 15; Col. 2.6; 3.7). In a slightly different vein, we also find Paul encouraging the believers in Corinth to walk or live according to the situation in life to which God has called them, whether that is as circumcised or not, as a slave or free, married or single (1 Cor. 7.17). Amidst the many references in the undisputed letters, one in particular stands out for it also employs εὐσχημόνως in connection with the use of περιπατέω: Rom. 13.13. However, the use of περιπατέω here is not exclusively to do with behaviour among outsiders, although the wider context shows that Paul is concerned about how believers relate with outsiders and how they are viewed by outsiders. We therefore find that the connection between the metaphorical use of περιπατέω and outsiders is rarely found in the undisputed letters, being explicit in 1 Thess. 4.12a and implicit in Rom. 13.13.

Nevertheless, when we turn to the disputed letters, there is quite a startling similarity found in Col. 4.5, where we find the author instructing the believers: Ἐν σοφίᾳ περιπατεῖτε πρὸς τοὺς ἔξω τὸν καιρὸν ἐξαγοραζόμενοι.[19] This is found in a passage that is conscious of the opportunities believers may have to evangelize: firstly, the believers are asked to pray for the apostles, that they might have the chance λαλῆσαι τὸ μυστήριον τοῦ Χριστοῦ (4.3), and secondly, after the believers are urged to 'walk' wisely among the outsiders, the hope is that their own words would always be spoken with grace, and having been seasoned with salt, that they would know how to provide an answer (4.6). The instruction to 'walk wisely' must be connected with their ability to engage in fruitful discourse about the gospel of Christ; the attention is undeniably fixed upon the outsider and the potential for a good response of the outsider to witnessing the behaviour and words of the believer. Interestingly, earlier in the letter the Colossian believers are instructed: περιπατῆσαι ἀξίως τοῦ κυρίου εἰς πᾶσαν ἀρεσκείαν (Col. 1.10; also 2.6). This echoes the instruction in 1 Thess. 4.1, where believers are περιπατεῖν καὶ ἀρέσκειν θεῷ. We find then that in both 1 Thessalonians and Colossians, the believers are to live a life that is worthy of and pleasing to God (1 Thess. 4.1; Col. 1.10) and also a life that is appropriate and good with regard to outsiders.

The use of the verb περιπατέω together with 'outsider' in 1 Thess. 4.12a and Col. 4.3 illustrates that although it is rare to find these two terms used together, there is a stream of consciousness that pervaded some early Christian thought and teaching that recognized the importance for believers not to hide away from the rest of society or even to form a self-enclosed ghetto, but rather to keep on 'walking' alongside unbelievers. Furthermore, from all of these passages, it is clear that the verb περιπατέω is a holistic term simply used to refer to the external life of the believer, in how they ought to 'live' *with reference to others,* whether that is with reference to God (and thus his desires) or with reference to outsiders (and thus what they would find respectful or beneficial). This can be accompanied with a further clarification – that believers are to live 'pleasing' God (1 Thess. 4.1) or that they should live 'wisely' (Col. 4.5), and in 1 Thess. 4.12a Paul uses the adverb εὐσχημόνως to describe *how* the believers are to visibly live among outsiders. We will turn now to explore this adverb.

2.3.1b Εὐσχημόνως

This word is only used three times in the NT, all in Pauline passages where there is a concern for the outsider, specifically for how the outsider views the believer. Thus, it is used in Rom. 13.13 where Paul urges the believers to behave in a way that is appropriate or decent (εὐσχημόνως περιπατήσωμεν) for the one who lives in the light in contrast to those who conduct their lives in 'works of darkness' (Rom. 13.12-13). The wider context here is that Paul is instructing the believers to behave excellently among one another but also towards outsiders including their persecutors (12.9-21; 13.8-10), to think of what is good in the eyes of all people (ἐνώπιον πάντων ἀνθρώπων, 12.17) and to behave so as to win praise from the rulers and leaders in society (13.3; we will explore all of this in more detail in Chapter 3). This adverb is also used in 1 Cor. 14.40, where Paul uses it to describe how the believers' worship should be conducted, commenting that πάντα δὲ εὐσχημόνως καὶ κατὰ τάξιν γινέσθω. This is a concluding statement after a lengthy chapter pertaining to the appropriateness of speaking in tongues or prophesying within gathered worship, where the believers are charged to conduct their worship carefully and peaceably giving thought to what an outsider might say or to how they might react to some forms of their worship (14.23-25).

Paul uses εὐσχημόνως in both of these passages to mean 'decently' or to denote 'blameless' behaviour, but the important point is that it is not just about what is considered to be decent in their own eyes, but in the eyes of the outsiders.[20] There is in these passages an exhortation to behave in excellent ways that are worthy of commendation not just from the fellow believer but also from the neighbouring outsider, and as such, Paul urges the believers to consider how their behaviour might be interpreted by the outsider (and adjusted accordingly, where necessary). Furthermore, the concern is set upon making sure that the interpretation is one that is good, whereby the outsider sees the decency of the believer in ways that they admire and value. As Greeven notes regarding the use of this term, 'there is agreement with non-Christians who might criticise Christian conduct' (1964: 770). In secular use of this term, it is used to refer to 'good external appearance', which is also 'applied to the whole external and internal conduct and attitude' (Greeven 1964: 771). Paul recognizes that there is an overlap between the insider and the outsider regarding what is considered blameless, or decent, but also when it is used as an adjective (εὐσχήμων) this word is used to describe someone who is 'considered especially worthy of public admiration' (Bauer et al. 2000: 414; see Mk 15.43; Acts 13.50; 17.12). It therefore carries with it not just a sense of 'decency' but also a sense of admirability – whosoever is found to be acting 'decently' or 'honourably' will also win public admiration.

2.3.1c Summary of 4.12a

Thus, turning back to our passage in 1 Thess. 4.1-12, the overall concern is for the believers to be ever more attentive to how they behave and conduct their lives, that they should strive to live ever more holy lives which will please God. However, Paul then connects their behaviour and conduct also with a concern for outsiders and uses εὐσχημόνως to urge the believers to pay attention to how they should live in a way that is not only considered decent in the eyes of the outsiders but also admired by outsiders. We therefore find not only a concern for outsiders but also a concern for how outsiders perceive and receive the behaviour of the believers; and underlying this there is also an acknowledgement that whatever constitutes decent or respectable behaviour is seen to be such by those who are believers *and* those who are outsiders. Indeed, if εὐσχημόνως does not refer to decent behaviour in the eyes of the *outsider*, then it is rather unnecessary to mention this at all. Paul could have instructed the believers to walk in 'holiness' towards outsiders (using ἁγιασμός as in 4.7); but the understanding of what holiness looks like in practice is anchored in and determined by the believers, and not the outsiders. The use of εὐσχημόνως, however, is a more general term that evokes an understanding that is anchored in a social norm, and it is this that determines what behaving decently should look like in practice. Behaving decently here is not defined by believers, but rather by outsiders, by what is already agreed to be socially acceptable behaviour.

Remembering Barth's theory that for interaction between groups there needs to be a reduction of difference across the boundary and a 'similarity ... of culture' (1969: 15), then what Paul articulates here in 1 Thess. 4.12 is precisely a point of 'similarity of culture'. However, this area of similarity becomes not just a contact point between insider and outsider where the two can have meaningful interaction without conflict, but also what I would term an *attraction point*. Believers living 'honourably' do not just avoid criticism or conflict – they attract admiration. And of course, with admiration comes the possibility that outsiders might also aspire to be like them, and Holtz asks if there is 'a missionary intention' behind this instruction ('Man wird annehmen dürfen, daß eine missionarische Absicht dahinter steht', 1986: 180). This might be so; but what demands our immediate attention is the fact that Paul identifies that this hope for believers to live honourably among outsiders is the result of them living according to the three short instructions in verse 11, namely that they should 'aspire to live quietly, to mind their own affairs and to work with their own hands'. It is to these that we shall now turn.

2.3.2 The way to walk honourably

It appears that the way in which the believer can walk honourably with outsiders is indicated in the three infinitive instructions found in v. 11, with which the believers have already been charged (καθὼς ὑμῖν παρηγγείλαμεν, v. 11), and which leads Paul to use ἵνα at the beginning of v. 12. Paul urges believers: 'aspire to live quietly and to mind your own affairs and to work with your own hands' (καὶ φιλοτιμεῖσθαι ἡσυχάζειν καὶ πράσσειν τὰ ἴδια καὶ ἐργάζεσθαι ταῖς ἰδίαις χερσὶν ὑμῶν, v. 11). However, these instructions have drawn a plethora of translations and interpretations, and it is not even agreed that all three instructions lead to the first purpose clause in verse 12 of the believers being able to 'walk respectably among outsiders'. Wanamaker for example argues that the third instruction 'to work with your own hands' is only connected to the final clause in v. 12, that 'you may have need of nothing' (1990: 163–4).[21] He refers to 2 Thess. 3.6-12 and 1 Thess. 5.14 to argue that there was a problem with self-sufficiency, where some believers were becoming lazy and relying on the goodness of others for their own needs. He suggests that in 1 Thess. 4.11 we see Paul's concern for not wanting the command to love one another to be 'exploited' whereby poorer members were over-reliant on wealthier members for financial help.

However, there is no evidence that this is a problem in this passage or in the wider letter; the encouragement to admonish οἱ ἄτακτοι in 5.14 is probably referring not to those who are abandoning their employment but to those who are 'disorderly, insubordinate' (Bauer et al. 2000: 148).[22] And, unlike Wanamaker, there are many other scholars who propose that the three instructions in v. 11 are all related and thus 'it would be artificial to separate them' (Malherbe 2000: 250). Before exploring how these instructions are connected to living honourably with outsiders, we will firstly examine the possible meaning behind each instruction in turn.

2.3.2a Living quietly and minding your own affairs

The first instruction in v. 11 is for the believers 'to aspire to live quietly' (φιλοτιμεῖσθαι ἡσυχάζειν). Both of these words are fairly rare in Paul's letters: Paul only uses this first word φιλοτιμέομαι for 'aspiring' or having 'ambition' in two other places: in Rom. 15.20 (where he describes his aspiration to proclaim the good news) and in 2 Cor. 5.9 (to describe his ambition to please the Lord). And the verb ἡσυχάζω is only found here in Paul's letters, and refers to living a quiet or peaceable life (Bauer et al. 2000: 440), one that is tranquil (Morris 1991: 131). As such, Best notes the oxymoron here in 1 Thess. 4.11, for the believers are urged to 'be ambitious to be ambitionless' (1972: 174). This could mean that the believers should strive not to be 'disruptive regarding the lives of others' (Fee 2009: 162), and hence this instruction is very much connected to the second instruction in v. 11, where Paul asks the believers 'to do your own things' (πράσσειν τὰ ἴδια). This is an encouragement to mind their own affairs, not to be concerned with or to interfere in those of another person.

Some scholars argue that the language used in these first two instructions is 'unmistakably political' (Hock 1980: 46) and that Paul's meaning can only be understood fully if we examine these words and idioms 'in the context of Greek social philosophy and practice' (Malherbe 2000: 246). Thus, Malherbe argues that φιλοτιμέομαι means 'to love or seek after honor' and provides examples from writers such as Aristotle, Epictetus, Philo and Plutarch to show that it came to be used to describe the 'endeavor of the ambitious man' who longed for fame and reputation and sought this through becoming involved in the political life and public affairs (2000: 246). Paul, however, instructs the believers to be ambitious about having a 'quiet life' and about 'minding their own affairs', which is 'diametrically opposed to Plutarch's view of things' (Malherbe 2000: 247) for it essentially encouraged believers to withdraw from 'active participation in political and social affairs' (2000: 247).[23] That Paul deliberately used this political language is important in Winter's theory that he was calling believers who were caught up in client relationships with patrons (or those who were tempted to enter into such a relationship), to leave the public and civic domain and the interests of their patron (1994: 48–50). It was impossible to live a 'quiet life' if, as a client, your responsibility was to make sure that your patron's name and generosity were well known throughout the political arena, and thus Paul calls the believers to turn away from this type of life and become self-sufficient.

However, whilst it is not necessary for us to get too drawn into this lengthy conversation here, there are several points of argument against the interpretation that Paul is deliberately using political language and therefore advising believers to withdraw from political life. Firstly, it is important to note that when Paul uses φιλοτιμέομαι elsewhere it is only used in the sphere of faith and not of politics (Rom. 15.20 and 2 Cor. 5.9); Witherington also shows how φιλοτιμέομαι evolved from its original sense of pursuing honour in political contexts to a later and 'lesser sense' of aspire, as we find in Paul's use of this term in 1 Thess. 4.11 (2006a: 121). Secondly, a concern over the believer's involvement in civic affairs is not seen elsewhere in the letter, and one would think that if this was a concern for Paul, he would explain it in more detail or at least revisit it throughout the letter, as he does with other concerns.

Thirdly, these instructions are given to all of the believers; if we are to believe that these are political instructions then this presupposes that most of the believers are involved in political and civic affairs, which is clearly not the case (also Holtz 1986: 176).[24] Fourthly, and more significantly, if many believers were involved in political affairs, the order to abandon their duty to the state or their civic involvement could potentially be seen as a passive-aggressive move that stated a withdrawal of concern for the wider society; this then would result in the opposite of 'walking respectably' among outsiders (v. 12) and would indeed increase tension between believers and outsiders. Hence, it is much more likely that there is nothing complicated behind these two instructions, and that Paul is simply calling the believers to be quiet rather than disruptive and to be diligent rather than nosey.

2.3.2b Work with your own hands

The third instruction in verse 11 helps to develop these goals, for Paul asks the believers to focus on keeping themselves busy with their own work: καὶ ἐργάζεσθαι ταῖς [ἰδίαις] χερσὶν ὑμῶν ('and to work with your own hands'). Scholars are divided over what type of work Paul is referring to here and there is little consensus regarding Paul's intention. Some argue that this idiom refers specifically to manual labour (e.g. Neil 1950: 88; Best 1972: 175), whereas Fee notes that it would rather refer to 'work of any and all kinds' (2009: 162 footnote 22), and Richard goes one step further and ascertains (without weighty evidence or persuasion) that it 'refers not to manual labor but to trades deemed proper by outsiders' (1995: 212). Manual work was valued and expected in Jewish culture, for it was understood as fulfilling 'a divine mandate going back to Genesis 1' and therefore a 'healthy work ethic was inculcated in Jewish literature throughout the ancient period' (Witherington 2006a: 123), although it was despised in Greek culture for manual work belonged only to slaves (see Neil 1950: 88; Best 1972: 175).

Hock, however, sees a similarity between Paul's exhortation here and attitudes found in Greek moralists, especially in Dio Chrysostom, and concludes that Paul's instructions 'to stand aloof from public life and to work at a suitable occupation' should be understood neither as an endorsement of the Jewish value of labour, nor because of idleness resulting from eschatological expectations, but rather 'as reflecting Paul's clear familiarity with the moral traditions of the Greco-Roman philosophers' (1980: 47). Witherington, though, rightly cautions against the uncritical use of ancient sources from rhetoricians and philosophers and he illustrates how there was not always a unanimous agreement on how to view work (2006a: 122).[25] It is almost impossible to know what specific work, if any, Paul was referring to in 1 Thess. 4.11, but the important point here is that Paul regarded work as something that was good and which the believers should be engaged with themselves.

However, how these instructions in verse 11 result in the believer living respectably among the outsiders has also been widely debated among scholars and there have been many attempts to interpret these instructions, to understand their underlying motivation(s), and how they are connected to verse 12. We will now turn to explore the connection between verse 11 and verse 12, specifically focusing on the importance of 'walking honourably with outsiders' and how this can be achieved.

2.3.3 Connecting verses 11 and 12

In attempting to connect verse 11 to verse 12, many scholars focus their attempts solely on the third instruction, which hinges on the idea of reputation: having a good work ethic leads to having a good reputation among unbelievers. For example, although Bruce, like Wanamaker (1990), imagines that some believers were becoming a 'financial burden on others' and were ignoring the apostles' 'admonition and example' to work hard and support oneself, he nevertheless concludes that 'those who were behaving in this way were not only being burdensome to their fellow Christians; they were incurring a bad reputation among non-Christians' (2015: 92; also Morris 1991: 133).[26] Neil goes slightly further, for not only should believers make sure they don't create a bad reputation, they should also in fact become 'an example to the rest of the non-Christian community ... and set the highest possible standard as honest hard-working citizens' (1950: 88). Indeed, they must not be charged with creating disturbances as the apostles had been when they were in Thessalonica earlier (see Acts 17.6-7), but should strive to be reasonable (1950: 88). As we will see below, most scholars agree that the type of life depicted in verse 11 will lead to the believers having a good reputation, and hence being able to walk honourably with outsiders (v. 12a). However, there appears to be a difference in understanding how Paul envisages the believers achieving this good reputation – whether it is by them living in a way so as to actively draw attention and admiration, or to live in a way that does not draw attention to themselves or to their differences.

2.3.3a Reputation: drawing positive attention

For Witherington the connection between work and reputation is about being able to *help* others in society: the command to love one another results in the believer firstly refusing to become parasitic, building unhealthy relationships of dependency on others, and secondly it motivates the believer not to 'stand idly by and watch the needy go hungry (cf. Eph. 4.28; 1 Tim. 5.3-8)' (2006a: 123). Given the hostility they were now facing, and the limited socio-religious opportunities they had to interact with unbelievers, Witherington argues that Paul therefore urges the believers to 'work hard, live quietly, and avoid entangling alliances while building up a positive Christian community known for its love and caring for each other' (2006a: 124). This reputation for demonstrating love and care to others acts as a counter-narrative to the one the outsiders have of the believers and which leads to hostility. This interpretation certainly seems to be plausible, and one could also look to 5.14 and specifically the instruction to 'uphold the weak' (ἀντέχεσθε τῶν ἀσθενῶν) to support the argument that this is about believers being able to help others rather than be in the position of seeking help.[27] It also seems a reasonable suggestion when one takes into account the learnings from SIT about the need for the ingroup to build up a positive social identity. Whereas Tajfel noted the fact that ingroup members might be tempted to join another group if a positive social identity is not achieved (Tajfel 1981: 256), in this interpretation, one could see Tajfel's theory working the other way, whereby if believers gain such a positive evaluation with regard to caring for others, then it could tempt outsiders to leave their group and join the believing community.

However, Witherington's interpretation encounters two significant pitfalls. The first is the obvious fact that Paul does not mention in this passage the motivation of being willing and able to help another person in need, or, as Witherington puts it, to feed the hungry. There is only the encouragement to live the type of life that would enable each believer to be in a position of independence and not dependence on another (v. 12b); it is another step still to say that they would then be able to help others who are dependent upon them, and it is this step that finds no support in the passage itself, and very little support in the wider letter. The second pitfall is the fact that if the motivation behind the endorsement to work with their hands is so that they can then help the needy and feed the hungry, then this is actually doing the very opposite of the other two instructions in v. 11 where believers are urged to aspire to live quietly and to mind their own affairs. We therefore see that whilst on the surface this interpretation appears to be quite conceivable, a closer look reveals that there is a disconnect with the rest of the instructions and a hermeneutical step is made which is unjustified by the textual context itself.

Richard offers another interpretation which attempts to make more sense of the immediate textual context, but in so doing falls into the same error. He begins by arguing that the command to work is a development of the command to love one another more and more (vv. 9-10); thus, Paul encourages greater 'Christian involvement in the socioeconomic context not because of idleness caused by exaggerated apocalypticism but for the reason underlying the entire section, namely, an expanded, outer-directed concept of love of others' (1995: 212). He also sees this as part of a missional concern, commenting that productive believers 'were to be productive members of the society in which they lived and their activity was to contribute to the well-being, unity, and outreach of the fellowship', and as such that they 'could have a profound impact on the lives of outsiders' (1995: 223). He does not elaborate on what this would look like, but the thrust of his argument is akin to that of Witherington's, that the command to be 'productive' is related to v. 12a because it produces believers who can then contribute to society and be a blessing to others. Again, this interpretation is not entirely out of place within the rest of the letter, for as we have seen Paul does encourage the believers to love all people, including outsiders (3.12), and to do good to all (5.15). However, in addition to the fact that the command to love one another in vv. 9-10 is specifically a call to love other believers (φιλαδελφία) and does not also specify outsiders, this interpretation once again seems to go against the essence of living quietly and minding one's own business and adds a layer of interpretation onto the text that simply is not there.

In the above interpretations it is evident that reputation is the key that unlocks the connection between a believer's work ethic and being able to walk honourably with outsiders. In other words, what connects these two verses is a realization that it is important to consider what others think, and these three instructions are motivated by this concern and shaped by what would result in a good opinion of the believers in the eyes of the outsiders. For Bruce (2015), Neil (1950) and Morris (1991) this reputation is created because working means the believers cannot engage in other activities or behave in other ways that would bring scorn (such as idleness, being 'busybodies', or depending upon charity). For Witherington (2006a) and Richard (1995) this reputation is created because working means that the believer is able to help others in need or be a positive influence in society. A good reputation is gained because of the outsiders being drawn to look at the believers' positive and outward-focused work. Hence, the thrust of these interpretations is on the believers being able to behave in a way that wins them good attention from outsiders.

2.3.3b Reputation: taking charge of visibility and interaction

However, as we have seen, these interpretations do little to take into account the other two instructions in v. 11, which convey the need for believers to behave quietly, being focused on their own affairs. If we take these three instructions together, I would argue that it is in seeking *not* to draw attention to themselves that creates the good reputation and the ability to walk honourably with outsiders. It has been seen that one of the major concerns in this letter is about the conflict that has arisen between believer and unbeliever. Therefore, contrary to Malherbe who writes that 'it is fundamentally wrong to view the passage as though the main focus were the relations between the church and a hostile society' (2000: 254), in a passage which specifically mentions 'outsiders' (v. 12a), it would not be unsurprising for Paul to have this conflict at the forefront of his mind. As such, whereas Trebilco remarks that there is no strategy in the letter to 'try to reduce disharmony by encouraging integration or the lowering of boundaries' (2017: 238), I would argue that the motivation behind verses 11 and 12 is precisely an attempt to reduce friction between the believer and the outsider. For, in reading verse 11 as a whole, it appears that there is a concern for the believers not to attract too much attention to themselves, to have the means to live independently, and to be as little a distraction as possible; and it is *this* that results in the believers being able to walk amongst the outsiders honourably. If the mere presence of believers in the community is enough to provoke hostility, then perhaps what is needed is for these believers not to promote or make more visible their presence in society, and to demonstrate that they are not a threat to the stability of the wider community. This in itself would enable them to walk honourably with outsiders. Ironically, the influence of being *with* outsiders causes the believers to reflect on their visibility among outsiders. Furthermore, if they are able to act as per the instructions in v. 11 whilst being persecuted, then their ability not to react and to stay resilient might have been considered admirable in the outsiders.

Barclay (1993) offers an interpretation that does much of what I have briefly proposed above, for it firstly seeks to bring together all three infinitive instructions in verse 11, it secondly seeks to offer a suggestion as to what prompted these three instructions, it thirdly argues that the goal of the instructions is about the believers being less obvious in their daily life, and fourthly it connects all of verse 11 to verse 12. Barclay begins by proposing that the reactions of the believers to their 'social harassment' might not always have been 'entirely passive' (hence the instruction in 5.15 not to repay evil for evil) but that they might have reacted in such a way as to 'heighten the social tensions between believers and non-believers' (1993: 520), and the main crux of his interpretation is that one of these reactions may have been an increased fervour in evangelizing aggressively among their neighbours, which would have involved them abandoning their daily work and interfering in the lives of other people (see v. 11). In proposing this situation, Barclay brings together two of the major themes or concerns in the letter: that of the imminent expectation of the eschaton and of the conflict and persecution. For, he argues that some of the believers have abandoned their work 'in order to engage in something altogether more urgent: the preaching of the gospel' (1993: 522) *and* that they have been doing so in a disrespectful manner, so that they are now giving their time 'to aggressive evangelistic activity', hence interfering 'too readily in the business of nonbelievers' and so living their lives in a way that 'could endanger the safety of the church' (1993: 522).

Barclay underpins his argument by firstly referring to Paul's remark earlier in the letter that 'the word of the Lord has echoed out from you not only in Macedonia but also in Achaia' (1.8), which for him suggests that they have been evangelizing further afield than their own community, and secondly by proposing that Paul's description of his own evangelistic activity (2.1-12) is an attempt to show the Thessalonian believers how they should rather seek to participate in mission, which includes acting in gentleness and supporting oneself economically (1993: 523). It is this backdrop that leads to the 'carefully framed instructions' in 4.11-12 (1993: 520), and he comments that these 'three concrete activities enjoined appear to belong together: living quietly will consist in minding their own business and getting on with their work' (1993: 521). Paul is understandably concerned 'that his converts should not behave indecently towards outsiders' (1993: 522).

There are huge merits in Barclay's proposal. Unlike the other interpretations we have looked at thus far, it keeps together the integrity of the whole of verse 11 and its connection to verse 12, and the suggested situation behind the instructions takes note of two of the major themes in the letter. It is entirely possible that loud and disruptive evangelism was increasing the conflict between believer and unbeliever, and this potential scenario would understandably give rise to the three instructions in v. 11 and result in the believers being able to walk more decently among their neighbours. Out of all the interpretations so far, this one honours the integrity of verses 11 and 12 as well as the wider explicit concerns in the letter. However, we need to ask if the character portrayal in Barclay's argument of the believers matches that of Paul's. Indeed, given the significant amount of space Paul gives to praising them (e.g. 1.2-10; 2.13-14, 19-20; 3.6-9; 4.1, 10), it would be surprising to find out that they are actually engaging in 'aggressive evangelism' for this seems to go against the character portrayal that Paul has already illustrated of them. For Paul writes that they are people of faith, love and hope (1.3; 3.6; 4.10), imitators of the apostles and of the Lord (1.6), examples to other believers (1.7), welcoming to strangers (1.9), vessels of God's work which is active in them (2.13), the crown of boasting of the apostles, their glory and joy (2.19-20), and pleasing to God (4.1). They are clearly not perfect: in some way their faith is lacking (3.10) and there are times when Paul appears to write in order to correct behaviour, or at least remind them not to be tempted to behave in a certain way (e.g. 4.6; 5.12-13, 15). However, the character portrayal built up in Barclay's thesis of zealous and aggressive evangelists, uncaring and thoughtless about how they behave towards other people, does not quite match that given by Paul himself in the letter.

Additionally, Barclay's proposal raises the question as to whether or not the instructions in v. 11 are attempting to stop the believers from living in the opposite way. As Hock observes: 'Few scholars doubt that there was an actual problem; they disagree only on the cause' (1980: 43). For Barclay the problem is that the believers are being disruptive, interfering, and abandoning a self-sufficient lifestyle in order to engage in aggressive evangelism. For others the problem is that believers are choosing idleness over production because of their belief in the imminent return of Christ (e.g. Best 1972: 175; Neil 1950: 87; Dobschütz 1974: 180–3), or because of the exploitation of the command to love one another and are therefore relying on the resources of others in the community (e.g. Wanamaker 1990: 163).[28] Malherbe suggests some believers are asking 'about the nature of brotherly love' (2000: 255) and how much they are required to help one another (2000: 256).[29] For Winter these instructions are needed to act as a deterrent to believers who already are, or who would become clients of wealthy patrons, for this would require them to be ambitious (hoping to secure for themselves gifts from their patron) and politically active and visible (1994: 48).

However, it is possible that these instructions are not intended to correct behaviour, but to encourage believers to persevere in what they are already doing. Chapter 4 begins with Paul urging the believers: περιπατεῖν καὶ ἀρέσκειν θεῷ, even though he remarks that they are already doing such, and he urges them to keep doing this and to do so 'more and more' (v. 1) by attending to the 'orders' they have already received (v. 2, 6). Paul then urges the believers to love one another 'more and more', and again admits that they are indeed loving πάντας τοὺς ἀδελφοὺς [τοὺς] ἐν ὅλῃ τῇ Μακεδονίᾳ (v. 10). Finally, he encourages them to aspire to live quietly, to mind their own affairs and to work with their own hands, and once again, comments that they have received this instruction already (v. 11). Although this verse lacks the remark 'as indeed you are doing', it would not be unusual for Paul to call the believers to do something they are already doing. Indeed, there is little in the rest of the letter to suggest that the majority of believers are not living quietly, or that they are interfering in the affairs of other people, or that they are abandoning their work. As such, the above scholars appear to be over-reading the text as reflecting a problem, whereas it may be simply reinforcing what is already happening.[30] It is possible that Paul is reminding them of the necessity of living in a way that will not provoke outsiders but rather will help believers to function well within their own community and to be seen as respectable members of society. Dibelius also argues that there is nothing in this letter that suggests that these instructions are in any way a warning against current bad practice and proposes that Paul is simply reminding believers of this way of life for the sake of new converts (1925: 20).

Having surveyed some of the diverse interpretations of verses 11 and 12, we have argued that there is no explicit evidence that Paul is giving these instructions as a corrective to unhelpful behaviour, that the wider backdrop of hostility between the two groups is at the forefront of Paul's mind here, and that the three instructions in verse 11 amount to the believers living in such a way that does not attract any unnecessary attention from outsiders, and rather builds up a picture of the believers simply 'keeping their heads down' and getting on with their life despite the conflict they are experiencing. It is a picture whereby they take charge of their visibility, ironically to live *with reference* to and among outsiders. Clearly, Paul envisages that outsiders would find this behaviour respectable and honourable, conceivably because they would then not have such a visible reminder of that which they perceive to be a threat to their own way of life. For believers to walk honourably *with reference to*, and *among*, outsiders, they need to take charge of their degree of visibility in the community, which in turn will lead to the type of reputation they hold in that community.

The final statement in v. 12b, that believers should not need to depend on anyone, strengthens this interpretation, for here Paul tells believers that they should take control of how much they do interact with outsiders. Schellenberg argues that if believers work hard then they show love for one another by taking seriously the responsibility to provide for and support one another by contributing to the 'shared resources of the assembly' (2018: 29), which in turn means they are not dependent upon anyone else (v. 12b). However, this also means that they are in control of their interactions with outsiders. Although the believers should not separate themselves from outsiders, they should also maintain a degree of control over how much, and what type, of interaction they have with outsiders. Paul's message to these believers living in a hostile environment is that they should not find themselves in a position where they become dependent upon outsiders, for then there is increased potential for the friction to escalate and for the relationship to be exploited.

2.3.4 Summary

A few scholars highlight the fact that in verses 11-12 Paul is clearly recognizing or presupposing an overlap area where both groups share similar group norms, and as such, he encourages behaviour that would 'be acceptable to social norms' (Malherbe 2000: 251; also Furnish 2002: 112; Schnelle 1990: 298).[31] As Chapter 1 indicated, although difference between groups is highlighted by SIT as being important for group formation, maintenance and identity, Barth did raise the argument that when social interaction between two groups happens the differences between the groups are 'reduced' for 'interaction both requires and generates a congruence of codes and values—in other words, a similarity or community of culture' (1969: 15). It is however not obvious as to what this 'community of culture' is as described in verse 11; it is more evident, however, that there is a concern for the believers not to overtly demonstrate their differences, if these specific differences are leading to persecution and threatening the survival of this faith community. As Horrell notes, 'the content of shared norms is here only minimally evident—essentially it is a matter of keeping inoffensively quiet' (2016: 285). Whilst the believers are not to erase their differences, they are, however, not to draw attention to them. Thus, Witherington writes regarding the first instruction that 'Paul is not talking about retirement but avoidance of conflict', and he argues that 'Paul is not countering apocalyptic lethargy' but responding to the persecution so that 'the lower profile they maintained the better it might go for them' (2006a: 121).

Paul observes that the behaviour of believers will be open to judgement by the outsiders, and as such, shows a recognition of, and sensitivity towards, what the social-scientist Jenkins argues: 'what people think about us is no less significant than what we think about ourselves' (2008: 42). Jenkins proposes that there is an ongoing interplay between 'self-image and public-image' (2008: 42), and whilst Paul spends many words building up a positive and glowing self-image of the believers in Thessalonica, he appears to be aware also of this 'interplay' and is cautious about the public image of this faith community. Thus, he discerns how the believers are to behave that would at least not offend any norms held in the wider society, and that would perhaps lead to a positive public image of the believers. In other words, Paul is encouraging the believers to do the opposite of what the majority of SIT focuses upon – for he is encouraging them not to go out of their way to illustrate their differences. This is perhaps all that is needed or all that can be expected to make an impression on the outsiders, and an impression that neither explicitly seeks commendation nor converts, but an impression that might just be enough to encourage an attitude of tolerance in outsiders towards insiders, and a recognition that believers are not radical fanatics who threaten the stability, traditions and unity of the community.

Verses 11 and 12 are therefore attempts to re-design the public image of the faith community. The instructions in verse 11 and the hope in verse 12 represent an attempt to influence how outsiders might label or stereotype insiders and an attempt to lessen any negative opinion outsiders may have of insiders. Paul is therefore concerned that the believers should notice the influence of 'with': that they are called to live in a way *with regard* to the presence, sensitivities and opinions of the outsider, and that living *with* outsiders will influence how the insiders should shape their lives, perhaps enabling them to discern which parts to emphasize and reveal, and which aspects not to specifically draw attention to, lest this should increase conflict, expose the faith community to harm, and threaten its very existence. As much as the believers are to be among outsiders, they should take charge in controlling their visibility and the interaction (and the type of interaction) that they have with outsiders. This is important: Paul very much encourages the believers to interact with outsiders when they are the ones offering love and good actions. But, he advises them not to be in a position where they might be reliant on outsiders for resources, and he clearly attempts to reduce the encounters where they would be the recipients of persecution.

2.4 Conclusion

When reading this letter to the Thessalonians, it is clear that a dimension of 'all' should be applied to the believers' way of life: they neither live as an isolated community, nor only for themselves, but for others, for 'all'. The presence of the outsiders reminds them that God is 'for all', not just their own faith community, and this in turn shapes their group beliefs and behaviour: thus, they are to love all abundantly (3.12) and know that how they love 'one another and all' will determine how their heart is seen in the parousia by God (3.13). And whilst the presence of outsiders might mean they are the recipients of evil, they are not to let stereotypes and categorization shape how they respond to others: even when persecution may force differences to the fore, they are to re-address this and instead point to the similarities, specifically in pursuing what is considered to be good for one another and for all (5.15). Even though these two verses are small, this does not indicate insignificance in how Paul sees believers interacting with and responding to outsiders. Rather, given the use of 'superabundance' to describe their love for all and of 'pursue' to describe how they should go about doing good for all, Paul identifies the importance of these two expectations in the identity (behaviour) of the believer, and he subtly integrates this into a larger understanding of God's way in the world, thus informing the believers' group beliefs.

The dimension of 'all', however, must be understood alongside the influence of 'with'. Abounding in love for all and pursuing that which is good for all needs to be linked with the recognition that the believers also need to live in a way that pays respect to how outsiders might view and receive them, but also to acknowledge the power that living *with respect to* outsiders has upon shaping their norms. Thus, Paul instructs them to 'walk honourably' with outsiders (4.12a), and I have argued that the use of περιπατέω conveys with it a sense of living in a way that acknowledges that there exists a relationship between the believer and the other (whether God, or the outsider) and also *with regard to the other*, considering the values, hopes and expectations of the other. Paul declares that the way they should live *among* and *with regard to the outsider* should pay attention to what the outsider would deem to be honourable or decent (εὐσχημόνως) which would additionally enable outsiders to view insiders with a measure of admiration. Through exploring verse 11, it became clear that living honourably with regard to the outsiders requires the believers to take charge of their degree of visibility within the community, and the type of interaction they would have with outsiders. Living so as not to draw attention to themselves or to emphasize their differences is, for Paul, a way that these Thessalonian believers can, in the midst of persecution, find a counter-narrative to the way they are perceived which has resulted in the conflict, and therefore challenge and transform their public image. What these outsiders think has a significant impact not only on the day-to-day lives of the believers but also on the bigger question of whether or not they will live or die for their faith.

As such, whereas SIT suggests the need for groups to emphasize their difference, Paul has discerned that here in Thessalonica these differences are creating tension and persecution to the degree that he is worried for the continued existence of the faith community – presumably either because the believers might begin to disown their faith, or because the persecution will eventually wipe them out. Believers are not to deny their differences, but nor are they to strive to make them visible. There is throughout the letter an explicit concern for how the hostility of outsiders directed towards believers might impact upon the believers' well-being and their faith, and in turn, shape Paul's own sense of achievement and faithfulness. For the strength and health of the believers' faith in some way is a reflection of his own work among them: they are his hope, joy and crown of boasting before Jesus Christ (1 Thess. 2.19). Paul is clearly motivated to try and reduce the tension between outsiders and insiders, and the way in which he encourages believers to live will hopefully function not only to reduce tension but also to create the potential for outsiders to hold a more positive opinion of them, and perhaps even to admire them. Clearly, a missional motive cannot be ruled out since a reduction in tension from asking the believers essentially to behave in ways which outsiders will find attractive and honourable could also lead outsiders to become insiders.[32] But the primary motivation seems to come from a deep recognition in Paul of the power outsiders have over the very existence of the faith community (to allow or deny it), over the strength and content of the faith of the insiders (their group norms and beliefs) and also over how the hearts of the believers are established at the parousia. Ironically, Paul's concern for the outsider is motivated by his concern for the insider; but this also sits alongside a profound respect for the presence and opinion of the outsider.

Notes

1. See also 2 Cor. 3.2 where Paul describes the believers as their 'letter of recommendation'.
2. The contrast between light and darkness has often been used to describe the difference between those who belong to God or not, or those who follow holy ways or not (e.g. in the *Testament of Levi* 19.1-2 and the *Testament of Naphtali* 2.7, 10). In the Qumran text *Community Rule* members are required to love the 'sons of light' and to hate the 'sons of darkness' according to their guilt (1QS 1.10).
3. See for example the chapter on 'Persecution and Martyrdom' in Lane Fox 1986: 419–92.
4. On the religious setting of Thessalonica, see Jewett 1986: 126-32.
5. Weima shows that Thessalonica went to all measures to ensure its favourable relationship with Rome was upheld, and hence that its leaders valued and protected without hesitation its favoured status (2014: 3–7).
6. Bruce explains the reasoning behind calling it a 'wish prayer' since the prayer 'is expressed in the optative rather than the imperative mood' (2015: 71) but that this is a stylistic move for there is little difference between the optative and the imperative (also Wanamaker 1990: 140). Witherington notes that Paul clearly has no doubt that God can accomplish his prayer (2006a: 103).
7. Interestingly, when commenting upon 5.15, which also has the added dimension of 'and for all', Fee has no qualms in accepting that Paul is urging believers to 'do good' to those outside the community of faith, which 'would include the very people who are doing their best to make life miserable for people like themselves, who have chosen to follow Christ' (2009: 213; see also Bruce 2015: 124).
8. His reasoning is based on his interpretation of whom Paul is referring to in 5.12 when he asks the believers to respect τοὺς κοπιῶντας ἐν ὑμῖν. Because Paul writes 'among you' rather than 'for you', Malherbe argues that 'the labor here is not directed to the congregation' (2000: 311) but rather that the workers are evangelists who are working among the unbelievers present in their meetings as they gathered together in a home (2000: 311–12). However, this argument fails to be persuasive and is lacking in evidence, and together with the fact that in the same verse Paul asks the believers to respect those who have charge over them and who admonish them, the likelihood is that Paul is simply referring to those people who are working among and for the believing community (also Weima 2014: 239). Whilst Trebilco seems to consider Malherbe's argument, he nevertheless writes that 'there is no need to limit the application of the language' to the unbelievers present in the congregation (2017: 240).
9. E.g. Richard 1995: 174; Witherington 2006a: 103; Neil 1950: 72; Best 1972: 149.
10. See also: Bruce 2015: 72; Horrell 2016: 289; Morris 1991: 109.
11. Verse 13 is the final clause of the prayer but its relationship to v. 12 is often debated. Fee puts weight on the fact that the verb στηρίζω is a 'strongly transitive

verb' (2009: 132) and therefore translates it as 'strengthen' (rather than 'establish') and concludes that v. 13 is not an 'immediate result of their increased love for one another' but that it is a separate prayer for strengthening which is '*in the context of their increased love*' (2009: 133). Wannamaker, however, argues that v. 13 is not a separate petition since it is an 'infinitival purpose clause dependent upon the main clause of v. 12 instead of a prayer-wish with an optative verb as in the previous two wishes' (1990: 143). As such, the intention behind superabundant love for believers and unbelievers is for the hearts of the believers to be *established* as blameless in holiness. Similarly, Richard (1995) argues for translating στηρίζω as 'establish' and hence that the goal of abundant love is to establish believers as blameless at the parousia. Verse 13 is therefore not a 'new petition' but rather 'a statement concerning the outcome of the Lord's increased gift of love and its actualisation in the lives of the new converts' (1995: 175). Clearly, the grammatical construction of v. 13 is complex, but I would argue for the reasons put forward by Wannamaker and Richard, that v. 13 is linked to v. 12 and expresses the *result* of offering abundant love to others rather than it being another separate petition. Additionally, v. 13 lacks the beginning phrase of 'and now God' found in verses 11 (δὲ ὁ θεὸς καὶ πατὴρ ...) and 12 (δὲ ὁ κύριος ...) as well as the optative form found also in the two previous verses (κατευθύναι in v. 11, πλεονάσαι in v. 12; cf. 5.23). It is also the only verse that has an eschatological orientation, whereas verses 11 and 12 are about present concerns and actions.

12   The prohibition of retaliation would not be an unusual instruction (e.g. Prov. 20.22; 24.29) and Jesus issued an instruction both to refrain from retaliating and to give generously when asked even by the person who treats you harshly (e.g. Mt. 5.38-42).

13   See also Richard 1995: 271; Bruce 2015: 124; Best 1972: 234; Neil 1950: 127–8; Morris 1991: 171; Fee 2009: 213; Furnish 2002: 111.

14   Ironically, this verb is often used for persecution or harassment (e.g. Rom. 12.14; 1 Cor. 4.12; 15.9; 2 Cor. 4.9; Gal. 5.11; 6.12).

15   For example, Matera writes that 'Paul is referring to moral conduct' without specifying what this might be (1992: 217). 'Doing good' for Cole means giving alms (1989: 232), and for Ngewa it is similarly about giving to those in need: 'No boundary of any kind should be placed between the one in need and the one with the ability to assist' (2010: 162).

16   See also 1 Pet. 3.9-12, where there is a similar command to avoid retaliation and instead to 'repay with a blessing' followed by a reminder that God turns his face away from those who do evil but that he is attentive to those who do good (v. 12).

17   Note the only two occurrences of ἵνα in 4.1 and 4.12.

18   It is not clear if Paul means for believers to walk 'with a view to' or 'in view of' outsiders but I would argue that it is not a question of 'either or' for Paul, but both: believers are to walk among and in view of believers (just as their 'walking with' God presumes a relationship between the believers and God), but also with regard for *how* outsiders might view them and therefore a corresponding desire to walk in a way that is considerate of the other.

19   Περιπατέω is also found twice in the disputed letter of 2 Thessalonians. However, here the references are not to believers 'walking' among outsiders but to believers who are 'walking' in a 'disorderly' manner (ἀτάκτως, Bauer et al. 2000: 148), and Paul instructs the wider congregation to stay away from such believers (2 Thess. 3.6, 11).

20   Thus, the use of this word as a noun and adjective in 1 Cor. 12.23-24 to describe the various parts of the body show that it is used to indicate what would be considered by

all to be 'decent'; in other words, it suggests and takes for granted what is considered acceptable in the eyes of all.

21 This last clause of verse 12, καὶ μηδενὸς χρείαν ἔχητε could be understood as Paul hoping for the believers to lack nothing (e.g. Wanamaker 1990: 163–4) or for them to have no need to be dependent on another person. However, Witherington astutely points out that 'if a person lacks for nothing essential then there is no reason to be economically dependent on another' (2006a: 124).

22 Jewett persuasively argues that the older translation or preference of 'loafers' for ἄτακτοι (by e.g. Best 1972: 230; Bruce 2015: 122) has mistakenly led to the idea that laziness is behind the rejection of self-sufficiency in these believers, and that ἄτακτοι should rather be understood as meaning those who are 'rebellious or insubordinate' (1986: 105; also Malherbe 2000: 317). Wanamaker's argument is also shaped by the fact that he believes that not only is 2 Thessalonians an authentic letter but also that it pre-dates 1 Thessalonians (1990: 37–45, 164).

23 On the political and social overtones, see also Richard 1995: 219–20.

24 See Best who argues that the first two instructions do not require for them to withdraw from public or civic life because they are not occupied with public affairs in the first place (1972: 175).

25 For example, whereas Dio Chrysostom defended work 'in the face of an elitist disdain for manual labor as well as for poverty', Plutarch distinguished between valuing work but despising the workman, and Philo comments upon Sophists who despise those who worked (Witherington 2006a: 122).

26 Although Morris concludes that the connection between the instruction to work and to walk respectably with outsiders is to do with reputation, he earlier argues that the idiom 'work with your own hands' refers to manual labour, and in so doing comments that it was not a respectable form of employment for those who were not slaves, but that this shows that 'the Christians refused to take their standards from the community in the midst of which they lived' (1991: 132). The corollary of this is surely then that it would attract scorn and derision from the outsiders; however, Morris does not see this logic for he goes on to argue that by engaging in this labour the believers are rather keeping the church from disrepute (1991: 133).

27 However, it is not immediately obvious who 'the weak' are, if they are the ones who are spiritually or morally weak, or those who are impoverished, and as such there is a plethora of interpretations: 'those who find the Christian way of life a hard one' (Richard 1995: 277); 'weak in faith' (Bruce 2015: 123; also Best 1972: 230–1); 'weak souls' (Morris 1991: 169 and Neil 1950: 124); those who have a 'physical weakness, perhaps as a result of abuse or persecution' (Witherington 2006a: 163), and Wanamaker writes that they could be those who are 'economically needy' but suggests that Paul left this term (and the others in v. 15) deliberately vague and as such 'he sought to give the whole community a sense of pastoral responsibility' (1990: 198). Regardless of who the weak ones are, we still find here a command for believers to be able and willing to help others (whether spiritually, morally, physically or economically), and as such be in the position of helper rather than dependent upon others for their own needs.

28 Although, as Barclay notices, neither of these proposals explains why the believers would be living 'loudly' or disruptively or interfering with the business of other people (1993: 521–2), and neither finds support from the text itself.

29 Malherbe accuses Barclay of finding 'a connection not found in the text' (2000: 254); ironically, this could be a charge levelled at Malherbe for there is no hint that some

believers are becoming frustrated with offering hospitality to other believers in the passage itself or in the rest of the letter.

30   Ironically, Barclay has written an essay on the perils of 'mirror-reading' but appears to be using this method in interpreting 1 Thess. 4.11 (1987: 73–93).

31   Schnelle writes: 'Dabei geht Paulus offensichtlich von einer Gemeinsamkeit ethischer Normen bei Heiden und Christen aus' ('Paul obviously starts from a shared sense of ethical norms among Gentiles and Christians', 1990: 298).

32   Some scholars argue that there is a missional motivation behind these verses (e.g. Richard 1995: 221; Wanamaker 1990: 143, 199). Holtz, commenting upon 3.12, suggests that the only way the believers could show love to outsiders would be by trying to convert them: 'In Wahrheit dürfte es nur eine wirkliche Form der Liebe der anderen gegeben haben, nämlich sie hereinzuholen in die eigene Gemeinde' (1986: 144). This, however, creates an unnecessary and unwarranted distinction between the type of love one might offer to a believer and an unbeliever, and is not supported by the text or the rest of the letter. Holtz, however, also concludes that the intention behind 'walking honourably' must be missionary (1986: 180). In contrast, for Furnish, there is no hint of Paul desiring for believers 'to be models of good behaviour in order to attract outsiders to the gospel' (2002: 132–3, also 124). Horrell, however, wisely remarks that, although there might not be a 'positive missionary motivation', there is at least a 'passive' one in the sense that the believers are urged to live in a way that would 'remove a hindrance to others' acceptance of the gospel' (2016: 284, 285).

3

In Pursuit of Peace and Praise: Re-Creating the Public Image in Romans 12–13

3.1 Introduction

Paul's letter to the Romans is a cascade of theology involving teaching, apologetics, diatribe and argument. It has often found itself at the centre of debate from the early church, through the Reformation to the contemporary church, where theologians have argued endlessly over matters of doctrine, ethics, ecclesiology and politics. Whereas Paul's first letter to the Thessalonians is a mere five chapters long, his letter to the Romans extends to sixteen chapters. And where Paul mainly focuses on local matters in 1 Thessalonians (albeit with a fixed eye upon the eschaton), in Romans he not only traverses across the local terrain dealing with immediate and contextual issues (e.g. 12.14; 13.1-7; 14-15; 16.17-20), but he also widens the focus to embed the local concerns into God's eternal time frame.

As such, he appeals to the beginning of creation (1.20), to God's early dealings with humankind and with the forefathers of Israel and the prophets (e.g. David in 1.3; Abraham and Sarah in chapters 4 and 9; Adam and Moses in 5.14; Rebecca and Isaac in 9.10; Elijah in 11.2-4), and he frequently refers to other parts of Scripture (e.g. the Psalms in 3.10-14, 18; 4.6-8; Isaiah in 3.15-17; Genesis, Malachi, Exodus and Hosea in chapter 9). Paul also gives a significant amount of time to his theology of the cross (e.g. Romans 5) and to how the cross impacts upon the daily lives of his readers (chapters 6–8), but he also looks to the future judgement of God (12.19; 14.10-12; 16.20) and the glory of God (5.2).[1] He is sure of his own call to the Gentiles (1.13; 11.13; 15.15-19) but also determined to explain the relationship between God, Jews and Gentiles (chapters 9–11).

Perhaps it is because this letter has such a wide focus of time and space that some of Paul's teaching has a more generalized feel to it than that found in 1 Thessalonians, where the readers of Romans are sometimes addressed because of their specific belonging to the local faith community in Rome, and sometimes because of their belonging to the universal category of 'believer', regardless of time and location. In terms of SIT, Paul appears to hold together a larger concept of what distinguishes believers from unbelievers on a global and even cosmic scale, but also what marks out the boundary between the believers and their local unbelieving neighbours in Rome. Thus, regarding the believers' more immediate and local identity, in the opening section of the letter

Paul describes his readers as 'called ones of Jesus Christ' (κλητοὶ Ἰησοῦ Χριστοῦ, 1.6) and he addresses his letter 'to all God's beloved in Rome, who are called to be saints' (πᾶσιν τοῖς οὖσιν ἐν Ῥώμῃ ἀγαπητοῖς θεοῦ, κλητοῖς ἁγίοις, 1.7a). The believers in Rome are reminded twice that their membership of the believing community is not accidental but is in fact ordained by God: Paul speaks of them as being 'called' and 'predestined' by God (1.6-7; 8.29-30). With strong echoes of the opening of 1 Thessalonians, Paul continues to edify his readers by stating that he thanks God for all of them because their faith 'is being proclaimed in all the world' (1.8; see 1 Thess. 1.2, 8), and that he longs to visit them in order to strengthen their faith, although he has so far been hindered from doing so (1.10-11, 13; 15.22-29; see also 1 Thess. 2.17-18; 3.1-2). He even suggests that the believers have something worthy to impart to Paul for the strengthening of his own faith (1.12; cf. 1 Thess. 3.10) and he recognizes that there is reciprocity in how they can edify one another in faith.

There is also an acknowledgement that the faith community in Rome is somewhat diverse, consisting of both Gentiles and Jews. It is clear that throughout the letter Paul is writing to Gentile believers (e.g. 1.5-6, 13; 11.13; 15.15-21), but there are other places where Paul seems to presume the presence of Jewish believers among those reading or hearing his correspondence (e.g. 1.7; 1.18–4.25; 7.1; 16.3-16).[2] Some scholars argue that, whilst Paul is mainly addressing his letter to Gentile believers, there is an acknowledgement that Jewish believers may have been present in the congregation.[3] Moo writes that 'the audience Paul addresses in Romans is made up of a Gentile-Christian majority and a Jewish-Christian minority' (1996: 13). Witherington (2004: 8) and Esler (2003: 115), however, argue that Paul was deliberately addressing *both* Gentile and Jewish believers.

Regardless of the proportion of Jews and Gentiles in the 'ingroup' of believers, this diversity determines some of what Paul deems necessary to write to this local faith community, which includes an attempt to explain how both Jews and Gentiles can belong together in the same ingroup of those who believe in Jesus Christ as the Son of God (e.g. chapters 9–11). It is for this reason that Esler argues that Paul is engaged with recategorization in bringing Jewish and Gentile believers together as part of one group (e.g. 2003: 144, 300). There is also clearly an element of conflict within the ingroup: in the final chapters Paul calls the believers to welcome one another, to live in harmony rather than judgement (14.1-6, 10, 13; 15.7; 16.2-16) and to adopt an attitude toward one another that would result in mutual edification and peace (14.15, 19, 20-21; 15.2; 16.17). Rather than a call to erase differences within the ingroup, it is a call to renew how they perceive their new identity as belonging to one another, and to realize the importance of how they view and act toward one another (the cognitive and emotional components of social identity).

However, Paul also refers to the ingroup in wider terms to describe their difference from the more general and universal outgroup of unbelievers. Paul describes the ingroup as 'all the ones believing' in response to seeing the 'righteousness of God' (3.22) which is not a local event but a universal and cosmic one. However, the caveat to this is that this universal group of believers shares something in common with all of humanity, for Paul then writes: 'for there is no distinction, for all have sinned and come short of the glory of God' (οὐ γάρ ἐστιν διαστολή, πάντες γὰρ ἥμαρτον καὶ ὑστεροῦνται τῆς δόξης τοῦ θεοῦ, 3.22b-23). Here, we see where the difference between ingroup and outgroup is *not* found, and Karl Barth, writing before SIT was articulated in the form that we have now, writes on 3.22b that Paul's 'mission did not erect barriers; it tore them down. God can be known only when men of all ranks are grouped together upon one single step' (1933: 100). Paul's use of πάντες shows that the believers' difference is not through their own goodness or merit (for they too are part of the indictment that all have sinned and all fall short of God's glory; see also Cranfield 1975: 204; Jewett 2007: 279), but only because of God's goodness, understood as his righteousness, seen through the sacrifice of Christ Jesus, received by the believers as a gift of grace, and owned by the believers through faith in this same redeemer, Jesus (3.21-25). The boundary between insider and outsider is not placed upon moral superiority but upon faith in Jesus Christ; they are therefore described as being 'in Christ Jesus' (ἐν Χριστῷ Ἰησοῦ, 8.1, 2). As Jewett writes, the 'threefold reference in Rom. 3.24 to the "free gift," to divine "grace," and to "redemption" through Christ makes plain that no one gains this honourable, righteous status by outperforming others or by privilege of rank, wealth, or ethnicity' (2007: 281-2).

Similarly, Paul refers to the unbelievers both on a universal and a local scale. In general terms, Paul describes outsiders as those who live 'according to the flesh' and who therefore have their minds set on the things of the flesh (8.5), which is death (8.6). These people are hostile to God and are not able to please him (8.7-8). In contrast, the believers live according to the Spirit and have set their minds on the things of the Spirit, which is life and peace (8.5-6); Esler has called this comparison 'an eruption of ingroup/outgroup differentiation' (2003: 245). Paul also calls the believers to 'put away the works of darkness' (13.12), indicating that these would include 'orgies and drunkenness, sexual immorality and debauchery, strife and jealousy' (13.13), and in so doing also builds up a negative stereotype of those outsiders who are unable to put on 'the weapons of the light' (13.12). Although moral superiority does not award someone membership of the ingroup, it should nevertheless be the expectation of belonging to the ingroup. However, these descriptions need to be framed by one of Paul's opening remarks, that it is possible for those who do not possess the law (of Moses) to still live according to God's ways (2.14-16).[4] Describing believers and unbelievers in contrasting terms of flesh/spirit and darkness/light helps to set up an understanding of the general distinction between these two groups, but experience also tells Paul that these general descriptions might not always be the case in practice, for he also acknowledges the potential for an overlap in behaviour to appear between both groups.

However, when it comes to describing the neighbouring local unbelievers, there is evidence that they regard the believers with hostility which may even lead to physical forms of antagonism. In chapter 12, Paul instructs the believers to be patient in affliction (τῇ θλίψει ὑπομένοντες, 12.12), and to 'rejoice with those rejoicing and weep with those weeping', which might also indicate an expectation and recognition of suffering in the community (12.15). Furthermore, believers are urged to be careful with how they respond to evil: they should bless and not curse their persecutors (v. 14), they should not respond to evil with evil but with that which is considered good by all (ἐνώπιον πάντων ἀνθρώπων, v. 17), they should attempt to live in peace with all (μετὰ πάντων ἀνθρώπων, v. 18) and they should seek to provide for their enemies when they are in need (v. 20). The believers are experiencing significant conflict from some of their unbelieving neighbours.[5] There is also an expectation in chapter 13, that, depending on how the believers behave among outsiders, they will either have reason to fear those in local positions of authority, or to anticipate praise (vv. 3-4).

There are also several references to suffering earlier in the letter. Paul proclaims that 'we boast in our sufferings' (καυχώμεθα ἐν ταῖς θλίψεσιν, 5.3) and in chapter 8 he poses a series of rhetorical questions (vv. 31-35), provoking the believers to realize that even if they have enemies and different challenges, including persecution or the sword (ἢ διωγμὸς ... ἢ μάχαιρα, v. 35), these are not powerful enough to separate them from 'the love of Christ' which gives them their identity (vv. 35, 37, 39). Paul can therefore proclaim that in all of these sufferings they are 'more than conquerors' (v. 37). Although these might be general references to the types of suffering that any believer might encounter, chapter 12 strongly suggests that the Roman believers are facing hardship in the form of persecution from their unbelieving neighbours.

This would not be unsurprising, as at the time of Paul's writing the believers are just a few years away from Nero's persecution, after he erroneously charged them with arson after a fire in the capital in July 64 CE (Tacitus, *Annals* 15.44). And, in order for Nero to make the believers a scapegoat, Adams argues persuasively that 'when scapegoating occurs, it is directed toward a group in society against whom there is widespread prejudice and upon whom feelings of hostility can easily be vented' (2000: 214). In other words, the believers 'must have been perceived as sufficiently *dangerous* and *subversive* as to make the charge of arson a plausible one', for 'arson was viewed as a revolutionary act' (Adams 2000: 215). This suggests that there was an acceleration of public suspicion, mistrust and resentment towards the believers and, together with evidence in Romans 12, that there were actual localized situations of persecution and conflict from outsiders before 64 CE. Paul emphasizes repeatedly throughout 12.14-21 that the believers are not to retaliate or to seek vengeance, but are rather to bless, to do good and to show mercy to their enemies (vv. 14, 17, 19, 20) and work for peace (v. 18). These commands all presuppose an actual situation of conflict with outsiders. As Adams writes, 'A warning against retaliation supposes prior provocation. A repeated warning not to strike back suggests a recurring pattern of provocative encounters' (2000: 216).

Thus, it appears likely that the believers in Rome, like those in Thessalonica, are facing hostility and conflict. In the previous chapter, we saw that Paul advises the Thessalonians to take charge of how visible they are (and to limit this where possible unless it is to show love and goodness to the outsider), and to control the type of interaction they would have with their outsiders, all the time showing sensitivity to how the outsiders might perceive and interpret them. Whereas the Thessalonians are not to go out of their way to attract attention, in Romans, however, it appears that the believers are to do the opposite, for they are not just to avoid criticism but are to seek commendation (Rom. 13.3). As such, although most of Romans is concerned with explaining ingroup identity on a local and a cosmic scale, Paul turns his gaze specifically to the local outsiders in chapters 12 and 13, showing a significant concern for what they think of the believers. It is to these chapters that we shall now turn.

3.2 Romans 12

3.2.1 Introduction: inward and outward orientation

In Romans 12 Paul turns to focus more on detailing the expected behaviour for the ingroup. The first section concentrates on how believers are to develop their relationship with God: they are to present their bodies 'as a living sacrifice' which should be 'holy and pleasing to God' (ἁγίαν εὐάρεστον τῷ θεῷ, 12.1; cf. 8.8), and to use their minds to discern God's will, which is 'good and pleasing and perfect' (τὸ ἀγαθὸν καὶ εὐάρεστον καὶ τέλειον, 12.2). The focus then turns to how believers should interact with one another and function as many members with different gifts in the one body (12.3-8). Passing over verses 9-16 for the moment, the focus of the final part of the chapter has a clear outward orientation, concentrating on how believers should respond to outsiders, and specifically, to those who view them with hostility (vv. 17-21). With overtones of 1 Thess. 5.15, the believers in Rome are told not to return evil for evil, but instead are to 'take thought for what is good before all people' (ἐνώπιον πάντων ἀνθρώπων, Rom. 12.17). They are also to strive to live in peace with all (μετὰ πάντων ἀνθρώπων, v. 18), remembering that God is judge (v. 19), and they should not hesitate to provide for their enemies in need (v. 20), believing that they can 'conquer evil with good' (v. 21). There is a gradual movement in this chapter from describing how the believers should relate to God, to one another within their believing community, and finally to those outside their group with a specific focus on those intergroup relationships marred with hostility.

However, the point at which Paul moves on to describe intergroup relations has been debated among scholars. There is no doubt that verses 9-13 are concerned with how believers should interact with each other, and with the type of attitude, prayerful character, and qualities they should aim to embody. Paul seems to particularly concentrate on how they should respond in a context of hardship, encouraging them to prioritize love in their relationships (v. 10), neither abandoning their hope, faith in prayer or fervour in serving 'the Lord' in the face of tribulation (vv. 11-12), nor their responsibility to support other brothers and sisters in Christ (v. 13). The next verse, however, switches abruptly to how believers should respond to those persecuting them, which we have already argued is referring to the outsider: εὐλογεῖτε τοὺς διώκοντας ὑμᾶς, εὐλογεῖτε καὶ μὴ καταρᾶσθε (v. 14). There is also a grammatical change in verse 14, for verses 9-13 consist of short phrases that are mainly constructed with a combination of nouns, adjectives and participles, whereas verses 14 and 15 lack nouns but consist of a collection of eight verbal forms: two short clauses made up of an imperative and a participle in v. 14, and two short phrases in v. 15 made up of an infinitive (which can function as an imperative) and a participle. As such, some scholars see that v. 14 signals a shift from internal relations to external ones, so that vv. 14-21 are all concerned with how believers should behave among outsiders (e.g. Cranfield 1979: 629; Dunn 1988b: 738–9, 755; Wilson 1990: 190; Witherington 2004: 295).

The difficulty with this proposal is that verses 15-16 are more likely to be referring to how believers should behave in their faith community. In verse 15 Paul asks the believers to 'rejoice with those who rejoice, weep with those who weep', which strongly resonates with another Pauline passage in which intragroup relations are envisaged. For, in 1 Cor. 12.26 Paul asks the different members of the one body to suffer or rejoice with one another: if one member suffers, then every member should suffer alongside this member, and if one member is honoured, all others should rejoice with them. Linguistically there is not a great overlap between 1 Cor. 12.26 and Rom. 12.15, but theologically there is the same understanding that what also binds members of the one body together is a corporate sharing of experience marked by empathy and compassion. This suggests that Rom. 12.15 is concerned with intragroup relations and is understandable, given Paul's desire to enable the members of this diverse faith community to recognize their shared identity.[6] In terms of SIT, it could also be seen as an important group norm to increase similarity within the ingroup, which functions to increase solidarity and in turn the perception of a positive social identity.

Paul's instruction in Rom. 12.16 also links with a wider concern in this letter to do with intragroup relations. He writes: τὸ αὐτὸ εἰς ἀλλήλους φρονοῦντες, μὴ τὰ ὑψηλὰ φρονοῦντες ἀλλὰ τοῖς ταπεινοῖς συναπαγόμενοι. μὴ γίνεσθε φρόνιμοι παρ' ἑαυτοῖς (roughly translated as, 'think the same thing towards one another, not thinking the proud things, but associating with the lowly. Do not become wise with yourselves' 12.16).[7] Firstly, it is important to note that Paul uses the reciprocal pronoun ἀλλήλους which he normally uses in the context of the believers to indicate the frame of reference as being within the body of Christ (e.g. Rom. 12.10; 14.13, 19; 15.7, 14; 16.16; 1 Cor. 7.5; 11.33; 16.20; Gal. 5.15, 26). This in itself is a strong indication that Rom. 12.16 has an inward focus. Secondly, Paul elsewhere in this letter refers to the hope that believers should in some way be of one mind but also not be inclined to think of themselves as more important or as wiser over and above another member (e.g. 11.25; 12.3; 15.5). He prays toward the end of the letter that God would give to the believers the ability 'to think the same thing among one another' (τὸ αὐτὸ φρονεῖν ἐν ἀλλήλοις, 15.5), which is essentially a plea to find harmony in the eradication of judgement and pride; this is found within a wider context that is concerned about hospitality, reconciliation and harmony within the body of Christ (15.1-13). This strengthens the argument that 12.16 is also inwardly focused, and concerned, like 12.15, with encouraging 'solidarity within the Christian community' (Peng 2006: 63).

Given the above, it appears more likely that Rom. 12.15-16 provide instructions regarding how ingroup members are to relate to one another, rather than specifically to outsiders. This means that verse 14, with its focus on outsiders, becomes a brief interruption in a passage that otherwise focuses on ingroup relations (vv. 9-16). The explanation that this is because of the loose nature of the passage (e.g. Schreiner 1998: 663) is not a convincing one, but the argument that verses 15-16 are about ingroup relationships leaves us with few other options rather than to conclude that for a moment, Paul took his eyes off ingroup relations to focus on outgroup relations. However, this is hardly problematic, and we have also previously seen in 1 Thessalonians that Paul can suddenly refer to outsiders within a passage that otherwise focuses on the ingroup (1 Thess. 3.12; 4.12; 5.15).[8] Neither does it come across as grossly out of place in the passage: Paul appeals to the believers to 'pursue' the giving of hospitality in v. 13 (τὴν φιλοξενίαν διώκοντες), and then instructs that they should bless those who 'pursue' them in v. 14 (εὐλογεῖτε τοὺς διώκοντας [ὑμᾶς]). They are both the subject of pursuing (with regard to offering hospitality to others) and the objects of pursuing (with regard to suffering from others).

As such, within chapter 12 we see that although the main thrust is to do with ingroup relations, there are significant verses towards the end of the passage that are concerned with how believers should behave among their unbelieving neighbours (Rom. 12.14, 17-21). The emphasis is now upon directing the actions of the believers towards those outside the believing community, and Schreiner describes this passage as 'exhortations for nonretaliation toward enemies' (1998: 663). However, there is a concern that the believers should consider what the *outsiders* value as good and what is beneficial to *them* (vv. 17, 20). They are to trust in God's judgement (v. 19), but as they wait, they are to actively seek and create peace between themselves and the outsiders (v. 18) and behave in a way that publicly reveals the injustice of their persecution (v. 20). It is to these verses that we shall now turn.

3.2.2 Givers of blessing (12.14)

In verse 14 Paul calls on the believers to behave in quite a remarkable way towards their persecutors, for they are to bless those that seek to bring them harm, and not to curse: εὐλογεῖτε τοὺς διώκοντας [ὑμᾶς], εὐλογεῖτε καὶ μὴ καταρᾶσθε.[9] The repetition of 'bless' serves to emphasize the importance of this response to the outsiders, and, correspondingly, to emphasize that the antithesis of blessing is prohibited. Perhaps, as Wilckens observes, it is because this instruction is so contrary to human inclination and so 'provocative' ('ja provokativ ist', 1982: 22) that Paul needs to repeat the command to bless. However, this echoes Jesus's teaching to the disciples: ἀγαπᾶτε τοὺς ἐχθροὺς ὑμῶν (Mt. 5.44 and Lk. 6.27-28). In Matthew's gospel they are then instructed to 'pray for those persecuting you' (προσεύχεσθε ὑπὲρ τῶν διωκόντων ὑμᾶς, 5.44), whereas in Luke the teaching is extended to include doing good to 'the ones hating you' (τοῖς μισοῦσιν ὑμᾶς, 6.27), blessing 'the ones cursing you' (τοὺς καταρωμένους ὑμᾶς, 6.28) before the instruction to pray for 'the ones mistreating you' (τῶν ἐπηρεαζόντων ὑμᾶς). The similarity in content and in vocabulary might suggest that in Rom. 12.14 Paul alludes to Jesus's teaching, and he returns to this in 1 Cor. 4.12: λοιδορούμενοι εὐλογοῦμεν ('being reviled, we bless').

However, not only is this teaching counter-cultural, where for Schreiner it is 'one of the most revolutionary statements in the NT' (1998: 667), it also powerfully reverses what the believers would have expected for those who carry out acts of evil. As Beyer writes, 'Originally blessing is for Israel and cursing for all its enemies. But it is increasingly realised that the blessings are only for those who keep God's commandments, for the righteous' (1964: 757). This is a strong thread that runs throughout most of the Old Testament. For example, in Deuteronomy blessings are given to those who keep God's commandments, and a curse to those who break them (11.26-28). The psalmist reassures those who have 'pure hearts' that they will receive not only a 'blessing from the Lord' but also vindication (Ps. 24.4-5; see also Rom. 12.19). Although Job's story seeks to uncover the complexities around blessing and cursing, in a slight twist Job is told by his wife to curse *God* because of the suffering God has given to him and his family (Job 1.9), and his friends perpetuate the belief that only the ungodly perish and therefore claim that Job's suffering is on account of his own sin and guilt (e.g. 4.7-9; 8.3-6, 13, 20; 11.1-6; 18.5-21). Even the sailors in the narrative of Jonah conclude that the storm threatening their lives is divine punishment upon a member on board their ship (1.7-10).

The blessing–cursing phenomenon was a deeply entrenched theological and social view, and a way of understanding an unpredictable and uncontrollable world by using a simple formula: goodness leads to blessing, wickedness leads to punishment. It also appears to have provided another way to categorize people into fairly crude groups whereby those who are suffering through illness or calamity are those who must be ungodly, and those without suffering are those pure in heart.[10] Thus, when the believers in Rome are told to bless their persecutors, doing so would not only prove difficult and go against the human inclination, but it also appears to reverse a deeply held theological belief. The faith community is asked to give to their enemies what should only be theirs by right; they should be the ones receiving blessings, not rewarding their persecutors for their evil. The type of response that Paul is urging the believers to adopt here is what Bertschmann would call the 'counter-intuitive' or 'asymmetric approach' to good and bad, where the response to an action is its opposite (2014: 238). And so, in this particular situation, the importance of the outsiders for the social identity of the faith community is the fact that they are causing the ingroup to review its theology and its praxis. Paul takes the opportunity to take a deeply held belief and reshape it so that it not only becomes a reformed belief but also a significant way of expressing faith. The outsiders help to reveal and reshape the blessing–cursing phenomenon and in so doing help to form some of the group norms that will be important in the maintenance of the ingroup.

Paul does not specify what he means when he asks the believers to bless their persecutors, and it appears that there are different dimensions to the concept of blessing. Beyer, for example, notes that in Greek literature εὐλογέω comes from εὖ λέγειν, and thus the verb carries with it the sense of 'speaking well of someone' (1964: 754). In other words, it means 'to praise', 'extol' or 'eulogise' (also Dunn 1988b: 744). This meaning is found towards the end of Paul's letter to the Romans when he reports that the false teachers have 'deceived the hearts' of some believers by their 'smooth speech and praise' (διὰ τῆς χρηστολογίας καὶ εὐλογίας, 16.18). Thus, in 12.14 Paul might be asking the believers to bless their persecutors by making sure they speak well of them, in the same way that he later asks the believers to seek the praise (ἔπαινος) of those in authority (13.3). However, it is more common to understand the act of 'blessing' as being that which transmits something physical to the recipient of the blessing. This is often seen in the OT as fathers give their blessing to their heirs just before their death, and it consists of the transference of what Beyer calls their 'mastery', which can include a title and possessions (1964: 756; e.g. Isaac and Jacob in Genesis 27; Jacob and Joseph in Gen. 48.15; 49.25-26).

But a blessing can also simply be understood as a gift or reward: when Caleb asks his daughter what she would like, she replies 'give me a gift' (Josh. 15.19 LXX, δός μοι εὐλογίαν) and she receives springs of water in the land in which she has been set. Likewise, after Naaman is healed of leprosy, he asks Elisha to accept a 'blessing', understood to be referring to a physical gift or payment, although Elisha refuses it

(2 Kgs 5.15 LXX, καὶ νῦν λαβὲ τὴν εὐλογίαν παρὰ τοῦ δούλου σου). In 2 Corinthians Paul refers twice to the collection of money for Jerusalem as a 'blessing', but he also points to the fact that the way in which it is given and the attitude behind the action also contributes to what makes something a blessing (9.5).[11] Therefore, it is possible that Paul intended the believers in Rome to bless their persecutors by giving them material gifts. This would fit well with the rest of his instructions, which largely focus on the believers giving something good and beneficial to the outsiders (Rom. 12.17, 20). There is to be a deeply practical and gift-giving element to the believers' relationship with their persecutors, and so it would be logical to understand that the instruction to 'bless' might refer to the giving of gifts.

However, the giving of a blessing can also be understood as praying for others, asking God to bestow upon another person that which would enable their flourishing and well-being (e.g. Jacob's blessing of Joseph in Gen. 49.25). This dimension of blessing is significant because it shows that 'The One who possesses and dispenses all blessings is God the Lord. This is the sacred knowledge underlying all OT statements concerning blessings' (Beyer 1964: 756). It seems that God's blessing involves imparting the gift of life, of fruitfulness, of dominion and greatness (Gen. 1.28; 12.2; 13.16; Deut. 28.1-13), and it is this understanding of blessing that most scholars refer to in their reading of Rom. 12.14. Thus, Cranfield writes that Paul's instruction is about 'praying for God's blessing' upon those who harm the believers (1979: 640). For Zerbe it is about calling down 'God's gracious power on someone' (1993: 241), and for Witherington it is about 'invoking' God into their relationship with their persecutors (2004: 295).[12]

In biblical thought, whilst cursing someone was 'perceived to inaugurate the process of divine judgment on a sinner' (Jewett 2007: 766) and thus 'bring disaster and/or spiritual ruin on a person' (Moo 1996: 780), blessing someone in prayer was to ask God to pour out his favour upon them, asking God to gift them with life, with fruitfulness and greatness. As such, in Rom. 12.14 'blessing implies seeking the well-being of persecutors, treating them with care, and interceding for them before God' (Jewett 2007: 766-7). The believers are to discern that which would be good for the recipients of their blessing: whether their blessing is seen as complementary speech, as the giving of gifts or time spent in prayer, our exploration above has revealed that the recipient of blessing should always be edified. This sounds obvious, but it is important to highlight what can often be missed (or rather, the significance of which can be overlooked), that Paul is asking the believers to behave in such a way that the outsiders will perceive and taste it as good and beneficial to *them*. The blessing needs to be in a form that the persecutors will indeed understand it to be a blessing: a gift, an act of generosity, a word of praise or a prayer for *their* benefit. This reveals the existence of an overlap area in what is thought of as good and of what leads to edification of the other. Contrary to SIT, the recognition of this similarity between insider and outsider is not to give the ingroup a better positive social identity, but primarily in order to advantage the outgroup.

Although Paul encourages the believers to give blessings and not to curse (12.14) or to seek revenge (v. 17), he does, however, later remind and therefore reassure them of the place of God's wrath and the role of God to judge (Rom. 12.19).[13] Paul refers to Deut. 32.35 to show that the believers are to behave in this way in the certain knowledge that God is still God: he will still execute judgement.[14] For God is still the 'guarantor of the moral universe' (Bertschmann 2014: 236). However, whereas God has the right and the power to display blessings or wrath (Rom. 12.19), the believers only have one choice, which is to seek and ask for the blessing of the other, and in this case, their persecutors. In so doing, they are to overlook the categories of godly/ungodly, overlook group boundaries, and instead should bless without regard to the boundary. As Witherington writes, 'Blessing is a boundary-removing act, just as cursing is a boundary-defining act' (2004: 295). In asking the believers to bless their persecutors, Paul redefines how the faith community understands blessing: a blessing is to say less about the recipient and more about the giver.

As such, believers are to be defined as givers of blessing; they are to understand their social identity not as those who have learned to discern who deserves a blessing or a curse, but as those who are the indiscriminate givers of blessing. The presence of the outsiders, including their negative opinion of the believers that has resulted in them persecuting members of the ingroup, has forced the believers to see and understand something about their identity that perhaps they would not have realized had the outsiders thought positively about them. Their identity is not as judge, and they are therefore not to be found 'usurping God's place' (Jewett 2007: 776) which, according to Klassen, would be 'the ultimate act of unbelief' (1984: 119). Instead, the presence of these particular outsiders sharpens the cognitive aspect of the ingroup's social identity: the understanding of the blessing–cursing phenomenon gains a new emphasis, which is placed not upon the recipient and what that says of their nature, but upon the giver, and what that says of their character. In the following verses, we will continue to see how the outsider influences and brings to the fore certain group beliefs and norms in the believing community, thus helping to shape the cognitive element of a believer's social identity.

3.2.3 Givers of good and pursuers of peace (12.17-18)

The idea that the believers should be engaged with discerning what would bless or edify their persecutors is continued through into verse 17, as is the acknowledgement that there exists an overlap area, a point of contact between the two groups, which can primarily be harnessed for the advantage of the outgroup (but also implicitly for the ingroup). For Paul continues by instructing the believers not to return evil for evil, but that instead they should consider what is deemed as 'good' by all and be prepared to give good to all: μηδενὶ κακὸν ἀντὶ κακοῦ ἀποδιδόντες, προνοούμενοι καλὰ ἐνώπιον πάντων ἀνθρώπων (12.17). The prohibition against retaliation in the first part of this verse presumes the presence of someone who is directing evil their way and is most likely another reference to the persecutors, emphasizing once more that the believer is not to cause or desire harm for those afflicting them. The warning against retaliation was not one that uniquely belonged to the faith community that followed Jesus, being also found throughout Jewish literature.[15] And, although Esler argues that Paul is urging a very different approach to that which was encouraged by the Stoics (2003: 327), Thorsteinsson makes a persuasive case that the demand for non-retaliation was apparent in most Stoic teaching, 'at least with a general reference to this demand', and gives examples from Cicero, Seneca, Musonius and Epictetus (2010: 167–8).

However, Paul develops the teaching on non-retaliation so that the response should not just be an absence of retaliation, but an active response.[16] The verb προνοέω normally means to 'think beforehand' or 'consider', and so in Rom. 12.17 Paul is calling the ingroup to look outwards and 'take into consideration' what all people perceive as good (Jewett 2007: 772) and to show a 'sensitivity to the views of others' rather than actually engaging in 'material provision' (Dunn 1988b: 748). However, the wider context reveals that it is not just about being sensitive to the views of others but also about *doing* what is perceived to be good (12.14, 20). Additionally, the verb προνοέω is used twice more in the NT, and on both occasions, it appears in its natural sense of 'consider' or 'taking forethought' but with the assumption that this will lead to action (2 Cor. 8.21 and 1 Tim. 5.8).[17] Thus, it is not just simply 'considering', but it is also about the action that flows from this: 'Προνοέω suggests ... thought which precedes and controls action' (Leenhardt 1961: 317) so that 'doing good to all is something to be planned and not just willed' (Käsemann 1980: 348). As such, the outsiders are not simply an audience; they are not merely to see and witness the good actions of the believers, but they are to be the recipients of this good as well. These concrete acts of καλόν, like the acts of blessing, are to be seen as such and received as such by all people. Furthermore, because Paul gives this instruction as the alternative to returning evil for evil, it is likely that he especially envisages the believers giving this goodness to the ones who dealt them evil.

This is not an isolated command: Paul also encourages the Thessalonian believers to refrain from retaliation and to actively 'pursue' doing that which is considered good by all and for all, including the outsiders (1 Thess. 5.15).[18] Furthermore, Paul makes it clear to the Philippian believers that they 'are responsible for recognising and doing *whatever* there is in the world's treasury of wisdom that can be reckoned morally excellent and praiseworthy' (Furnish 2009: 146–7). Paul writes that the believers here must consider (with the implication also of 'doing') 'whatever is true, whatever is honourable, whatever is righteous, whatever is pure, whatever is pleasing, whatever is commendable' (ὅσα ἐστὶν ἀληθῆ, ὅσα σεμνά, ὅσα δίκαια, ὅσα ἁγνά, ὅσα προσφιλῆ, ὅσα εὔφημα, 4.8). Although this verse lacks the significant phrase in Rom. 12.17 of 'before all people' (ἐνώπιον πάντων ἀνθρώπων), the repetition of ὅσα functions to emphasize that the scope for considering that which is true, honourable, commendable, etc., is limitless and not just restrained to the boundaries of the church community. Thus, Furnish continues: 'Here the apostle is presupposing that at least some of what is esteemed as good conduct in the civic community can be accepted as such also by the believing community' (2009: 146–7).

However, for Cranfield, since Paul 'was well aware of the darkening of men's minds' (1979: 646) he could not be referring to discerning 'those things which are agreed by all men to be good' (1979: 645), but rather they are to 'seek, in the sight of all men those things which (whether they recognize it or not) are good, the arbiter of what is good being not a moral *communis sensus* of mankind, but the gospel' (1979: 646; also Morris 1988: 452). But this view ignores the deliberate recognition by Paul that there is some common ground between the believers and the outsiders regarding what is considered to be 'good'. Thus, as Dunn notes, the fact that Paul is using the more general words of κακός and καλός (rather than, for example, asking them to respond with 'holiness') shows that Paul is appealing to 'a widespread sense of what is morally right and fitting' (1988b: 748).[19] Paul's use of καλός is to denote 'a quality of beauty (physical or moral) which would receive general approbation in people of sensibility' (Dunn 1988b: 748; also Schreiner 1998: 672 and Fitzmyer 1993: 656-7). Keck acknowledges the tension here with Paul's description of unbelievers elsewhere, but nevertheless concludes that in chapter 12, 'Evidently not being conformed to this age (v.2) does not require total rejection of all the values in the culture' (2005: 308).

At this point we return to the juxtaposition outlined in the first chapter: that although Paul uses negative stereotypes to describe the outsiders in a way that polarizes ingroup and outgroup members (suggesting no similarity regarding morality or spirituality), when instructing the ingroup to relate to the outgroup there is a recognition of shared values and a concern for the believers to demonstrate behaviour that is commendable among outsiders. Romans 12.17 belongs to these passages, for the believers are to respond to evil with that which is understood as καλός by all people. Thus, Constantineanu writes that 'Paul's point here (v.17) is that wherever there is good in a culture which is universally recognized, they [the believers] should be committed to that good' (2010: 161), and it therefore follows on that in doing so, the believer must then 'perform good deeds, which will be recognized as such by those who are the object of them' (Leenhardt 1961: 318). As such (and given the close parallel to the wording in 2 Cor. 8.21), when Paul writes, 'before all people' (ἐνώπιον πάντων ἀνθρώπων), we must understand ἐνώπιον as 'before' in the sense of seeking approval.[20] Although Schmithals emphasizes the outsiders as onlookers (referring to other NT instructions that call for believers to make sure that their good is visible; see Mt. 5.13-16; 1 Pet. 2.12, 15; 3.13ff; 4.12ff), he is also correct in concluding that 'the members of the congregation, by publicly doing good, are to silence the ignorance of the foolish people who slander them as offenders' (1988: 453). Thus, instead of giving their persecutors 'like for like', they are to offer them that which is received as 'good'.

As Schmithals suggests, there is a possible underlying motivation concerning a desire for the outgroup to see the ingroup in a new way, and thus change their opinion of them. What others think is important here because their thoughts and opinions are clearly leading to suffering and persecution of the ingroup. However, Paul is not willing simply to instruct the believers to do whatever is good for their persecutors and hope that this positive interaction from ingroup to outgroup is enough to lead to a positive opinion in the outgroup towards the ingroup. For he continues to urge the believers: εἰ δυνατὸν τὸ ἐξ ὑμῶν, μετὰ πάντων ἀνθρώπων εἰρηνεύοντες (12.18). Hopefully, blessing their persecutors and offering to them not evil but that which will be received as good, should work towards deconstructing the negative opinion of the believers in the minds of the outgroup, and thus lead to the reduction of hostility. However, Paul makes it clear that, although peace might not always be the outcome, it is something that the believers need to seek actively; it is not just a pleasant side-effect of the believers' positive interaction with outsiders through blessing them and offering good acts. The seeking of peace is in itself a command which is not gained by living a quiet lifestyle, seeking to limit interaction (see 1 Thess. 4.11), but is rather something that is pursued, and as such the creation of peace here is a social achievement, not just an absence of friction or conflict. Once more, the presence of these particular outsiders sharpens up the cognitive element of the ingroup's social identity: they are to be peacemakers. This ultimately involves reconciliation in relationships marked by conflict, and the building up of trust and positive relationships with the other. This does not happen by doing nothing; rather, this is an intentional, thoughtful and committed approach to relating within and to the wider society. This also touches on the 'emotional' element of social identity (the attitudes or feelings the ingroup may have for the outgroup) since the act of pursuing peace requires the believer to value the unbeliever and their relationship with the unbeliever, and a desire not to cause the other any offence, as far as possible.

In this way, what others think of the believing community might also be a sign that the believers are managing to achieve an important group norm or expectation that is part of their social identity. If being a believer means seeking peace with all people, including outsiders, then the achievement of this involves a radical transformation of relationships so that there is a positive one with outsiders. The formation of good relationships, however, is built upon good opinions of the other; difference between groups can still remain but a positive opinion of (or at least attitude towards) the other group needs to be more salient than perceived difference. This will lead to the desire for, and the attainment of peace across boundaries. Thus, what others think is in itself an indication of whether or not believers are able to live out one aspect of their identity in being those who pursue and create peace in a society.

3.2.4 Providing for your enemy and changing the narrative (12.20)

Thus far, we have seen that Romans 12 reveals a concern for the way in which believers should interact with outsiders, and a sensitivity regarding outsiders that shapes how the believers should discern what would be received by them as a blessing and as good. In this way, not only is a 'similarity or community of culture' recognized (Barth 1969: 15) but also the importance of discerning 'what others think'. In the process, believers are prompted to reshape some of their theology around blessing–cursing and thus gain a greater appreciation of their identity as givers of blessing, and also as doers of good and pursuers of peace. Whilst not directly indicated, clearly these aspects of the believers' identity, focusing on their relations with outsiders, will in turn impact upon what outsiders think: there is an unstated hope that they will be able to transform how the persecutor looks upon them so that instead of finding hostility at the boundary between the two groups, peace and positive relationships are found. As such, there is a cyclical dynamic whereby what others think impacts upon the believers' understanding of their social identity (and their group behaviour), which in turn influences what others think. The outsiders' view of the insiders shapes but also redefines the believers' understanding of their own identity and calling.

Thus, after warning the believers not to assume the identity of the one who judges and who avenges, for this is God's role (v. 19), Paul again encourages the believers to show concern for the outsider and to respond appropriately in providing for their needs to promote and protect their welfare. He writes, 'but if your enemy hungers, feed him; if he thirsts, give him a drink' (ἀλλὰ ἐὰν πεινᾷ ὁ ἐχθρός σου, ψώμιζε αὐτόν, ἐὰν διψᾷ, πότιζε αὐτόν, 12.20a).[21] Given what has just been instructed in previous verses, this comes as no surprise: the believer cannot aim to bless their persecutors (v. 14) whilst returning evil for evil (v. 17); the believer cannot return good for evil (v. 17) and yet ignore their enemy's destitution (v. 20). Thus, Cranfield is surely right to point out that 'to fail to do to our enemies the good they stand in need of, when it is in our power to do it, is "a kind of indirect retaliation"' (1979: 648, quoting from Calvin). Furthermore, these instructions to give food and drink to those who need them may intentionally be reflecting a universal ethic that was held in society at that time, concerning the type of behaviour or co-operation that was essential for healthy community life. Josephus, for example, describes how one must give 'fire, water, and food to all who request them ... and that the decisions made even towards enemies should be kind' (*Against Apion*, Book 2: 211). This is also found in Greek teaching and literature, in what is known as 'the curses of Bouzyges', which denounce those who do not adhere to the unwritten laws of humanity concerned with how to help one's neighbour.[22] These include duties such as sharing fire and water and giving directions to a stranger. Hence, in asking the believers to provide food and drink to their neighbours, Paul is appealing for them to ensure that they show no partiality when doing what is universally considered to be good and essential for healthy relationships in the community.

However, unlike in the previous instructions to bless, to offer what is good and to pursue peace, Paul does issue an underlying motivation for this instruction, which does come as a surprise: 'for by doing this you will heap burning coals upon his head' (τοῦτο γὰρ ποιῶν ἄνθρακας πυρὸς σωρεύσεις ἐπὶ τὴν κεφαλὴν αὐτοῦ, v. 20b). The intention behind the visible act of generosity and care appears at first glance to have a somewhat darker side in the interaction between believer and unbeliever. Paul does not explain this imagery, but it is often used throughout the OT and apocryphal works to carry a range of symbolic meanings, which seem to have developed over time. For example, David uses the image of 'glowing coals' (ἄνθρακες ἐξεκαύθησαν) or 'coals of fire' (ἐξεκαύθησαν ἄνθρακες πυρός) coming from God to describe God's anger towards David's enemies (2 Sam. 22.9, 13). And the psalmist, in writing of his desire for his violent enemies to be stopped in their evil (Ps. 139.9, LXX) and for them to 'rise no more' (v. 11b), cries out: 'Let burning coals fall upon them!' (πεσοῦνται ἐπ' αὐτοὺς ἄνθρακες, v. 11a). This imagery of burning coals is used by God's people to describe or call for God's anger or judgement towards their enemies, in order to bring about an end to unjust suffering in the believer at the hands of their enemies. It is used to describe God's power and anger in reaction to the psalmist's cry for help ('glowing coals flamed forth from him', Ps. 17.9, 13 LXX) and the image of 'burning coals of fire' (ἀνθράκων πυρός, Ezek. 1.13 LXX) is also part of a vision given to Ezekiel which displays the 'glory of the Lord' (δόξης κυρίου, v. 28). However, in Sirach, 'burning coals' are used to describe the identity of the sinner, not that of God. Thus, there is a prohibition against kindling 'the burning coals of sinners' (8.10a, μὴ ἔκκαιε ἄνθρακας ἁμαρτωλοῦ), otherwise that person may 'be burned in their flaming fire' (8.10b, μὴ ἐμπυρισθῇς ἐν πυρὶ φλογὸς αὐτοῦ). Burning coals seem to identify sinners but are also linked with their ultimate destruction.

In the apocryphal work of *6 Ezra* (*2 Esdras* 15–16) we find this image being used in a similar way, but with the addition that the coals are placed on the *heads* of sinners, like that in Rom. 12.20.[23] The author declares that 'God will burn coals of fire on the head of him who says, "I have not sinned before God and his glory"' (16.53, in Charlesworth 1983: 559). Here, the burning coals are a sign of sin, and when the author later warns about God making 'a public spectacle' of those who have sinned, it is possible that the image of burning coals is used to refer to a *public* identification of those who are sinners (v. 64). However, there is an eschatological element within these verses, for the author refers to the sinners being revealed as such 'on that day' (v. 65), and he therefore calls them to 'cease' from their sins so that God will deliver them (v. 67).[24]

The image of burning coals has long been used to identify sinners and to indicate God's judgement of sinners, and although *6 Ezra* is written after Paul's letter to the Romans, it might have also acquired the sense of shaming by the time Paul wrote this letter. However, one striking difference in Rom. 12.20 is the fact that it is the believers rather than God who will be the ones putting burning coals onto the heads of their enemies. The motivation for offering assistance and supporting those in need seems to be in order to increase the certainty of the outsiders (especially their persecutors) receiving God's wrath. This, however, sits uncomfortably with the attitude that Paul is attempting to engender in the believers towards the outsiders: that of mercy, grace, and generosity in order to desire for the blessing of their enemies and to offer goodness in return for evil. Furthermore, Paul's use of the verb σωρεύω ('to heap') seems to emphasize this action.[25] Understandably, this has led some scholars to interpret ἄνθρακας πυρός in a new way, so that Paul is using it as a sign of 'the burning pangs of shame and contrition' (Cranfield 1979: 649). This is because the good acts of the believer cause their enemies to feel a sense of shame, which in turn will lead to their repentance; burning coals are now a sign that the enemy has been reconciled to the believer. Barrett goes further and writes, 'If an enemy is treated in this way he may well be overcome in the best possible fashion – he may become a friend' (1991: 242-3).[26]

In proposing this interpretation, scholars have often referred to a possible Egyptian religious custom where a sinner carried a tray of burning coals on their head as a sign of their repentance.[27] Klassen explores this possibility quite thoroughly, and he links this Egyptian ritual with the custom of putting ashes on one's head as seen in 2 Sam. 13.19 by Tamar after she is raped by her brother Amnon and sent away. Although Klassen acknowledges that Paul would probably not have known of this Egyptian custom (1963: 347), he argues that the understanding of burning coals to mean repentance fits better with the context of Romans 12, rather than meaning revenge (1963: 345). He remarks that the believers are not intended to sit 'nursing' their wounds and pleasing themselves with thoughts of their enemies being punished, but should instead busy themselves with the power of love, and showing their enemies that they desire good for them rather than punishment (1963: 346). He concludes that the coals of fire are a 'dynamic symbol of change of mind which takes place as a result of a deed of love' (1963: 349). In his later writing, Klassen emphasizes the importance of the command to provide food and water to their enemies (which, he argues, would infer that the believers actually ate with their enemies) and thus sees the instruction of hospitality as a way to even prevent such people from becoming enemies in the first place (1984: 120).

However, not only is this interpretation using the image of burning coals in a different way to that found in the OT or Apocryphal texts, the scholars above have also introduced into the Romans text a desire for friendship that is not justified by the passage. Furthermore, the scholars who propose this reading are often too quick to equate burning coals with punishment and destruction (e.g. Dunn 1988b: 750–1; Adams 2000: 204). We have, however, seen that burning coals may *signal* the destruction of the unrepentant sinner, but are not always themselves the act of destruction. The overriding use of this image is to identify the one who has turned away *from* God, rather than one who has turned *to* God. As such, through their good actions, the believers are not so much heaping up *punishment* on their enemies, but are rather revealing the *sins* of their enemies. The believers are heaping up *evidence* of the unfair hostility of the enemies (and therefore a sign that they are liable to God's wrath) but not the *execution* of that wrath itself (which is an action reserved to God). In other words, the merciful and generous actions of the believers, which are also actions that will have a positive impact on the wider society, are to demonstrate the *difference* between insiders as those who are blameless and those who are wicked.

However, this difference is one that has not been proven by an appeal to religiosity but by appealing to a commonly held view that one should seek to provide for another person when they are hungry and thirsty. Presumably, those who persecute believers would not offer such care to believers who might be in need of help; they therefore have burning coals heaped on their heads because of social judgement. For, in giving food and drink to their enemy, the believers are not only inviting their enemy to reciprocate with a similar positive act of goodness, but are also revealing and classifying the hostility of the persecutors as unnecessary and unjust. If the believers give in this way, then they are truly exposing the sin of their enemies, because they are showing that they are not deserving of acts of hatred. The persecutors believe they are right to be acting in such a way towards the believers, but the believers' actions of kindness, goodness and mercy will function to change the narrative and reinterpret the situation. However, this only works if the actions of the believers are indeed understood by all as good; it is crucial that the believers are unified in acting in ways that are seen and interpreted as good, kind and merciful by the wider society, by the outsiders.

3.2.5 Summary

Within a wider passage where Paul reveals the norms and expectations for the ingroup (which would result in a strengthening of ingroup cohesion by increasing the similarities *within* the ingroup), Paul turns his attention to the outsiders – not just to their hostile presence, but to the need for the believers to engage with them across the boundary in a certain way. We find that the presence of these particular outsiders causes certain understandings of the believers' identity to come to the fore (the cognitive aspect of social identity) and that implicit in these instructions is therefore a concern for how the believers view the outsiders (the emotional aspect). It is only in viewing the outsiders in a certain way that the believers can achieve their group norms; the instructions require the believers to view the outsiders with mercy and kindness but also in a way that values their presence. However, in doing so, Paul also encourages the believers to discover the areas where the boundary is blurred, where there is a 'community of culture', which here centres on a universally acknowledged view of what is 'good'. Thus, it is crucial that the believers are to recognize and align themselves with the shared norms of καλός.

Clearly, it is also crucial that the outsiders are to see this, and perhaps the actions of blessing, of doing that which is good, of seeking peace and of offering welfare assistance will be enough to change the narrative held by the outsiders regarding the insiders that has led to hostility. There is a desire for the ingroup to influence the emotional aspect of the outgroup's identity, in other words, how the outsiders view the insiders. Believers are to show by their actions (which belong to a universal ethic) the injustice of their experience as ones persecuted in the wider community. Thus, although not denying aspects of the believer's counter-cultural identity, those aspects that set them apart as different from outgroup members, Paul is rather emphasizing (or at least specifying) that part of a believer's identity is *not* counter-cultural, and shares some similarity with an unbeliever's identity. For Paul this creates an opportunity for positive interaction with outsiders. Whereas SIT suggests that groups need to lean on difference to protect their identity and existence, Paul believes that the ingroup needs to lean on their similarity with the outgroup in order to re-create their public image, but also to ensure survival.

3.3 Romans 13

3.3.1 Introduction

In chapter 13 Paul continues to outline some of the important group norms and expectations of believers in relation to the outsider. However, rather than continuing to refer to those outsiders who are persecutors or enemies, he instead turns to look towards those outsiders who have received authority from God to rule over society (13.1-2). How the believers should be concerned about this relationship with outsiders is discussed in verses 1-7, before Paul reminds them of the law of love and some of the Ten Commandments that particularly guide social relationships (vv. 8-10). The chapter ends with yet more expectations for how believers should behave in general (vv. 11-14), referring to some specific moral decisions and using the image found in 1 Thess. 4.12 of 'walking honourably' (Rom. 13.13), and appealing to the coming eschaton (13.11-12). Clearly all three of these sections will impact on their relationships with outsiders and how they are seen by them. But it is the first section that reveals an explicit concern regarding a particular group of outsiders: whereas Paul uses general terms in the second section which allow for the interpretation that he still has an eye on the outsider (μηδενί, v. 8a, ὁ ἕτερος, v. 8b; ὁ πλησίον, vv. 9, 10), it is Paul's focus on those in authority in verses 1-7 that will be the centre of attention in the remainder of this chapter. However, the identity of the outsiders mentioned in vv. 1-7 has been debated, and so we will first briefly turn to examine this before exploring Paul's expectations for believers interacting with these outsiders.

3.3.2 Defining the outside authorities

Paul appears to use many different terms in Rom. 13.1-7 to refer to a particular subgroup of outsiders. For, he instructs believers to be 'subject' (vv. 1, 5) to 'the governing authorities' (ἐξουσίαις ὑπερεχούσαις, v. 1) who have been appointed by God, and as such 'the authority' (τῇ ἐξουσίᾳ, vv. 2, 3) should not be resisted. However, they could be feared, for 'rulers' (οἱ ἄρχοντες) do not punish good but bad conduct (v. 3).[28] Therefore, it is possible for the believers to receive praise from 'the authority' (v. 3) by doing good, for the person in this position of authority is 'a servant of God' (θεοῦ διάκονος, twice in v. 4) whom Paul also describes as 'an avenger for wrath' (ἔκδικος εἰς ὀργήν, v. 4).[29] They are 'public servants of God' (λειτουργοὶ θεοῦ, v. 6). And in the last instruction in this section, Paul widens the scope to include 'all people' (ἀπόδοτε πᾶσιν τὰς ὀφειλάς, v. 7). Some of these descriptions are used elsewhere in Romans: Paul refers to God as having 'authority' like the potter over the clay (ἐξουσία, 9.21), and to Christ, and then to Phoebe, as 'a servant' (15.8, 16.1, διάκονος), and himself as a 'servant of Christ Jesus' (λειτουργὸν Χριστοῦ Ἰησοῦ, 15.16).[30]

Most scholars are persuaded that Paul is referring to those in civic authority.[31] Thus, whereas Cullmann (drawing on Dibelius 1909) argues that Paul is both referring to the state and to the 'angelic powers that stand behind the State government' (1951: 195; 1957: 100), Käsemann points out that 'in the authentic Pauline letters, unlike Heb. 1.14, angelic powers are not spoken of as servants in the work of the divine creation but as forces which are hostile, or at least dangerous, to the community and the faith' (1980: 353), and Schreiner rightly argues that 'elsewhere Paul forcefully contests the idea that believers should be subservient to angelic powers (cf. Col. 2.8-15)' (1998: 682). Nanos however has proposed that Paul is referring to the authorities of the Jewish synagogues. He argues that Gentile believers were meeting in synagogues and therefore that Paul is concerned that they should adopt and commit to accepted behaviour in the synagogues which includes submitting to the Jewish (non-Christian) leaders and paying the temple tax (1996: 291, 293, 295-6, 309). His fundamental premise that the believers were still closely associated with the Jewish synagogues, however, goes against what Romans 16 suggests, that the believers were rather meeting in the houses of fellow disciples of Christ (see Esler 2003: 331). The rest of his argument fails to thoroughly engage with the interpretation that Paul is referring to civic authorities, and so he neither undermines this interpretation nor strengthens his own.

The passage itself, however, gives a strong indication that Paul is concerned with local authorities, since verse 6 refers to the believers paying taxes (φόρους). Paul's use of 'because of this' (διὰ τοῦτο) at the beginning of this verse functions to join it with the preceding verses, where Paul explains the function of the 'rulers' and 'the authority' (vv. 3-4), and the reasons for the believers to be subject to them (v. 5). Additionally, although Paul normally uses terms such as διάκονος and ἐξουσία to refer to himself and his co-workers, it is clear that this is *not* the case in 13.1-7, since Paul never describes his own role as 'bearing the sword' or himself as 'an avenger of wrath' (13.4). Rather, ἐξουσία is often used throughout the NT to refer to the possession and the exercise of power, and often to refer to civic authorities or their power (e.g. Mt. 8.9; Lk. 7.8; 12.11; 19.17; 20.20; 23.7; Jn 19.10, 11; Tit. 3.1).[32] As Moo notes, it can be used in a 'typical' way (e.g. Mt. 28.18) to denote 'a sphere over which authority is exercised' (e.g. Lk. 23.7), or to refer to the person or divine being who exercises authority (1996: 795).

Furthermore, this passage in Rom. 13.1-7 has strong connections and similarities with other passages in the NT, where the relationship between believers and civic ruling authorities are in view. The strongest connection is with 1 Pet. 2.13-17, where believers are also instructed to submit (using the same verb of ὑποτάσσω as in Rom. 13.1) to 'every human institution because of the Lord' (1 Pet. 2.13). The author continues to explain that these human institutions include 'a king as being in authority' (βασιλεῖ ὡς ὑπερέχοντι, 1 Pet. 2.13; cf. ἐξουσίαις ὑπερεχούσαις, Rom. 13.1) and 'governors, as being sent by him for vengeance [on] evildoers but praise of ones doing good' (ἡγεμόσιν ὡς δι' αὐτοῦ πεμπομένοις εἰς ἐκδίκησιν κακοποιῶν ἔπαινον δὲ ἀγαθοποιῶν, 1 Pet. 2.14). Both passages explain the source and function of the power of those in civic authority as coming from God, and both refer to vengeance (ἔκδικος/ ἐκδίκησις), evil or evil-doers (κακός/κακοποιός), praise (ἔπαινος) and good or good-doers (ἀγαθός/ἀγαθοποιός).[33]

There are also clear connections with two passages in the Pastoral Epistles. In 1 Timothy, the Author urges the believers to pray not just for all people (πᾶς ἄνθρωπος, 2.1) but also for 'kings' (βασιλεῖς) and 'all those in authority' (πάντων τῶν ἐν ὑπεροχῇ, 2.2; cf. ἐξουσίαις ὑπερεχούσαις, Rom. 13.1). And in Titus, the Author also commands the believers to be subject (using the same verb as in Rom. 13.1, ὑποτάσσω) to rulers and to authorities (using the same titles as in Rom 13.1, 3). The Author does, however, take this command one step further than that found in both Romans 13 and 1 Peter 2, for the believers are also to be obedient (πειθαρχέω). Once again, believers are instructed 'to be ready for every good work' (πρὸς πᾶν ἔργον ἀγαθὸν ἑτοίμους εἶναι, Tit. 3.1, also v. 8), although there is no mention this time of winning praise through doing such, nor a warning of doing evil and the subsequent fearing of wrath.

These passages in the Pastoral Epistles and 1 Peter, where the focus is on how believers should view and relate to civic authorities, show clear connections with Rom. 13.1-7 in vocabulary and in thought, which strongly suggests that the outsiders in Romans 13 are also those of the ruling earthly powers. This theme of submitting to established earthly authorities, and of the belief that the existence of these authorities was dependent upon God, however, is also seen in the OT, particularly in Daniel. Thus, in one of Nebuchadnezzar's dreams he hears the proclamation that, 'the Lord is the Most High of the kingdom of mortals and gives it to whom he will' (ὅτι κύριός ἐστιν ὁ ὕψιστος τῆς βασιλείας τῶν ἀνθρώπων καὶ ᾧ ἐὰν δόξῃ δώσει αὐτήν, Dan. 4.17, LXX; also 4.25, 32; 5.21). It is clear that even though Nebuchadnezzar was given 'kingship, greatness, glory and majesty' from 'the Most High God' (5.18, LXX), it made him neither infallible nor exempt from God's judgement (5.21; also 2.21, 37-38). Similarly, in the Wisdom of Solomon, kings and judges over the earth are addressed (6.1) and are explicitly told that their dominion and sovereignty are from God and are thus reminded that he is the superior ruler, the 'Most High' (v. 3, LXX). However, unlike in Romans 13, there is also a judgement upon them, for they have been found not to act rightly and so God will come upon them 'terribly and swiftly' (v. 5, LXX).

3.3.3 What the insiders think of the outsiders

Whereas these OT passages portray the belief that no ruler is exempt from human frailty or divine judgement, Paul offers an uncritical description of the authorities and rulers in Romans 13. He instructs the believers to be subject to their governing civic authorities without also clarifying any exceptional circumstances, such as when these same authorities do not keep God's will and themselves become evildoers rather than avengers of evil. As Kim points out, this passage is devoid of Paul's 'critical view of the rulers of this world that he expresses elsewhere (1 Cor 2.6-8; 6:1; 15.24-25; 1 Thess. 2.18; etc.) and the unjust treatment that he himself has received from some of them (1 Cor. 4.9-13; 2 Cor. 1.8-10; 6:5; 11.23, 25a; 1 Thess. 2.2, 18; etc.)' (2008: 38). Rather, he pronounces that they have been appointed by God (αἱ δὲ οὖσαι ὑπὸ θεοῦ τεταγμέναι εἰσίν, Rom. 13.1).[34] Paul only uses this verb τάσσω here and in 1 Cor. 16.15 where he describes the household of Stephanas as having 'devoted themselves' (ἔταξαν ἑαυτούς) to the service of the saints. It is used fairly frequently throughout Acts in the sense of appointing someone, some people or something to a specific role or task (15.2; 22.10; 28.23), having been 'destined' to receive something (13.48) or in the sense of a command that has been issued (18.2). The act of appointing often presumes that a correlating action will be undertaken by those who have been appointed. And thus, Paul continues in Romans 13 to outline that they function as a 'terror not to good conduct but to evil' for to good they will give praise (ἔπαινος, v. 3). It is in this context that Paul describes them as 'servants of God', continuing to expand upon their function by writing that they are those who 'bear the sword' and act as 'avengers of wrath' to the one who does evil (v. 4).

This uncritical description of these particular outsiders has led some scholars to emphasize the fact that Paul was writing at a particular time, in a particular context and to a particular community, and they thus appeal to the 'situation-bound nature of the passage' (Kim 2008: 38).[35] This appears to lift the pressure from understanding how these instructions can be applied to all contexts in all ages. However, Elliott argues that even if this passage is understood simply in its own situation and context, this in itself is not enough to explain 'the benign, even benevolent characterization of "the governing authorities"' (1997: 196). Elliott is right in noticing the 'contradiction' between Paul's negative description of the Gentile world earlier in the letter and his 'generous characterization' here (1997: 186). However, what can often go unnoticed is that this 'generous characterization' is in the context of issuing the believers with a series of instructions on how to behave among the authorities. This was the apparent contradiction highlighted in Chapter 1, that although Paul gives negative descriptions of unbelievers elsewhere, when he instructs believers to behave amongst or respond to the unbelievers, he acknowledges their positive character or attributes by recognizing that there exists a shared understanding of morals and values between the two groups. Here in Romans, Paul shows an appreciation that the unbelievers are still part of God's sovereign plan in ordering the ways of the world. Thus, whilst Kim acknowledges the aspects of the 'Roman imperial system' that Paul would have easily criticized, he also suggests that Paul 'may have appreciated the *relative* order and justice of the Roman Empire' which he preferred 'to chaos and anarchy' (2008: 42–3).

Additionally, it should not be overlooked that Paul bases the believers' submission on two main points: that the authorities are appointed by God (and thus answerable to him, v. 1), and that it is the intention for them to do the divine work of encouraging good and dissuading evil (vv. 3-4).

Furthermore, the effect of describing the authorities in such a glowing way would have impacted upon how the believers viewed these specific outsiders. It is surely intentional that Paul describes them without criticism in order to encourage the believers to see them in the best possible light. In other words, if the main message Paul wants his audience to take away is that they should work and live well with outsiders, then clearly he will only give a partial view of 'the authorities'. Perhaps, as Käsemann suggests, some believers in Rome were viewing 'earthly authorities with indifference or contempt' (1980: 351). If so, it is even more important for Paul to emphasize the divine appointment and work of those in authority. Paul's concern is not to give a full thesis on the nature of earthly rulers, but clearly to persuade believers that they should look on these outsiders with positivity and respect and respond accordingly. They are to see that, although they are 'outsiders' in the sense that they do not believe in Jesus as Lord, they are in some way still connected to the insiders in the sense that God has appointed them to carry out his work of distinguishing good from evil. Although they are outsiders in terms of what they believe (or not), God nevertheless relates to them and appoints them to act on his behalf. Moreover, it is the way in which believers acknowledge and respond to this that creates the potential for the ingroup to be viewed in a positive and even praiseworthy way (v. 3).

As such, one important observation on this passage is that Paul is concerned with how the ingroup sees the outgroup: what the insiders think of the outsiders is as important as what the outsiders think of the insiders. If the insiders view the outsiders with the kind of admiration that might follow upon knowing that these outsiders in effect work for God, then this will make them more likely to submit to these outsiders, but also increase their concern for what these outsiders think of them. On the other hand, what the outsiders think of the insiders will also affect how they respond to the insiders, which Paul is very clear about: if the outsiders praise the insiders then the corollary is that they will not unfairly punish the insiders, contrary to the persecutors. In terms of SIT, Paul is trying to influence the emotional component of the social identity of both the ingroup and the outgroup. In Romans 12 Paul did not attempt to influence how the believers saw the outsiders as sinners and ungodly, undeserving of their grace but recipients of it nevertheless. However, in chapter 13 Paul describes these outsiders in a positive light and connects them to God's sovereignty. The boundary between believer and unbeliever is still there, but there is no boundary in relation to those with whom and through whom God works, and those among whom he is present.

3.3.4 What the outsiders think of the insiders

As we have already noted, Paul is also concerned about what the outsiders think of the insiders. As such, Paul is trying to ensure that the believers behave among these outsiders in such a way that means they will receive their praise and admiration, rather than their wrath. Specific norms for the ingroup are therefore emphasized to achieve this result. The first one is that they are all to 'be subject' to the ruling authorities (13.1, 5). Paul uses this verb ὑποτάσσω elsewhere in Romans and in 1 Corinthians and in doing so identifies the one with the authority and power (e.g. Rom. 8.20; 10.3; 1 Cor. 14.32, 34; 15.27-28; 16.16). However, he also uses it to signal the expectation that the behaviour of the one who submits will be shaped accordingly. As such, women in the congregations in Corinth are to submit, but the surrounding description of what their behaviour should look like (namely being silent) is clearly connected to their submissive disposition (1 Cor. 14.34-35; also 16.16). When the verb ὑποτάσσω is used in the disputed epistles, there also often follows a description of the subsequent behaviour. Believers are told in Ephesians 5 that they should submit 'to one another' (v. 21), but then the description goes on to focus upon wives, who should submit to their husbands 'in everything' (ἐν παντί, 5.24). In other words, how they shape *all* of their actions and thoughts should be orientated around the position of submission to their husbands (see also Col. 3.18; Tit. 2.5). This is also true of the slave, who in submitting to their master, should be aiming to please them in all things, being faithful, respectful and honest (Tit. 2.9-10).

Thus, contrary to Adams who, when referring to Rom. 13.1 writes that the 'call to submit is a call to recognise one's place in this order' rather than 'a call for unqualified obedience to rulers' (2000: 206), I would argue that although Paul does not call the believers to 'obey' the authorities (cf. Tit. 3.1), it can be seen from the above references that ὑποτάσσω is used to signal the expectation that this submission impacts upon behaviour, which is sometimes described, and other times left as an assumption. Thus, in Romans 13 Paul is calling the believers to recognize the authority and power of the civic authorities, to recognize their place in this relationship, but also to acknowledge that this informs and shapes their behaviour towards them. It is the posture of submission that shapes the behaviour of the ones submitting. Verses 2-7 then provide the detail as to what this submission looks like in practice. For, the posture of submission means that they will not 'oppose' or 'resist' these authorities, and the consequence for doing so is receiving judgement (v. 2).[36] By presenting submission and opposition as the two ways for the believers to choose from in acting towards outsiders, Paul is adding a subtle quality to the act of submission so that it is not simply about doing whatever the authority figure asks of you but also in some way taking the stance that they are correct in what they instruct; they are not to oppose but to affirm. Their submission is not just out of duty, or because of hierarchy, but because they should concur with what those in authority are working to achieve in society – namely, encouraging good works rather than evil (v. 3).

Thus, although Wright sees 'counter-imperial hints' in this letter, he does conclude that Romans 13 is motivated by a desire to 'steer Christians away from ... civil disobedience and revolution', for even though they are 'servants of the Messiah, the true Lord, this does not give them carte blanche to ignore the temporary subordinates whose appointed task, whether (like Cyrus) they know it or not, is to bring at least a measure of God's order and justice to the world' (2005: 78–9). The submission of the believers to these authorities is, according to Paul, one way of contributing 'to the realization of God's plan' (Leenhardt 1961: 323; also Ziesler 1989: 309). As such, the believers are not only to hope for the outsiders to simply stop in their acts of persecution, but for the outsiders to praise and commend them: τὸ ἀγαθὸν ποίει, καὶ ἕξεις ἔπαινον ἐξ αὐτῆς (13.3c).

Once again, believers are to 'do good' (cf. ἀγαθός in 12.9, 21; καλός in 12.17), and specifically that which is understood and appreciated as good by these outsiders, if they are to win praise from them, or find approval from them. Winter argues that Paul is referring to believers acting as benefactors by paying for public resources in order to 'enhance the environs of their cities', and that the rulers were expected to publicly honour and praise such people (1994: 26, see also 26-40). However, it is clear from the contrast made between doing 'good' and 'evil' that Paul is referring to believers living according to what is accepted as ethically and morally good, in contrast to living in a way that is dishonourable and destructive; this also runs through chapter 12. It is similarly clear that Paul expects *every* member of the believing community to 'do good' and thus command praise from the rulers; this rules out Winter's proposal since only wealthy citizens could be benefactors, and whilst it is possible that the believing community had wealthy members, there would have been those who had no personal resources to give to the community in this way. Rather, Paul has the expectation that *every* member is capable of winning praise from the authorities, and indeed, that every member *should* command respect and praise from such people. The way to do this was to consider what was seen as 'good' in the eyes of the outsider, and here, specifically, in the eyes of those in authority. Paul is aware that what might be considered 'good' by one person might not be received as such by another (Rom. 14.16), and so he urges the believers to consider what is perceived as good by outsiders.

Thus, whereas in 1 Thessalonians the believers are asked to live quiet lives, doing what would be considered as good in the eyes of the unbelievers, but being as independent as possible, in Romans the believers are to go out of their way in publicly showing the goodness of their lives. As Schmithals writes: 'Verstecken weckt Mißtrauen gegen die Christen; ein vorbildliches Leben in der Öffentlichkeit läßt dagegen Vertrauen entstehen' ('hiding arouses mistrust of Christians; on the other hand, an exemplary life in public gives rise to confidence', 1988: 453).[37] The lifestyle they must adopt is a very public display of what is considered as καλός by all. They are to be conspicuous not because their counter-cultural lifestyles threaten the stability of society, but because they are praiseworthy citizens who seek to uphold peace and who show through their lives what is approved as good, honourable and essential in the rest of society. Paul's instructions force the believers to be as integrated into their community as possible, as known by their neighbours as is reasonable, and as visible in their streets as is practical.[38] It is crucial that the believers recognize that there is common ground in the ethical values held by believers and outsiders, and act accordingly. Conversely, it is crucial that outsiders also recognize this common ground, for this will in turn positively influence their view and opinion of believers, hopefully resulting in praise.

Paul does not elaborate on what this praise might look like from the authorities. Dunn notes that it can carry the sense of 'complementary address' (1988b: 763) which can also be public. For example, in Ps. 21.26 (LXX) the psalmist exclaims that his praise comes from God amidst the great congregation (παρὰ σοῦ ὁ ἔπαινός μου ἐν ἐκκλησίᾳ μεγάλῃ).[39] Paul also mostly writes of the praise that comes from God, which is in preference to winning the praise of other men and women. As such, the 'inward

Jew' will find their praise (ἔπαινος) not 'from others but from God' (Rom. 2.29). Similarly, when talking of Christ's return, Paul teaches the Corinthians that Christ will reveal the motives of all hearts and 'then each one will receive praise from God' (ὁ ἔπαινος γενήσεται ἑκάστῳ ἀπὸ τοῦ θεοῦ, 1 Cor. 4.5). However, in Philippians he calls the believers to take thought of anything that is worthy of praise (ἔπαινος), along with whatever is true, honourable, righteous, pure, lovely, and also whatever is 'well-spoken of' or 'commendable' (ὅσα εὔφημα, 4.8). Although this verse does not specify the source of this praise, it appears from the context that Paul was asking the Philippians to consider behaving in a way that would be considered praiseworthy, not just among the faith community but also among outsiders. According to Preisker, here 'it implies general human recognition' (1964: 587).

It can be seen from the above verses that normally praise is something that comes from God in response to seeing the faithfulness of the believers. Whilst Phil. 4.8 probably envisages the believers behaving in a way so as to win praise from all people, Rom. 13.3 is the only verse in the Pauline corpus that specifically instructs believers to behave so as to win praise from outsiders. This is, however, the expectation in 1 Pet. 2.14, that the believers will submit to the authorities (2.13) who have been sent by God to deliver punishment upon those who do evil, and praise upon those doing that which is good (2.14). It is clear that the praise envisaged in Rom. 13.3 and 1 Pet. 2.14 is a response from the outsiders when they see believers acting in a good way, but since these authorities are acting on behalf of God, then to be praised by the authorities is akin to being praised by God. As such, Paul protects himself from any counter-arguments that would voice the view that believers should not strive for the praise and commendation of others, but only that from God.[40] To Paul, striving for an excellent and praiseworthy opinion in the eyes of these outsiders is also motivated by a desire to win praise from God. It is therefore important what the outsider thinks, and how they evaluate the believing community, because in some way this will mirror God's own opinion of the believing community. Rather than the believers having a negative stereotype, Paul is urging them to build up a positive stereotype of themselves not just among those who persecute them or among their unbelieving neighbours (Romans 12), but even among those in positions of civil authority. The focus on striving for praise (from doing good) will naturally mean they avoid the wrath intended for the one doing evil – and as we have already seen, the authorities, as God's servants, are tasked with punishing the wrongdoer (Rom. 13.4).

Perhaps this link between God and the authorities is why Paul returns once more in verse 5 to the idea of submitting to the authorities, but also why he refers to the conscience of the believers: διὸ ἀνάγκη ὑποτάσσεσθαι, οὐ μόνον διὰ τὴν ὀργὴν ἀλλὰ καὶ διὰ τὴν συνείδησιν ('therefore it is necessary to be subject, not only because of wrath but also because of conscience'). Paul uses 'conscience' (συνείδησις) fairly infrequently (only in Romans, 1 Corinthians and 2 Corinthians), but he seems to understand that the conscience both acts to weigh and discern the goodness in something or someone else (e.g. 2 Cor. 4.2; 5.11) but also to reveal to the outside world the inner moral state of that person. As such, when referring to those Gentiles who have the νόμος written on their hearts, Paul describes their 'conscience' as bearing witness to this (2.15), and he declares that his own conscience bears witness to the fact that he is 'speaking the truth in Christ' (9.1).⁴¹ In these two references the conscience is that which testifies to the inner moral character of a person *and* to the outer moral actions that are produced by such. This is why Paul can defend his ministry and that of his companions by appealing to (and boasting in) 'the testimony of our conscience' (τὸ μαρτύριον τῆς συνειδήσεως ἡμῶν, 2 Cor. 1.12; see also 1 Pet. 3.16; 1 Tim. 3.9; 2 Tim. 1.3). The conscience is that which testifies to the honour and sincerity of the believer or the goodness of a person. It is something that cannot be fabricated; it is a window to the true nature of the soul.⁴²

Thus, in turning to Rom. 13.5, it is easy to see how the reference to the believer's conscience carries both dimensions. Paul urges the believers to submit to the authorities not just because of fear of receiving wrath from doing evil (vv. 4-5) but also because their conscience should be able to discern the fact that they are acting as God's servants to promote goodness. Their conscience should tell them that the authorities are carrying out a divinely appointed role, and as such, they should be able to concur with the messages from such people regarding good and evil (see Moo 1996: 803). 'Therefore', Paul says, believers should submit because they know that their actions and words should be 'good', which is precisely what the authorities are asking them to do, on behalf of God. Additionally, they should submit because in doing so they are revealing and testifying to their good, inner moral framework – it is important that outsiders see this.⁴³ Whilst Jewett argues that Paul is urging the believers to avoid the painful 'conscience-pang' which results from doing what is evil (2007: 797), here I would propose that Paul is reminding the believers that their conscience should be guiding them to recognize the rule of God channelled through the authorities (and therefore that they should submit) but also that their conscience should be guiding the outsiders to recognize the goodness in the believers. The appeal to the conscience reminds believers of the importance in how the insider views the outsider, and how the outsider views the insider.

It is 'because of this' (διὰ τοῦτο) that they pay taxes (v. 6).⁴⁴ This is not simply an illustration but a 'practical point' (Jewett 2007: 798; also Dunn 1988b: 766); they pay taxes because they recognize Paul's point in verse 4, and repeated here in verse 6, that the authorities are God's servants who will reward or punish. Paul continues in verse 7: ἀπόδοτε πᾶσιν τὰς ὀφειλάς ('give to all people what is due to them').⁴⁵ Here, Paul includes 'all people' whether or not they are working for the local authorities, but the context suggests that Paul is still focusing upon this particular group of outsiders.⁴⁶ For, he expands and highlights four obligations: τῷ τὸν φόρον τὸν φόρον, τῷ τὸ τέλος τὸ τέλος, τῷ τὸν φόβον τὸν φόβον, τῷ τὴν τιμὴν τὴν τιμήν ('to the one [requiring] the tax, [give] the tax, to the one [requiring] the indirect taxes, [give] indirect taxes, to the one [requiring] fear, [give] fear, to the one [requiring] honour, [give] honour'). Paul is urging the believers not to be in debt to anyone (see Rom. 13.8a). As well as simply reminding the believers of the 'moral recognition that obligations should be paid' (Dunn 1988b: 767), perhaps there is also an element of encouraging the believers not to be dependent on anyone so that they can control the level of contact and type of relationship with their outsiders, as was found in 1 Thess. 4.12.

There is an obvious cross-over with Jesus's own teaching: Τὰ Καίσαρος ἀπόδοτε Καίσαρι καὶ τὰ τοῦ θεοῦ τῷ θεῷ ('the things of Caesar give to Caesar and the things of God [give] to God', Mk 12.17). This has led some to conclude that the reference to φόβος in Rom. 13.7 is intended to be understood as giving reverence to God (e.g. Cranfield 1979: 670–1; Ziesler 1989: 314–15). However, given that it is used earlier in Rom. 13.3-4 with reference to the rulers and authorities, Paul would have surely been clearer in identifying a change of reference in verse 7.[47] Given this though, Cranfield is right to acknowledge the 'certain awkwardness' regarding the fact that in verse 3 believers are told that fear of the authorities results from doing what is evil and can be avoided by doing good, and now in verse 7 they are instructed to give fear to those due fear (1979: 670). Perhaps therefore Paul in verse 7 is reminding the believers of the consequences of their actions, and not necessarily giving a command to fear the authorities at all times. Clearly, what is important in these obligations is not just the moral duty of repaying what is due, but the respectful attitude towards, and honouring of, outsiders (also Peng 2006: 91). Paul is urging them not to judge or look down upon these outsiders, but rather that they should show their submission to those in authority, their willingness to work within these hierarchical structures, their faithfulness and integrity in honouring the rulers and recognizing that they will command fear if the believers disregard what is perceived of as καλόν by all. Once again, Paul is counselling them to behave towards the outsiders as if they were in fact 'insiders'. The call to honour the outsider to whom honour is due (13.7) reminds us of the call to honour one another in the believing community (12.10); for Paul, the believer is to honour both fellow believer and fellow outsider. However, this will all (positively) shape how outsiders view insiders.

This is to some extent continued through in verses 8-10, where Paul summarizes the instruction to pay taxes and to pay to all whatever is due to them (vv. 6-7) with a swift statement, 'owe no one anything' (v. 8a).[48] He then connects this with the expectation that for believers, the one exception to this rule is that they will always owe love to the other person, and this theme of love continues until verse 10.[49] As Cranfield writes, for the believers, love is 'an unlimited debt which we can never be done with discharging' (1979: 674), and as we have seen in 1 Thess. 3.12, Paul does not just restrict the love of believers to other believers, for it should cross the boundary between insider and outsider. However, whereas the use of μηδενί signals that *all* people are in view, Paul then immediately uses ἀλλήλους (v. 8b), which is often reserved for referring to the believers (e.g. Rom. 1.12; 12.5, 10, 16) unless he specifically expands it to include outsiders (e.g. 1 Thess. 3.12; 5.15). He then refers to 'the other' in verse 8; when Paul uses ἕτερος with the article elsewhere, the context usually makes clear whether this other person is within the community of faith (e.g. 1 Cor. 6.1) or outside it (1 Cor. 14.17), although on occasions it is unclear but seems to be used for anyone regardless of religious identity (e.g. 1 Cor. 10.24). Cranfield argues that the definite article when used with 'other' has a 'generalizing effect' so that Paul uses it to refer to anyone regardless of boundary (1979: 676; also Dunn 1988b: 777). And in verse 9 Paul refers to the 'neighbour' in reminding the believers of the command to love 'the neighbour' (πλησίον) which is more likely to be intended to be referring to anyone.[50]

The oscillation between using terms reserved for believers and universal terms to include all people in vv. 8-10 raises an element of uncertainty about who exactly Paul is viewing in this middle passage, and Dunn concludes, 'Perhaps it would be best to say that Paul has fellow believers particularly in view but not in any exclusive way'

(1988b: 776).⁵¹ However, it would not be unusual to find the expectation that believers are to be indiscriminate in their giving of love and honour, and if, as we have seen earlier in Rom. 13.1-7 that outsiders are not altogether 'outsiders' with regard to God's laws regarding good and evil, then neither are they outsiders with regard to God's laws of love. Therefore, since love is a fulfilment of the law (v. 10b), Paul also believes that to be sincere in keeping these commandments the believers need to show outsiders not only whatever is good (Rom. 13.3; also 12.17, 21) but also whatever is an outward expression of love (13.8-10). Paul is concerned not just with how insiders view (and therefore behave towards) outsiders but also with how outsiders view (and respond to) insiders.

3.3.5 Summary

Paul gives the outsiders a positive stereotype: they are servants of God, acting on his behalf to reward good and punish evil. However, in creating this positive stereotype, Paul is also creating a link between the two groups where God is the linchpin: both groups are tasked with the divine calling to uphold what is good. In one sense, Paul is revealing an overlap between the groups by indicating that even the outsiders are found within the sphere of God's reign. This therefore changes the believer's perception of the outsiders – whatever else they might think, these outsiders in particular are authorized by God to carry out part of the divine work on earth. This should in turn motivate a certain response in the insiders to these outsiders. And contrary to SIT, their reaction to the outsiders should neither be of discrimination nor of opposition, but rather they should show respect, and approval of their work. However, from the perspective of the outsiders, if the believers are seen to be respecting them and doing what is considered good, then this also in turn forces them to acknowledge that the believers are not an entirely distinct group in complete opposition to their own, but that they too, in sharing a common agenda for good, tread over the line between who is 'in' and who is 'out'. Paul hopes that in this way the believers have the potential and the power to win the praise of the outsiders, and as such, that the outsiders may now have a positive stereotype of the believers. As Peng observes, 'there is a concern about Christians' social image in the public eye behind the injunction for doing what is good in the sight of the authorities' (2006: 97).

However, it is also clear that, because Paul emphasizes throughout these verses the belief that God is behind the work of these outsiders, then although the praise is audibly coming from the authorities, its true source of praise is from God. As such, in this case the importance of what others think lies in the fact that it is also an indication of what God thinks of the believers. The authorities, as servants of God, are channels of his wrath or his praise. There is therefore a theological rationale for the behaviour of the believers – underpinning their submission, seen through their acts of good and of paying back whatever is due to another person, is the fact that this is good in God's eyes. The explicit rationale is to seek a good opinion in the eyes of the outsider, although the implicit one is to seek the approval of God. However, for Paul, here, you cannot have one without the other: to find the praise of the outsiders, is to find the praise of God. The importance of the outsiders in this passage is that they point the believers to God. Ironically, it is the unbelievers, the apparent outsiders, who remind and direct the attention of the believers onto God and the divine expectation for doing that which is good and avoiding that which is wrong. The importance of the outsiders is that they remind the believers of one of their core norms, to seek and do good, which is attached to one of their core beliefs, that God is judge.

3.4 Conclusion

It is clear that in Romans 12–13 Paul shows a sensitivity to the outsider and a concern for how they experience and view the insider, and as such, he not only shows a recognition of the importance of the opinion of the outsider for the identity and well-being of the believing community, but he utilizes this insight in how he instructs the ingroup in order to re-create its public image. The work of SIT is helpful in providing the language and the framework that enables a specific analysis of how Paul sees the ingroup and the outgroup and their respective identities, and how intergroup relationships constantly influence their own perception of their identity. In this chapter we have used the language of boundary and of group beliefs and norms in discovering how the presence of the outsiders influences, sharpens and perhaps even redefines how the ingroup understands its own identity and distinctive characteristics: this is the 'cognitive' aspect of social identity, as explained by Tajfel and Turner (1979: 40) and developed by Bar-Tal (1998: 93–113). We have also recognized that Paul is concerned with how the insiders view the outsiders (the 'emotional' component), which in turn is intricately connected to the believers' ability to carry out their group beliefs and norms, and thus live according to their specific identity. In contrast to SIT, which presumes that the ingroup will look upon the outgroup in such a way that will lead to discrimination, Paul is keen to stress the need for the believers to look on the outgroup positively and to treat them as if the boundary was not there.

In fact, Paul's thoughts as expressed in Romans 13 would suggest that not only should the believers not allow the boundary to negatively affect how they treat outsiders but they should also consider where other boundaries are found, with regard to God. For, Paul's description of the function of the local rulers and authorities, as acting on behalf of God, begins to connect insiders and outsiders together in one superordinate group where both subgroups are part of God's divine order and ordering of the universe. In the language of SIT, this is recategorization. In doing so, Paul is demonstrating that the two subgroups, although different, still have superordinate goals: both groups aim for good acts rather than evil ones to occur within wider society. Gaertner et al. argue that this recategorization often happens when there is an attempt to reduce intergroup conflict, since it 'shapes relationships, social perceptions, group attitudes and the treatment of others' so as to 'initiate more harmonious interpersonal and intergroup relations' (2000: 148). Given the implicit and explicit references to conflict and the instruction to strive for peace, it is reasonable to suggest that the creation of more 'harmonious' intergroup relations was a significant motivating factor for Paul. Indeed, Adams notes that most of Paul's instructions to the believers are an attempt to reveal that they are neither disruptive nor a political or social threat to the stability of the wider community, that they are neither subversive nor antisocial (2000: 217–18). It would be natural for Paul to have had fears over this escalating from local disturbances to major acts of persecution under the governance of the local authorities. Hostility between believers and outsiders was not uncommon; however, what was unique here was the role and identity that Rome held in the wider empire. If the persecution escalated in Rome, then other faith communities further afield could be put at risk. The safety of believing communities across the Roman Empire would have been a concern for Paul, and therefore most likely a significant motivating factor underlying some of these instructions (see also Dunn 1988b: 738; Campbell 2006: 74).[52]

However, it is when the third component of social identity (the evaluative component) is applied to Romans 12–13 that an interesting dynamic in Paul's theology and understanding of intergroup relations is revealed, also indicating how SIT can be developed. According to SIT, the ingroup normally compares itself with other outgroups, particularly choosing dimensions which would result in a positive comparison for the ingroup (Tajfel 1978: 63; Tajfel and Turner 1979: 40; Tajfel 1981: 229, 255). In order to compete with the outgroup, difference needs to be emphasized which will hopefully lead to a positive evaluation for the ingroup and therefore a sense of superiority over the outgroup. Paul clearly recognizes the difference between the ingroup and outgroup in Romans 12–13: whereas the outsider can be the one who persecutes and causes damage to the believer, the believer should be the one who blesses, who tries to cause flourishing, by divine intervention, to the outsider (12.14). Whereas the outsider gives evil, the insider should give thought to (and then do) what is considered good by all (12.17); whereas the outsider causes conflict and tension, the insider should strive to live in peace with all (12.18); whereas the outsider is revealed as the sinner, unjustly persecuting the believers, the insider is revealed as righteous and good. Whereas the local authorities are to reward good with praise and wickedness with punishment, the believers are to indiscriminately give goodness and blessing to all. It could be said that the importance of the outsider to the insider is that they reveal what the insider should *not* be like.

Nevertheless, Paul does not use this recognition of difference specifically to compare the groups in order to promote the ingroup over the outgroup. Rather, in revealing the difference between the members of each group, he also appeals each time to a widespread sense of what is right or good and what is wrong. As such, when he calls the believers to bless, to do good, to give food and water and to owe no one anything, we have seen that Paul is calling upon a universal agreement of what would be considered 'good' (and therefore also what is evil). Every time there is a nod to difference, there is a larger signpost to similarity between the groups. As such, whilst there is a recognition of difference and a confidence in the distinctiveness of the believers, there is a constant reference to, and therefore emphasis upon the *similarity* between the two groups. Barth wrote about the need for there to be 'a similarity or community of culture' (1969: 15) in order to enable interaction, and in Romans 12–13, this 'community of culture' is created partly from a social agreement on what is good and what is required of decent human behaviour towards someone in need (e.g. 12.17; 20; 13.6-8), but there is also a divine dimension to this agreement, as seen in chapter 13 where Paul notes that God has appointed those in civic authority to reward that which is good and to punish the wrongdoers (vv. 1-7). What is considered as good by all might be contained within traditional cultural values, but Paul also recognizes that God is the ultimate source of discerning what is good. Thus, Peng concludes that Paul's instructions are concerned not only with 'human ideals' but with their 'acceptability in front of God' (2006: 132).

But whereas Barth considered these areas of similarity important for interaction, I propose that Paul also recognizes their importance because they hold great potential for shaping the opinion of the other. For this community of culture is the ideal ground where the outsiders can view those group beliefs and norms of the ingroup that they admire. This then generates and influences the type of 'acquaintanceship' between the groups (Bar-Tal 1998: 111). Hence, Paul is concerned to search for an acquaintanceship that comes from outsiders seeing *similarity* in the ingroup, for this in turn has the power to transform the outsiders' response to the believers. This connects with Jenkins' theory that there is always an 'internal–external dialectic' in the formation of identity (2008: 40, 42), and that outsiders have a role in constructing the ingroup's identity so that 'the external moment can be enormously consequential' (2008: 96). Paul is keen to make sure that the 'external moment' happens at the point of similarity, so that a positive acquaintanceship is created, resulting in peace and praise, rather than in persecution and penalties. It is important to note what others think *now* (which largely seems to be a negative opinion of believers) in order to stress the type of ingroup behaviour and group beliefs that would particularly result in a *future* positive opinion of the believers. The opinions of others cannot be underestimated in the formation and maintenance of the identity of the believers: for Paul, these opinions significantly determine those elements of the ingroup's beliefs and norms that should be brought to the fore, and they determine how the ingroup will be treated by the outgroup, which can result in the protection and praise of the ingroup, or conversely in its extinction.[53]

In essence, the opinion of others influences how the ingroup views itself and its vocation, how it lives out its norms, and its ability to simply exist. Whereas Walters argues that these instructions should be viewed as 'the communication of a missionary intervening in a crisis, not that of a theologian composing a systematic doctrine' (1993: 65), I would propose that Paul is rather offering a general and important understanding of how believing communities should view not only themselves but also outsiders, of the importance of positive intergroup relationships, and of the significance of what others think. Although Horrell does argue that these instructions are concerned with a moral responsibility for all believers regardless of their situation (2016: 277–83), the general nature of these instructions is not necessarily in the detail but in the underlying rationale – that it is important to know your outsiders, to know what they think and then to discern how to reveal an area of similarity which will generate a positive acquaintance with outsiders, a positive opinion, and a positive and peaceful existence between the groups. Therefore, whereas SIT emphasizes the importance of difference in creating and maintaining group boundaries, an exploration of Paul's writing to the believers in Rome suggests that similarity is equally, if not sometimes more important, in forming and maintaining group boundaries, for what others think is crucially important for the existence of the ingroup.

Notes

1 This is an eschatological hope: hope of being transformed fully into 'Christ's glorious image at the resurrection' (Witherington 2004: 135, see also Rom. 8.18, 23-25), and hope of 'eschatological salvation' (Fitzmyer 1993: 396; Wilckens 1978: 290).

2 The list of greetings in 16.3-16 appears to include the presence of Jews (e.g. Prisca and Aquilla), although this is debated among scholars. See Moo (2018: 932-43) who identifies which people might be Jewish and the different arguments involved.

3 E.g. Barrett 1991: 6-7, 23; Schreiner 1998: 13-14; Dunn 1988a: xlv, 18-19; Schmithals 1988: 52; Fitzmyer 1993: 33; Keck 2005: 30-1, 46.

4 As Moo writes, 'Paul's point is that Gentiles outside of Christ regularly conform in their behaviour to basic moral norms as reflected in the law of Moses' (2018: 160; see also Fitzmyer 1993: 310; Bruce 1985: 97; Dunn 1988a: 98; Morris 1988: 124-5; Schreiner 1998: 120-4). Although some scholars think that Paul is referring to Gentile Christians (Barth 1959: 36; Cranfield 1975: 156; Jewett 2007: 213), given that in chapter 13 Paul argues that unbelievers in positions of authority know at least part of God's will (and indeed even enforce it; 13.1-7), it seems he understood that Gentile unbelievers can still have a sense of divine moral standards.

5 Yinger, however, argues that the persecution is coming from within the ingroup, for he believes that there is little evidence of persecution against the believers in the letter itself and instead points to chapters 14-15 where there is evidence of internal conflict (1998: 91). However, Paul does not repeat the designations of 'those persecuting you' and 'your enemy' in chapters 14 and 15 which would suggest he is referring to different sources of hostility and conflict. Zerbe also notes that διώκειν elsewhere in Paul 'refers only to hostility from outsiders, never from insiders' (1993: 227). Yinger also argues that some (but not all) of the instructions in 12.14-21 reflect a traditional Jewish response to conflict within the community. He turns to six Second Temple texts to try to illustrate this point (1998: 77), but admits that three of these texts might not be referring to community conflict after all. His argument is not persuasive, and, as Esler notes, since we know that the believers were being persecuted by outsiders in this period, if Paul intended to limit the instructions in 12.14, 17-21 to intragroup relations he would have signalled this more clearly (Esler 2003, 329).

6 Moo (1996, 782) and Schreiner (1998, 667-8) conclude that Rom. 12.15 reverts back to ingroup relations.

7 Some interpreters understand τὸ αὐτό as meaning 'same mind', a unity of thought (Moo 1996: 783; Cranfield 1979: 643; Schreiner 1998: 668). However, this raises a slight awkwardness with how to translate the phrase. It is more probable that τὸ αὐτό refers to 'the same thing', whereby Paul is encouraging his readers to think the same thing toward each person, i.e. to view each other as equal members of the one body (regardless of ethnicity). This would also suggest that μὴ τὰ ὑψηλὰ φρονοῦντες refers to the believers not thinking highly of themselves over and above other members, and that ἀλλὰ τοῖς ταπεινοῖς συναπαγόμενοι refers to them being willing to associate with those considered by others as 'lowly'. Scholars are divided over how to translate τοῖς ταπεινοῖς συναπαγόμενοι, since ταπεινοῖς can be neuter (and thus mean 'humble tasks', see Sanday and Headlam 1902: 364; Witherington 2004: 296) or masculine (and thus mean 'unimportant, lowly persons', see Cranfield 1979: 644; Käsemann 1980: 348; Schreiner 1998: 668). However, the latter meaning fits well with

the context, so that believers are exhorted to associate with those of a lowlier status, since Paul has been concerned about believers relating to one another and turning away from pride. In every other reference of ταπεινός in the NT it is also used to refer to people (Mt. 11.29; Lk. 1.52; 2 Cor. 7.6; 10.1; Jas 1.9; 4.6 and 1 Pet. 5.5), and this would support its function here as referring to 'lowly persons'.

8   After careful consideration of the structure of this passage, Peng also concludes that verses 14 and 17-21 are concerned with relations with outsiders. He points out (with reference to Rom. 1.25b and 9.25b) that it is not 'uncommon for Paul to deviate from what he is talking about to another topic' (2006: 64, note 114).

9   Some manuscripts omit ὑμᾶς (P[46] B 6 424[c] 1739 vg[ww, st] Clement) but whether it is included or not makes no difference to the interpretation of the verse (Cranfield 1979: 640; Schreiner 1998: 670). If it is omitted then the instruction could acquire more of a general sense, but since we have already noted the many signals throughout the letter to a real situation of opposition, then it would be natural to supply it and understand the verse as a reference to specific persecutors.

10 This understanding is seen when Jesus heals the crippled man by firstly pronouncing forgiveness of his sins (Lk. 5.17-26) and he seems to equate forgiveness with healing (v. 23), although when Jesus's disciples ask him why the man born blind is so – is it because of his own sin or that of his parents? – Jesus answers that it was not to do with anyone's sin but in order to show God's power (Jn 9.2-3).

11 See Martin (1986: 285–6) for a discussion of the meaning of πλεονεξία as referring not to how the gift is given (as an extortion versus a voluntary act) but to the attitude in which it is given (grudgingly as opposed to generously).

12 Cranfield also comments that v. 15 is an explanation of v. 14: 'for truly to bless one's persecutors must surely involve readiness to take one's stand beside them as human beings' (1979: 641). However, this interpretation of blessing does not correspond with that which we have found in other OT and NT sources.

13 See also Heb. 10.30. Although Paul does not specify that the wrath the believers need to give place to is God's, the context surely determines that this is what is meant, in addition to Paul's earlier language regarding the wrath of God (e.g. 1.18). The theme of God's vengeance is common in the OT (see Moo 1996: 787, who refers to Jer. 5.9; 23.2; Hos. 4.9; Joel 3.21; Nah 1.2). Keck (2005: 309) also notes that the prohibition of seeking revenge is seen throughout the OT (e.g. Lev. 19.18), the Apocrypha (e.g. Sirach 28.1) and Jewish literature (e.g. *Testament of Gad* 6.7). See also Jewett 2007: 774.

14 Paul slightly edits the text from Deut. 32.35 to add λέγει κύριος, which surely serves to emphasize 'divine authority and sovereignty' in the realm of judgement (Jewett 2007: 776).

15 See Proverbs (e.g. 17.13; 20.22 and 24.29) and Sirach (27.22–28.26). The *Apocalypse of Sedrach* attributes this prohibition to God (7.7, πῶς ἔπας, κύριε, κακὸν ἀντὶ κακοῦ μὴ ἀποδώσῃς), and there is also significant cross-over between Rom. 12.17 and *Joseph and Aseneth* 28.14, where we read: μὴ ἀποδιδόντες κακὸν ἀντὶ κακοῦ τινι ἀνθρώπῳ. For more examples of Jewish wisdom material that endorse non-retaliation, see Wilson 1990: 192–3.

16 There are parallels with Prov. 3.4 (LXX): καὶ προνοοῦ καλὰ ἐνώπιον κυρίου καὶ ἀνθρώπων, although if Paul is using this proverb then he has chosen to omit 'the Lord' and insert 'all' people. This adaptation functions to emphasize the need for the believers to discern what is good in the opinion of *all* people (not just their fellow

believers), and as such it 'takes account of the "good" in the values of human beings everywhere' (Jewett 2007: 772).

17 Polycarp also instructs οἱ πρεσβύτεροι not to neglect widows (and he also includes the orphan and the poor) and uses προνοέω to describe how they should take care to 'provide that which is good before God and all people': ἀλλὰ προνοοῦντες ἀεὶ τοῦ καλοῦ ἐνώπιον θεοῦ καὶ ἀνθρώπων (*Letter to the Philippians*, 6.1). Once again, this use of προνοέω is to give an instruction concerning *action*.

18 See also 1 Pet. 3.9, where acts of non-retaliation are to be followed by believers giving a blessing, which as we have noted, quite often refers to the physical act of offering a gift, i.e. giving something good to edify the other person.

19 Engberg-Pedersen also comments on this, but he then argues that because Paul does not speak of love in his instructions on how to relate to outsiders, then the appeal for the believers to, e.g. live at peace and not retaliate, 'allows for a sizeable portion of lack of *love*' towards one's enemies (2000: 269).

20 Also Moo (1996: 785) and Dunn (1988b: 748), but against Cranfield (1979: 645) who understands it in the sense of 'in the sight of' all people.

21 Here Paul uses a new term for the outsider (ὁ ἐχθρός), which almost certainly refers to the persecutors referred to in v. 14, although it is not limited by this designation. This instruction is nearly an exact quote from Prov. 25.21-22 (LXX), the only differences being that Paul inserts ἀλλά at the beginning of the quote and omits the last half of Prov. 25.22 which reads: ὁ δὲ Κύριος ἀνταποδώσει σοι ἀγαθά. See also 2 Kgs 6.22-23.

22 Williams writes, 'It is well known that on a certain festival of Demeter at Athens a member of the *genos* of the Bouzygai uttered solemn curses against those who trespassed against certain norms of good-neighbourliness which could not be enforced by law, but were nevertheless of such importance for civilised living that they enjoyed sanctions of the most venerable nature' (1962: 396). He argues that Menander's play, Δύσκολος (written around 317 BCE), reveals knowledge of and provides evidence for these curses.

23 This Christian text may have been written towards the end of the third century CE as an appendix to *4 Ezra*, where the backdrop is one of persecution and where the author attempts to instil confidence in the believers that God 'will eradicate sin and oppression along with sinners and oppressors' (Longenecker 1995: 114).

24 Bergren raises the question as to 'whether the polemic against "sin" and "sinners" in *6 Ezra* is directed against the "opposition" in the form of pagan persecutors of Christianity, or whether some of it may in fact be applicable to parties within the author's own community who are responding to the challenges of persecution in ways that he feels are inadequate' (1998: 23). In the case of 16.53, 63-67, Bergren argues that the sinners referred to are those from within the believing community, primarily because of the assurance in v. 67 that if they 'give up their sins' then God will deliver them and free them from tribulation.

25 This verb is only used one more time in 2 Tim. 3.6 to describe the women who have been 'captured' by the teachings of the heretics, as those who have been 'laden' or 'overwhelmed' with sins.

26 See also Leenhardt 1961: 320; Constantineanu 2010: 162; Morris 1988: 455; Wilckens 1982: 26.

27 See Cranfield 1979: 650; Käsemann 1980: 349; Dunn 1988b: 751; Klassen 1963: 343.

28 The term ἄρχων is only used elsewhere in 1 Cor. 2.6 to describe 'the rulers of this age who are doomed to perish'.

29 This description of 'avenger' is used only once more in the Pauline corpus in 1 Thess. 4.6, and this time it is used to describe God as an avenger (ἔκδικος κύριος).
30 The word διάκονος is used many times throughout the Pauline corpus to describe Paul and his co-workers (e.g. 1 Cor. 3.5; 2 Cor. 3.6; Phil. 1.1), but also to describe the false teachers as 'servants of Satan' (2 Cor. 11.15, 23). We only find the phrase 'servant of God' in 2 Cor. 6.4 where Paul describes himself and his companions, and in 1 Thess. 3.2 whilst some texts describe Timothy as συνεργός (with or without τοῦ θεοῦ), e.g. B D*, many others describe him as διάκονος τοῦ θεοῦ, either instead of συνεργός (e.g. ℵ A P) or in combination with that term (e.g. D² F G K L). See also Phil. 2.25 for the use of λειτουργός to describe Epaphroditus as Paul's own minister.
31 E.g. Cranfield 1979: 656; Leenhardt 1961: 323; Käsemann 1980: 352–5; Dunn 1988b: 760; Moo 1996: 795; Schreiner 1998: 681–2; Jewett 2007: 787–8; Keck 2005: 313.
32 Scholars have also commented that Paul is using here 'vocabulary of Hellenistic administration' (Käsemann 1980: 353; see also Moo 1996: 793–4 and Strobel 1956: 67–93).
33 Other similarities include the command to honour (1 Pet. 2.17; Rom. 13.7); to love (1 Pet. 2.17; Rom. 13.8, 10), and the theme of fear (1 Pet. 2.17; Rom. 13.3, 4).
34 For Jewett, Paul's assertion that the Roman authorities have been ordained by 'the God and Father of Jesus Christ' whom they had crucified, would have been viewed by such authorities as 'thoroughly subversive' (2000: 66). No doubt the authorities might not have appreciated this description, but Paul is clearly writing *not* to encourage hostility between believers and unbelievers, but rather peace and mutual respect (see 12.18; 13.3).
35 See also Stuhlmacher 1994: 198–208; Dunn 1988b: 768–9; Fitzmyer 1993: 662–3.
36 Although Paul sees this judgement coming from the authorities (v. 4), the implication is that the source of this judgement is God (see 12.19).
37 Cf. Dunn (1988b: 738) and Witherington (2004: 291) who believe that the ingroup is called to live quietly.
38 It is difficult to know why Paul encourages the Thessalonians to try to limit their interactions (although not entirely – they are still also required to pursue that which is good and to love all), whereas the picture built up in Romans is for the believers to be more visible and conspicuous; perhaps Paul is more confident of a positive response from the outsiders in Rome in achieving praise and peace.
39 In contrast, those who fashion false idols have 'escaped the praise of God and also his blessing' (Wisdom of Solomon, 15.19, ἐκπέφευγε δὲ καὶ τὸν θεοῦ ἔπαινον καὶ τὴν εὐλογίαν αὐτοῦ).
40 Philo writes that seeking praise from others is the act of foolish and boastful teachers (τῶν πολλῶν θηρώμενος ἔπαινον, *On the Posterity of Cain and His Exile*, 141).
41 Similarly, it is recorded in Acts that when Paul is making his defence before the council, the high priest and the Jews, he points to his own conscience, for this will truly show that he is without blame, and it will reveal the integrity of his goodness and motivations (Acts 23.1; 24.16).
42 I will also explore in our next chapter how Paul can refer to the conscience as that which provides an interpretation of a particular situation, which is then used to discern what is right or wrong, which in turn determines the action(s) of a person (see 1 Corinthians 8, 10).
43 Although Paul does not use συμμαρτυρέω along with συνείδησις as in Rom. 2.15 and 9.1, the theme of witnessing is already apparent in the context (vv. 3-4).

44 It is more likely that τελεῖτε is indicative rather than imperative since, as Moo notes, Paul always uses γάρ to 'introduce the ground or explanation of a previous statement' (1996: 804; see Dunn 1988b: 766; Jewett 2007: 798).
45 There is a notable parallel here with 12.17, where Paul previously uses ἀποδίδωμι in a warning whereby the believers are instructed *not* to return evil for evil, and this acts as an important clarification of the instruction in 13.7 to 'give to all people their dues': if a person deserves evil, the believer should not be the one who gives it, for this is the role of the authorities acting on behalf of God.
46 See Moo 1996: 805; Jewett 2007: 801.
47 We see this in 1 Pet. 2.17 where the author specifically identifies the object of each response or attitude of the believer: 'honour all, love other believers, fear God, honour the emperor'.
48 See Jewett who refers to a grave inscription of a pagan Roman woman, and an excerpt from a letter of a son to his mother, where owing nothing to anyone was clearly a virtue to be esteemed and praised (2007: 805).
49 Scholars mostly agree that εἰ μὴ (v. 8) is to be translated as 'except' rather than 'but' (e.g. Cranfield 1979: 674; Dunn 1988b: 776; Moo 1996: 812; Jewett 2007: 806) for this shows that for Paul, loving one another is a 'responsive obligation' (Dunn 1988b: 776).
50 Also Moo 1996: 816; Dunn lists occasions where 'the neighbour' is used in the general sense rather than specifically other believers in Jewish writings (1988b: 779). This general sense is surely intended in Jesus's teaching in the parable of the Good Samaritan, Lk. 10.25-37.
51 Also Moo 1996: 813; but contra Jewett 2007: 807 who argues that the command to love one another simply refers to other believers alone. He therefore interprets the whole of this passage as pertaining only to fellow believers.
52 In commenting on underlying motivations for the concern for a positive witness, some scholars suggest that Paul is concerned over the reputation of the gospel (e.g. Keck 2005: 308; Barrett 1957: 242), and even over his own reputation (Theissen and Gemünden 2016: 128). However, neither of these is indicated in these passages or indeed even in the wider letter.
53 Strangely, although Esler recognizes that the instructions in Rom. 13.1-7 might be part of a 'survival strategy' (2003: 333) and thus he indirectly acknowledges the importance of outsiders, his treatment of Rom. 13.1-7 is little more than two pages within which he mainly focuses on arguing against Mark Nanos's theory (1996) than on how these outsiders are forming and focusing the ingroup's own theology and norms. Thus, he makes no mention of SIT in this section, despite his commentary explicitly attempting to explore Romans via the lens of SIT (Esler 2003: 331-3).

4

That They Might Be Saved: 1 Corinthians

4.1 Introduction

Whilst the tone of Paul's letter to the Thessalonians could be thought of as largely encouraging, although 1 Corinthians is not *discouraging*, it nevertheless seems to be written in a spirit of frustration. Many chapters in 1 Corinthians address division within the believing community (e.g. 1.10-17; 3.1-23; 4.6-7; 6.1-8; 8.9-13; 11.17-22; 15.12), and believers are chastised for the immaturity of their faith (3.3). The letter begins using familiar language describing believers as those who have been 'called' and who are now 'saints' (e.g. 1 Cor. 1.2, 9, 26; see Rom. 1.7; 15.25, 31; 2 Cor. 1.1; 13.13; Phil. 1.1; 4.22), and Paul, as in Romans, reminds these believers that they are part of a larger 'ingroup' of believers that extends to 'every place' (1 Cor. 1.2; Rom. 1.5-6). But whereas Paul reveals that he also gives thanks for these Corinthian believers (1.4), unlike in 1 Thessalonians and Romans he does not continue to say that their faith in God has become known in other parts of the world (Rom. 1.8; 1 Thess. 1.8), nor does he praise them for having become an example to other believers (1 Thess. 1.7).

He similarly describes himself as their spiritual father (1 Cor. 4.15; see 1 Thess. 2.7, 11) and they as his 'beloved children' (4.14), but the nature of his relationship as father to these believers is characterized by the need for him to admonish them (4.14). Indeed, it quickly becomes clear that he is concerned about the internal dynamics and divisions within the ingroup. What is troubling Paul is that although they have received an abundance of spiritual gifts from God (1.5-7), they are also living in a way that ignores the demands of holiness and the way of Christ. As Thiselton writes, 'what is at issue is the anomaly of Christians who are nominally or in principle focused on Christ but *in practice and in stance still focused on the interests of the self*' (2000: 293).

As such, as early as 1 Cor. 1.10-17, Paul identifies the divisions that have arisen, and he returns to this again in chapter 3. The Corinthian believers are aligning themselves to their specific leaders, whether that is Apollos, Paul or Cephas (1 Cor. 3.4; also 1.12), and are ignoring their common identity in Christ, that it is God who has brought them together and that they belong to God (3.5-9). In terms of SIT, they seem to have failed to create one large believing community and have made smaller subgroups that are now competing against each other for the best positive social identity, and are doing so by comparing their status according to the identity of their leader. Paul's great anxiety is that in quarrelling they are behaving more like unbelievers, like 'mere humans' (Fee

1987: 123). Significantly for our study, Paul therefore accuses them of living (using περιπατέω) according to the ways of humankind (1 Cor. 3.3).

This appears to be the crux of the issue for Paul: the believers are living as if they are not members of the ingroup and have permitted conflict and division to exist within their ingroup. Whereas SIT proposes that similarity within the group leads to cohesion and stability, the believing ingroup in Corinth is rife with difference and division and seemingly does not know how to resolve its own conflict. Thus, Paul chastises them for their practice of taking their disputes to courts to be judged before the ἄδικοι (6.1) and ἄπιστοι (6.6), and for appointing as judges those who are not well regarded by the church (6.4, τοὺς ἐξουθενημένους ἐν τῇ ἐκκλησίᾳ).[1] His frustration is that the believers are asking unbelievers to do that which they should be more than equipped to do themselves, although Paul was surely aghast at the reputation the believers were building up for themselves in the eyes of the outsiders.[2] The struggle to live harmoniously among each other within the ingroup is seen in their understanding of eating meat (8.4-13), in sharing in the Lord's supper, (11.17-19, 20-22), in using their spiritual gifts in worship (14.5, 12, 26) and in understanding the power of resurrection (15.12).

Paul is evidently frustrated at the lack of unity within the group and the lack of commitment its members show to the group norms. As we saw in our first chapter, although Paul is clearly disturbed that 'there is sexual immorality' among these believers (1 Cor. 5.1), the greater sin for Paul is that the community has ignored this behaviour and has not removed the immoral brother from the ingroup (v. 2). Thus, the danger for Paul is not that the believers are associating with unbelievers (1 Cor. 5.9-10), but that they are associating with believers who *look* like they are unbelievers. Such believers threaten to confuse and oppose their social identity. For, in acting outside their group norms, they are disturbing and challenging the understanding that a washed, sanctified and justified believer should behave according to the Spirit (the cognitive aspect), that they should be distinguished from unbelievers by adhering to and *going beyond* what are considered to be the universally held values and ethics (evaluative aspect) and that they should view and love each other as part of the one body of Christ (emotional aspect). If they associate with an immoral brother or sister their community risks becoming 'indistinguishable from the world around it' (Hays 1997: 87).

Thus, Paul counsels the ingroup to 'purge out the old leaven' (5.7) and to judge one another according to their ability (or inability) to live holy lives (in other words, according to their group norms). They are to remember that they are the sacred dwelling place for the Holy Spirit, and that this belief should shape their practice (6.19). Thiselton calls these group norms, 'house rules', and perceptively notes that these are not only important for the believing community's unity in 'expressing a distinctively *Christian* (or *Christ*-like) corporate identity', but also for its witness and 'mission to the world' (2000: 416). As such, Paul is keen to ensure that the believing community should be a distinctive group within the wider community, and he endeavours to instruct that their distinctiveness lies in the strength and depth of their holiness.

In contrast, Paul uses the term ἄπιστος eleven times in this letter, meaning 'without faith, disbelieving, unbelieving' (Bauer et al. 2000: 103).[3] Hurd notices this frequency and comments that it shows Paul had an 'unusual interest in the unbeliever'

(1965: 221), although, as this book highlights, this is perhaps not such an unusual interest. Trebilco proposes, however, that it was natural that this term would be used to designate outsiders in contrast to believers, since faith became 'an essential definition of what it means to be an insider' (2014: 190).[4] As such, many scholars translate ἄπιστος as 'unbeliever', referring to all those who do not have the same belief as the ingroup, and who are therefore 'outsiders'.[5] For Paul, the key difference between the insider and the outsider is 'faith', and specifically faith in Jesus Christ.[6] In contrast, Lang argues that the term οἱ ἄπιστοι in the Corinthian correspondence is not referring to 'the undifferentiated mass of humanity who are unworthy to be called ἀδελφοί' (2018: 981) but to a specific category of *insiders* who have 'intimate social ties to the believers' (2018: 984). However, he clarifies that 'although the ἄπιστοι are unquestionably "outsiders" in terms of exclusive loyalty to Christ, they are also unquestionably "insiders" in the most socially serious ways' (2018: 985). Central to Lang's argument is that the word ἄπιστος usually means 'unreliable' or 'disloyal', and he contrasts this with Paul's use of πιστός in the Corinthian correspondence, referring to 'loyalty' or 'fidelity' (2018: 986). As such, he proposes that:

> Paul reserves this designation for a special class of affiliates, even sympathizers, of the Corinthian ἐκκλησία. These individuals are in significant ways internal to the community's life, yet they resist exclusive loyalty to Christ-devotion, even if they may perhaps be attracted to it. The social profile of the ἄπιστοι in Corinth is thus one of deviant insiders who sustain thick social bonds with the community but, because they fail to extract themselves from pagan ritual life, remain outside the "temple of God" (1 Cor 3:16–17, 2 Cor 6:16).
>
> (2018: 986)

Although Lang clearly understands these ἄπιστοι as being 'outsiders' with regard to (lack of) faith in Jesus Christ, and hence he follows the many other scholars who identify the ἄπιστοι as outsiders, it is his constant description of them as *insiders* that is unhelpful and that creates unnecessary complexity. Whether they are 'deviant insiders' or 'disloyal insiders' (2018: 986, 1001), it is the title of 'insider' that is problematic. He points to two different dimensions in terms of social relationships and in terms of exclusive loyalty to Christ, but he then conflates these two very different dimensions, but with an emphasis on the social dimension, so that these people become 'insiders'. For Lang, the social ties of the ἄπιστοι with the believers are more important in defining them as insiders than their lack of faith in Jesus is in defining them as outsiders. He therefore creates a new category of 'insiders'. Lang wants to describe οἱ ἄπιστοι both as insiders and as outsiders, and because of his certainty that this term does not refer to all outsiders in a generic way as those who are unfaithful or unbelievers, but to a specific category of unbelievers who have strong social ties with believers and who are tolerant of them, he therefore seems to emphasize the importance of their social closeness to the believers, which for Lang, means that they are therefore also 'insiders'.[7]

However, Lang creates a social boundary that determines who is 'in' and who is 'out', which, as well as appearing to be a one-dimensional understanding of regulating identity, is a boundary that neither Paul, nor SIT would use for this purpose. For

Paul, the line between the two groups is about the redeeming work of Christ. It is not about social relationships. Those who have *not* been washed, sanctified and justified ἐν τῷ ὀνόματι τοῦ κυρίου Ἰησοῦ Χριστοῦ καὶ ἐν τῷ πνεύματι τοῦ θεοῦ ἡμῶν (6.11) are οἱ ἄδικοι on one side of the line (who will therefore not inherit God's kingdom, 6.9, 10; also 1.18; 2.6) and those who have received this divine act of redemption are the Corinthian believers on the other side of the line (who have become temples of the Holy Spirit, 6.19). The earlier part of chapter 6 also makes it clear that for Paul, οἱ ἄδικοι, whom the believers are appointing as judges over their disputes (6.1) and who are (or who should be) 'despised' by the church (6.4), are οἱ ἄπιστοι whom he refers to in 6.6, who are involved in the judging between believers.[8] As such, οἱ ἄδικοι and οἱ ἄπιστοι are firmly located (spiritually) on one side of the boundary, and the believers on the other. Furthermore, one of the core beliefs or key marks for οἱ ἀδελφοί is that they can proclaim, 'Jesus is Lord' because of the Holy Spirit (12.3), who dwells in them (3.16; 6.19); this contrasts with their pre-conversion days, when they followed idols (12.2). Again, these verses reveal that for Paul, there is a line between those who confess Jesus as Lord and those who follow idols; Lang's creation of a new group of insiders who are 'Christ-sympathisers' and yet who follow other idols is simply not possible for Paul. As Trebilco writes: 'Being "in" is designated as being "a believer" or "a brother or sister", and all those who are not "in" are "out"; there is no middle ground. The boundary is constructed around πίστις, so those who are out are defined as ἄπιστοι, a term that is comprehensive and includes all outsiders' (2014: 187).

Paul recognizes that there is significant social interaction or a social dimension across these two groups, but this is not in itself a boundary that creates insiders and outsiders. Paul seems content for this social dimension to continue but nevertheless he is confident and articulate about defining the boundary between believers on one side (as insiders), and unbelievers on the other side (as outsiders), even if this means that the latter category is significant in size. And as we explored in Chapter 1 with regard to 1 Corinthians 5, if an 'overlap' area is found where the two groups agree on a matter of morality, then Paul still creates in this overlap an opportunity for the believers to distinguish themselves even more strongly from the outsiders. Paul's exclamation that the specific sexually immoral act of the brother is not found even among the Gentiles (οὐδὲ ἐν τοῖς ἔθνεσιν, 5.1) betrays a recognition that there is an overlap between believers and unbelievers regarding what is permissible or not in the realm of sexual ethics. It is the recognition of this overlap that allows in part for a distinctiveness between the groups to be created, for the believers should not only adhere to these shared norms, but go beyond them and therefore achieve a superior and more positive social identity than those who do not belong to this community.

Additionally, if Paul thought of οἱ ἄπιστοι as 'deviant insiders', then it is more likely that his attitude towards them would not have been as tolerant – I will shortly argue that Paul's attitude towards οἱ ἄπιστοί in chapters 7, 10 and 14 is one that values their opinion, and propels him to charge the believers to make sacrifices for the benefit of these outsiders. However, in contrast to this, Paul is ready to admonish the believers (4.14, 21) and, as we have seen, is not tolerant of behaviour and attitudes that do not align with the core expectations for those who belong to this community of believers (e.g. 5.1-5) and calls for a 'cleaning out' of the 'old yeast' (5.7). It seems highly unlikely that Paul would allow for those who still worship idols to be part of this community in a way that they, and others, understand and identify them as 'insiders'. He is clear that idolaters belong to 'those outside' and not within the faith community (5.9-13). If anyone inside is found to be called an idolater, the rest of the community should not associate with them, or even eat with them (5.11); ironically for Lang, Paul specifically says that insiders should not share the same social space with another insider who is an idolater, but he permits sharing the same social space with outsiders who might be idolaters.[9] Defining an insider, a member of the faith community as a 'deviant insider' who is permitted to remain as such is a complete oxymoron – what defines an insider for Paul is exclusive devotion to Christ as Lord, which carries with it clear expectations for behaviour, as well as expectations for inter- and intragroup relations.

Clearly, it is how Paul expresses these expectations for intergroup relations that will be the focus of this chapter, and we will specifically look at chapters 7, 10 and 14. However, before this, it is important to briefly highlight the fact that in this letter, Paul describes how he himself hopes to relate to different outgroups, and as such, offers his own strategy for engaging with outsiders with the intention of 'winning' them so that they might become true insiders. In chapter 9, Paul describes how he has made himself a 'slave to all' so that he 'might gain more' (9.19) and 'save some' (v. 22). In his own missionary practice, Paul shows a concern for how other groups regard him and what they think of him, and how this might affect their reception of his message and thus the possibility of their conversion. Thus, he writes that 'to the Jews I became as a Jew … to those under law as under law … to those without law as without law … to the weak I became weak … to all I have become all things, that by all means I might save some' (9.20-22).[10] The use of γίνομαι (v. 20 and twice in v. 22) indicates that Paul's missionary strategy is not merely concerned with *associating* with different people, but rather with *adopting* certain values, practices, experiences and norms that belong to members of another outgroup, and most importantly, making these known to members of the outgroup. This strategy is about showing the outsider where the common ground either naturally and already exists between the believer and the unbeliever, or where it has been created by the adoption of certain practices or values.[11] It is this common ground that may potentially change how the outsider views the believer, where the hope is that this will be a positive change. Paul is convinced that this then enables outgroup members to hear and experience the gospel in a way that they are more likely to receive it positively; hearing the gospel from someone you would negatively stereotype is going to be different to hearing it from someone whom you perceive to be closer to your own social identity.

However, Paul clearly gives thought to how he can maintain his own Christological identity whilst also considering how he can step out of his other more cultural or economic identities in order to inhabit carefully chosen ones of an outsider. As such, cultural and social adaptability is a conscious policy that recognizes not only the translatability of one's own cultural pattern of life, but the merit of cultural flexibility as part of the missionary endeavour. With regard to SIT, this is precisely what Barth argued: that, when interaction occurs between members of two different social groups, the differences that help to identify and maintain the boundary between ingroup and outgroup are reduced, whilst the similarities (of 'codes and values') become more important, and are in fact essential for interaction (1969: 15). He also argues that the shared codes and values that are necessary for this interaction are specific to the nature of that interaction, and do not need to extend 'beyond that which is relevant' to the interaction (1969: 16). This helps to explain how and why Paul is able to show flexibility, choosing to reveal or adopt those particular similarities between himself and the outsiders that would be most relevant to his presentation of himself as an apostle and to his proclamation of the gospel, which is the difference that Paul maintains and upholds, and is confident that this difference will 'win' particular outgroup members.[12] When the primary objective is to evangelize, to create or develop a relationship with an outsider not for social reasons but for missional reasons, then the evangelist intends the perceived similarity to be the catalyst precisely for the opening up and exploration of the difference.[13]

Thus, returning to how Paul instructs the Corinthian believers in their relationships with outsiders, not only does Paul describe his own intergroup interactions but he also expects the believers to imitate him especially in this area (e.g. 1 Cor. 10.32–11.1). He clearly desires for the believers *not* to dissociate from outsiders (5.10), and encourages meaningful intergroup relationships (e.g. chapters 7, 9, 10, 14). Paul dedicates a significant amount of space to explain how the believers should behave among outsiders, and *why* they should behave in such ways. Furthermore, these instructions reveal a concern to think always about the outsider, and a concern for their spiritual, physical and emotional well-being, but also, and significantly, a concern for how the outsider views the believer. We will turn to these instructions now, beginning with the instructions in chapter 7 concerning marriage between a believer and an unbeliever.

4.2. 1 Corinthians 7.12-16

4.2.1 Introduction: the marital overlap between insider and outsider

Chapter 7 is a long chapter that covers issues concerning marriage and divorce, singleness (for virgins and widows), self-control and passions, affairs of the world and devotion to the Lord. Paul indicates that some instructions are from the Lord (7.10) and some have arisen from his own opinion (7.12, 25, 40), but it appears that all of them have been prompted by the questions or matters that the believers themselves have raised in previous correspondence to him (7.1). However, it is in the middle of this complex chapter that we find mention of unbelievers, for Paul turns his attention to the believer who is joined in marriage to an unbeliever (7.12-16, ὁ ἄπιστος). Unlike the rest of the chapter, there is no mention here about 'acts of fornication' (e.g. 7.2) or about self-control (e.g. 7.5, 9). Neither is there an instruction for the believer to remain as they are in this relationship (e.g. 7.17, 20, 24), nor, given Paul's anxiety about how much a married believer can focus their attention on the Lord, is there an instruction for them to prioritize their desire to please the Lord over their desire to please their spouse (e.g. 7.32-35). Rather, this short section is motivated by a concern for the believer to listen and to submit to the opinion of their unbelieving spouse, giving them significant power in the relationship.

Furthermore, Paul attests that this union brings great spiritual benefit to the unbelieving spouse (and their children), and, although he refrains from instructing the believer to remain in the marriage (for this is a decision to be made by the unbeliever), his highlighting of the positive benefits for the unbeliever can only be seen to encourage the believer to continue in this relationship. In this passage, Paul appeals not to an overlap area between believer and unbeliever regarding ethics or societal values, but to an overlap area that exists because of marital union. The area of similarity or point of contact lies in the fact that a believer and an unbeliever are joined together in marriage, and he therefore discusses this area of overlap, focusing upon the opinion of the unbeliever, but also upon their present and potential future edification.

4.2.2 The unbelieving spouse: the importance of their approval

Paul begins this section (7.12-16) by admitting that the following instructions regarding the marriage between a believer and an unbeliever are rooted in his own opinion and observations, rather than in teaching that comes directly from the Lord (7.12a; cf. 7.10). Whilst Paul knew of Jesus's teaching that prohibited divorce (which he refers to in 7.10-11; see Mt. 5.31-32; 19.3-12; Mk 10.2-12; Lk. 16.18), he appears to judge that this command does not apply to marriages where one spouse is a believer and the other an unbeliever. For, unbelievers are free to leave and divorce their believing spouse (7.15a): it is the opinion and desire of the unbeliever that has the final word on the future of the marriage. And so, Paul instructs believing husbands *and* believing wives that if their unbelieving spouse chooses to live with them, then the believer should not leave their unbelieving spouse: εἴ τις ἀδελφὸς γυναῖκα ἔχει ἄπιστον καὶ αὕτη συνευδοκεῖ οἰκεῖν μετ' αὐτοῦ, μὴ ἀφιέτω αὐτήν· καὶ γυνὴ εἴ τις ἔχει ἄνδρα ἄπιστον καὶ οὗτος συνευδοκεῖ οἰκεῖν μετ' αὐτῆς, μὴ ἀφιέτω τὸν ἄνδρα (7.12-13). On the contrary, Paul later explains that if the unbelieving spouse desires to separate from their believing spouse, then they should be free to do so: εἰ δὲ ὁ ἄπιστος χωρίζεται, χωριζέσθω (7.15a) for the believing spouse 'has not been enslaved in such matters' (7.15b). In both scenarios it is the believer who should respect the choice of the unbeliever.

In verses 12-13, Paul uses συνευδοκέω to describe the choice of the unbeliever, often translated as 'consent'. Thus, if the unbeliever 'consents' to remain in the marriage, this is the course of action that should be followed.[14] However, although συνευδοκέω is used only a few times in the NT, it is always used in the sense of 'to approve' and to show approval for the *behaviour* of *another* person or group of people. Thus, in addressing the lawyers, Jesus remarks that they 'approve of the works of their fathers' who killed the prophets (Lk. 11.48), and in Acts we read that Saul 'approved' of Stephen's murder, stoned to death by a crowd bringing false accusations against him and before the high priest (8.1). Paul himself later admits that not only was he 'standing by' as Stephen was killed, but that he also was 'agreeing and protecting the garments of those killing him' (Acts 22.20). And finally, in Romans, Paul chastises those people who 'know the just requirements of God' and yet not only take part in ungodly acts but who also 'approve' of others who do so (Rom. 1.32). We therefore see that συνευδοκέω is used when a person approves of another's behaviour, and in the case of Saul, approval also led to him enabling the actions of those of whom he approved.

This suggests that when Paul uses συνευδοκέω to describe the potential response of an unbeliever to living with their believing spouse in 1 Corinthians 7, it refers not simply to them agreeing or consenting to remain in the marriage but also to approving of the marriage, which implies that the believer remains acceptable as a spouse, even as a believer. If the unbeliever approves of the marriage then there is an implicit assumption that they have a positive view of their believing spouse. As such, it is not merely about the unbeliever consenting (Thiselton 2000: 527), being 'content' (Barrett 1971: 164) or 'willing to maintain the marriage' (Hays 1997: 121), but about the unbeliever being pleased to remain in the marriage and pleased to live with their believing spouse (also Garland 2003: 285–6). And, Paul writes, if this is the case, then the believer should not seek to divorce their unbelieving spouse. This reading is significant as it recognizes the importance not only of the opinion of the unbeliever regarding their marriage but also the opinion the unbeliever has of their spouse as a *believer*. Accordingly, it reveals and anticipates the possibility for the unbeliever to allow or even approve of the behaviour of a believer; there is realistic scope here for believers to express their faith freely.

In contrast, Lang argues that Paul must be referring to marriages between believers and those who are already socially embedded 'within the ecclesial network' and who have 'a shared sympathy for Christ-devotion' (2018: 988). For Lang, it is impossible for a believer to be married to someone who is neither another believer nor a 'deviant insider', for the believer's refusal to take part in other rituals of the household 'would have destabilized the functioning of the home and risked social disgrace', especially if the believer was a woman (2018: 987).[15] This is a good point; but it needs to be considered alongside the wider context of the letter, which suggests that in Corinth there was perhaps quite a unique degree of tolerance shown towards believers and their abandonment of some social expectations. First, unusually for Pauline correspondence, there is no mention of persecution or any suggestion of tension existing between believers and unbelievers.[16] Furthermore, they also appear to have achieved an element of 'social acceptability' within the wider society (see Barclay 1992: 58). For Paul exclaims (somewhat sarcastically) that ahead of the apostles these Corinthian believers have already become rich and are like kings, and that, whereas Paul and his colleagues are despised, they are rather honoured (4.8-13). Additionally, Paul appears to advocate singleness and celibacy (7.8, 25-26, 32-35) which was usually considered to be highly counter-cultural, especially for those living under the Augustan marriage laws which encouraged marriage and procreation, and penalized those who remained celibate.[17] Since Paul gives no indication that this would result in intergroup conflict, or at least damage their honourable reputation, it is possible to assume that this is another indication of high levels of tolerance shown by outsiders to the believers.[18]

All of this suggests that it is not as impossible as Lang proposes for believers to be married to unbelievers and for them to excuse themselves from other (idolatrous) household rituals without attracting public conflict and shame. It also suggests that Paul's hope for the unbelieving spouse not only to remain married to a believer, but to approve of and perhaps even respect the believer's exclusive loyalty to Jesus Christ, is realistic and informed.

4.2.3 The unbelieving spouse: their sanctification and salvation

Paul continues in verse 14a to state that the unbelieving spouse is 'made holy' by being married to their believing spouse: ἡγίασται γὰρ ὁ ἀνὴρ ὁ ἄπιστος ἐν τῇ γυναικὶ καὶ ἡγίασται ἡ γυνὴ ἡ ἄπιστος ἐν τῷ ἀδελφῷ. Paul does not elaborate on how he envisages the unbeliever to be 'holy', or even how this happens by being united to the believing spouse, and there has been a plethora of interpretations around this verse. Usually, Paul uses ἁγιάζω to describe those who have become believers (1 Cor. 1.2; Rom. 15.16; 1 Cor. 6.11), and as such, Procksch writes that 'sanctification is a state' (1964: 112). However, Paul also appears to understand that not only is God the one who sanctifies (see also 1 Cor. 1.2; Rom. 15.16) but also that it is a process, since he writes to the Thessalonian believers that he desires for God to 'sanctify you entirely' (1 Thess. 5.23). Being sanctified involves being associated with God and with the community of believers, but also with certain expectations of living (1 Thess. 4.1-7; Rom. 6.19-22). Being called to the state of sanctification 'imposes a demand which must be met if the title of "saint" is not to be evacuated of all meaning' (Murphy-O'Connor 2009: 47).

In an unusual turn then, Paul in 1 Cor. 7.14 writes that the unbelieving spouse is caught up in this state or process of sanctification not because of their union with Christ (1 Cor. 1.2) but because of their union with their believing spouse. They are sanctified 'in' their believing husband or wife. Many scholars comment that, in this situation where an unbeliever is united physically in marriage to a believer, then this 'consecrated' nature of the believer is also 'imparted' to the unbeliever (Moffatt 1938: 81).[19] This is because where one is in a relationship that is ordained as good by God (see 1 Tim. 4.3-5), the power of divine holiness in the believer is more powerful than its absence in the unbeliever, and thus somehow it is passed on to the unbeliever (see Moffatt 1938: 82; Fee 1987: 301; Hays 1997: 121). Hays describes the 'holiness' of the believer as being 'contagious' for it is 'more powerful than impurity' (1997: 121), and Hauck, on writing of the 'clinging and infectious force' of impurity, argues that holiness in the believer also becomes such a force (1965: 429). Schweitzer, however, sees that this sanctified status is not just transmitted because it is a 'force' but because of the 'mystical doctrine of physical union' that believers have with Christ (1931: 127). Thus, he argues that through the 'bodily connection' that the unbelieving spouse has with their believing spouse, they also share in their spouse's physical union with Christ (1931: 128). Murphy-O'Connor, however, proposes that the unbeliever is considered holy simply because they show 'a pattern of behaviour that is analogous to the conduct expected of the *hagioi*' (2009: 49). This 'pattern of behaviour' is their 'consent' to remain in their marriage which is 'the intention of the Creator', as opposed to asking for divorce (2009: 49). For Murphy-O'Connor, 'holiness' is only predicated on actual behaviour, which may or may not result from an internal faith (2009: 50).

However, if, as we argued in the interpretation of 1 Cor. 7.12-13, the decision of the unbelieving spouse to remain in the marriage is not just simply a decision *not* to separate, but a stronger decision, which entails approval or at least tolerance of the behaviour of their spouse as a believer, then we can understand the reason for the holiness as being *both* the fact that they are united to their believing spouse (Moffatt 1938: 82; Fee 1987: 301; Hays 1997: 121) and also because they have rejected the option of divorce (Murphy-O'Connor 2009: 49-50). Although the state of being sanctified is not synonymous with being saved, the unbelieving spouse has nevertheless been 'set apart in a special way that hopefully will lead to their salvation (v.16)' (Fee 1987: 301). What is significant for our study is that Paul is not just stating why divorce is not necessary, but he is offering a positive benefit for staying married, which is solely and primarily focused upon the unbeliever. The final decision is in the hands of the unbeliever, but Paul gives the believers a reason to make the marriage work: that the unbeliever benefits from this relationship.

Furthermore, Paul then appears to provide an additional argument supporting his proposal regarding the holiness of the unbelieving spouse (and for the continued holiness of the believing spouse): ἐπεὶ ἄρα τὰ τέκνα ὑμῶν ἀκάθαρτά ἐστιν, νῦν δὲ ἅγιά ἐστιν (7.14b). Paul presents the assumption that the children of this marriage are holy without any explanation; however, the function of this assumption is primarily to provide evidence or further reasoning for the transformation of the unbelieving spouse as having been sanctified by their union with a believer (also Garland 2003: 289). For Paul, the holiness of the children shows that the husband and wife must also be holy. He is concerned to show that in this scenario of a marriage between a believer and an unbeliever, what prevails is not any unclean nature of the unbeliever, but the holiness of the believer, and that this holiness then covers the unbelieving spouse and the children of the marriage. When the believer is united to an unbeliever in marriage, then there is a very different consequence to when a believer unites with a prostitute (1 Cor. 6.15-17): not only does the believer maintain their holiness, but the unbeliever assumes this holiness. The logical deduction is that the resulting children from this union are therefore also holy, but Paul's use of ἐπεὶ ἄρα means that he rather uses the holiness of the children to provide an additional argument for, or proof of, the holiness of the spouse. There is a reassurance here to the believing spouse that their marriage to an unbeliever has not threatened their own identity, nor is their marital union any less holy than that between believers. As Fitzmyer writes, 'God's sanctifying power is greater than any unbelief' (2008: 301).

Therefore, if the unbelieving spouse decides to separate then so be it, and the believer is released from this marital union – but it must not be the decision of the believer to separate from their unbelieving spouse, for this presumably would terminate the status of the unbeliever as being holy. The believer would therefore consciously be pushing the unbeliever further away from God, or at least from being associated with God. Later in the letter Paul makes it clear that believers should only strive for unbelievers to encounter God, rather than putting a stumbling block in their way, and that they should cause no offence to anyone and should seek for the advantage of the other, which for Paul ultimately means their salvation (1 Cor. 9.19-23; 10.31–11.1; 14.23-25). As such, Paul reminds the believers that, although the unbeliever might choose to separate, their calling is to pursue peace, which, far from being the absence of conflict, is concerned with the reconciliation and bringing together of different parties. Thus he writes, ἐν δὲ εἰρήνῃ κέκληκεν ὑμᾶς ὁ θεός (7.15c).[20]

It is possible that Paul uses the particle δέ here in an emphatic or consecutive sense ('and', 'now', or left untranslated; see Rom. 9.30) to explain or establish further the preceding statement. If so, Paul would be acknowledging that peace might not always be possible in such a marriage and therefore reassures these believers that rather than living in marital conflict, they are called to peace, gained by the unbeliever deciding to separate. As such the verse would read, 'but if the unbelieving one separates, let him/her separate; in such a case the brother or sister is not bound; indeed, God has called you to peace' (1 Cor. 7.15). If it is understood in this way, then the corollary is that verse 16 is read negatively, where Paul is highlighting the fact that the believer may not even be able to save their unbelieving spouse anyway, should the marriage be maintained: 'how do you know wife, if you will save your husband? Or how do you know husband, if you will save your wife?' (v. 16).[21]

However, it is more likely that Paul uses δέ here in the adversative sense ('but', 'rather', e.g. 1 Cor. 1.23; 7.15a) of opposing the preceding statement.[22] In this case, whilst one scenario envisages the unbeliever deciding to leave the marriage (v. 15a), the other scenario is where the believer works for peace within the marriage (v. 15c). Thus, Paul reminds the believers that, whilst unbelievers have the choice of staying or separating, the only option for which believers should desire is to stay as they are and be committed to that which God has called them: to bring about peace and reconciliation. As such, the verse would read, 'but if the unbelieving one separates, let him/her separate; in such a case the brother or sister is not bound; on the other hand, God has called you to peace'. This corresponds with our previous work on Rom. 12.18, where creating peace between believer and unbeliever is an important group norm. Whilst he acknowledges that this might not always be possible, Paul's call to peace is about pursuing a better relationship with another person which also has an element of reciprocity about it. For, when Paul urges the divided faith community to 'pursue' both 'the things of peace' and 'the things of building up', it is 'for one another' (Rom. 14.19).

This interpretation of v. 15c would in turn mean that verse 16 is read in an optimistic way, where Paul highlights the potential benefit to the unbeliever resulting from the believer's dedication to peace and reconciliation in and through marriage: 'wife, for all you know, you might save your husband; husband, for all you know, you might save your wife' (v. 16).[23] Thus, Schrage writes that this verse is 'not an expression of resignation, but of encouragement' ('Der Vers ist nicht Ausdruck der Resignation, sondern der Ermutigung', 1995: 112). Similarly, after presenting how τίς οἶδεν εἰ is found in the LXX in 2 Sam. 12.22, Joel 2.14, Jon. 3.9 and Est. 4.14 (cf. τί οἶδας εἰ found twice in 1 Cor. 7.16) to express hope rather than doubt, Jeremias argues that this gives weight to reading 1 Cor. 7.16 as an optimistic expression (1954: 255–60). He also rightly observes that a pessimistic reading 'would in no way correspond to the missionary confidence of the apostle', or to 'the positive assessment of the mixed marriage in v.14' (1954: 259). Paul is continuing to show confidence in the blessings that a marriage to a believer brings to the unbelieving spouse. But he also shows confidence in the believer to live in a way that reveals the attractiveness of the gospel to their spouse, so that the unbelieving spouse not only desires to remain in the marriage but also, eventually, to become a full member of the believing community themselves. Clearly, the 'optimistic' reading and interpretation of vv. 15c-16 is contextually more appropriate, since the main thrust of the wider passage is Paul urging the believers not to desire separation from their unbelieving spouses, and to emphasize the benefits of staying in the marriage for *unbelievers*.

4.2.4 Summary

Deming argues that in this passage 'Paul is addressing the fear of *moral* pollution via *physical* association with non-Christians' (2004: 132), where perhaps some of the Corinthian believers were objecting to their marriages with unbelievers. As such, Paul is reassuring them that this union does not pollute the believer, but rather 'decontaminates' the unbeliever (2004: 130). However, there is no evidence that the Corinthian believers themselves were expressing this fear; to the contrary, there is evidence that they are only too happy to associate with unbelievers and see no harm in doing so (1 Cor. 6.1-6; 12-18; 10.27; 14.23). Furthermore, if this was the driving force behind the passage in 1 Cor. 7.12-16, then the focus would surely be on the believer, emphasizing *their* protection from the 'pollution' of their unbelieving spouse and how *their* positive identity, as those who are sanctified, remains intact and protected, as well as their salvation. Rather, the emphasis is on the sanctification and possible salvation of the *unbeliever*. As Eubank remarks: 'the expected movement is in the direction of the inclusion of the unbelieving spouse rather than the loss of the believer' (2017: 46).

Paul's concern for the sanctification and potential salvation of the unbelieving spouse is predicated on the believing spouse's desire to work for peace, their willingness to give voice and the power of decision to the unbeliever, and their recognition of the clear benefits and blessings that come to the unbeliever and to their children through this marital union. The corollary is that the *opinion* the unbeliever has of their believing spouse and their lifestyle is important, because this will determine whether or not they choose to remain married to them, and therefore, whether or not they have the opportunity to become a full member of the faith community through the hope of salvation. In the same way that the author of 1 Peter reveals that a believing wife can 'win over' (3.1 κερδαίνω) her unbelieving husband when he sees her behaviour (3.2), so too must Paul believe that the believing spouse can show the attractiveness of their faith-shaped behaviour to their unbelieving spouse. This is vitally important for it will lead the unbelieving spouse to agree to continue living with the believer *and* with their lifestyle, keeping hold of the positive social identity they secure through it (of being sanctified), and living with the opportunity of fully accepting the whole identity of one who is redeemed in Christ. The importance of the opinion of the outsider in this situation rests upon the fact it will determine the status of their marital union with their believing spouse, which in turn will establish an open door to attaining sanctification and the potential of salvation.

4.3 1 Corinthians 10.23–11.1

4.3.1 Introduction: the decision over food

The encouragement in 7.12-16 for the believing spouse to consider the thoughts and preferences of their unbelieving spouse before their own, and to conduct themselves in a way that will give maximum scope for unbelievers to find their own hope of salvation, is, I believe, the driving force behind the practical instructions Paul gives to all believers at the end of chapter 10 (vv. 23-33). This passage looks as if it is a continuation of the concerns in chapter 8 regarding food and how the decisions of one person may impact upon another. However, at the end of chapter 10 Paul takes this concern but sets it within a larger framework which now includes outsiders.

As such, this passage begins and ends with a reminder that the believers should always take thought for how their behaviour impacts others, and how they should seek the advantage of the other person (1 Cor. 10.23-24; 31-33). Thus, in verse 23, Paul writes: Πάντα ἔξεστιν ἀλλ᾽ οὐ πάντα συμφέρει· πάντα ἔξεστιν ἀλλ᾽ οὐ πάντα οἰκοδομεῖ (see also 6.12). The next verse goes further to explain that not only should actions be taken that are advantageous and edifying, but that 'the other person', ὁ ἕτερος, should be the recipient of these good consequences of the believers' actions: μηδεὶς τὸ ἑαυτοῦ ζητείτω ἀλλὰ τὸ τοῦ ἑτέρου (10.24). Seeking the other believer's edification is not unusual in Paul's letters (e.g. 1 Cor. 14.4; 1 Thess. 5.11), and given the use of οἰκοδομέω in 1 Cor. 8.1, 10 where the relationship between believers is the focus of the argument, then it might seem to suggest that here too, in 1 Cor. 10.23-24, Paul is encouraging the believers to take thought for what would build up the whole faith community.

However, the rest of the passage suggests that 'the other' is not restricted to the fellow believer but is also to include the outsider. For, not only does Paul continue by envisaging a scenario that involves οἱ ἄπιστοι (v. 27), but the final verses in this chapter also explicitly reveal that Paul is concerned with how the believers behave among, and towards, *outsiders*. In verse 31 he revisits and expands verse 23 by stating that *whatever* it is they do, they should do πάντα εἰς δόξαν θεοῦ (v. 31), *and* they should not be a hindrance (ἀπρόσκοποι) 'to Jews and to Greeks and to the church of God' (v. 32). The actions included under whatever is considered lawful (πάντα ἔξεστιν, v. 23), which might cover (but are not limited to) eating and drinking (v. 31), should not just be judged as appropriate on their ability to edify the other person (v. 24) but also on their nature as being 'pleasing' to all people (v. 33). Once more, we see in operation an overlap area in which there are recognized patterns of behaviour that are edifying and spiritually harmless to both insider and outsider, regardless of religious or cultural identity. Paul is appealing to the believers to recognize this and behave accordingly. However, the motivation behind this is to lead others to salvation (v. 33). Paul reveals his own concern to please all people in all things and not to seek his own advantage 'but that of the many' (ἀλλὰ τὸ τῶν πολλῶν, 10.33), and it is clear from the motivation given (ἵνα σωθῶσιν, 10.33) that 'the many' are unbelievers. Furthermore, Paul expects all believers to follow his example and 'imitate' his behaviour towards and concern for those yet to be saved (11.1).

These final verses function to extend the narrative of seeking what is good or advantageous for the other person. For, I will argue that having started by demonstrating what this looks like within the believing community, Paul then develops his thesis by stating that this should also encompass the *outside* community. There is a gradual overlap whereby we see Paul focusing on 'the other' in the faith community and then 'the other' in the unbelieving community, and at points there are debates among scholars as to whether Paul is referring to insiders or outsiders. This is reminiscent of what we found happening in Rom. 13.8-10 as explored in our previous chapter, where there is an oscillation between focusing on the insider and the outsider, and where vocabulary is used that can refer to either believer or unbeliever (Section 3.3.4). However, in

1 Cor. 10.23–11.1, the crucial verses that directly alert us to the fact that Paul also has an eye on outsiders, are verses 32-33. These verses not only indicate that, for Paul, the policy of thinking about others before oneself is not limited to ingroup relationships, but they also raise our awareness of the fact that Paul chooses to introduce a scenario that involves an unbeliever (10.27), which in turn raises the question as to how much this unbeliever is part of Paul's further teaching in verses 28-30, and specifically, if Paul is concerned about the conscience of the unbeliever (v. 29).

This is undoubtedly a complicated passage, where the complexity is sometimes heightened by lack of clarity around some of the social and historical factors which are alluded to here.[24] Within the text itself, there are questions around what Paul means by 'conscience' (συνείδησις), and whose conscience is being referred to in vv. 25, 27, 28-29, the identity of the person who reveals the food as having been offered in sacrifice (v. 28), and whether or not Paul is simply expanding on his argument from chapter 8, focusing on the 'weak' believers. Within the context of our current study, what is important is not so much exploring the discussion that was raised in chapter 8 and which is now revisited in a slightly different way here in chapter 10, but rather the impact the believer's freedom may have on another person, and specifically, on the outsider.[25] Thus, we will address how Paul's concern for the outsider (and their opinion or interpretation of the believer) comes through in this passage, and how, as a consequence, Paul shapes his instructions to the believers and shows how their behaviour may even lead to the salvation of the unbeliever.

4.3.2 The importance of conscience

As we have already seen, Paul begins this passage by reminding the believers to pay attention to the fact that not all actions are beneficial or edifying (10.23) and that believers should not be seeking their own advantage but that of 'the other' (v. 24). He then paints two scenarios that demonstrate how this group norm comes to fruition in different ways. One scenario depicts believers eating food from a market (Πᾶν τὸ ἐν μακέλλῳ πωλούμενον ἐσθίετε, v. 25a) while the other depicts believers eating food at a meal (in a home) at the invitation of an unbeliever (εἴ τις καλεῖ ὑμᾶς τῶν ἀπίστων καὶ θέλετε πορεύεσθαι, πᾶν τὸ παρατιθέμενον ὑμῖν ἐσθίετε, v. 27a).[26] However, there is a condition that applies to both scenarios, for in eating from the market and at the invitation of the unbeliever, the believers are to do so μηδὲν ἀνακρίνοντες (vv. 25b, 27b), in other words, without 'investigating its history' (Garland 2003: 490). The reason Paul gives in both scenarios is simply to do with conscience (διὰ τὴν συνείδησιν, 10.25c, 27c), and in between these two scenarios Paul explains, 'for the earth and its fullness are the Lord's' (v. 26; taken from Ps. 24.1; see also 1 Tim. 4.3-5). Whereas in chapter 8 Paul reminds the believers that there are no idols, only the one God (8.4-6), here he reasons that all food comes from and belongs to the Lord (10.26). Their conscience does not need to seek clarification because all they need to know is that this food belongs to the Lord (see Conzelmann 1975: 176–7).

Paul's concern for conscience continues, however, as he considers the conscience of other people and how this might alter whether or not the believer decides to eat of this food (vv. 28-29). For Paul adds a twist to the second scenario of eating in the home of an unbeliever.²⁷ He imagines another possible scenario where, although no questions have been raised about the food, someone nevertheless reveals that the food is offered in sacrifice. This time, because of this public revelation, and because of conscience, the believer should *not* eat it: ἐὰν δέ τις ὑμῖν εἴπῃ, Τοῦτο ἱερόθυτόν ἐστιν, μὴ ἐσθίετε δι' ἐκεῖνον τὸν μηνύσαντα καὶ τὴν συνείδησιν· (1 Cor. 10.28). The identity of the one who reveals the news is not clear and is debated among scholars. Some argue that it is one of the 'weak' believers, present in their role as a household slave or as a 'puritanic fellow-guest who had been asking nervous questions' (Moffatt 1938: 144; also Hays 1997: 177; Barrett 1971: 242; Horrell 1996: 147). Witherington also claims that 'Christian sources' use ἱερόθυτον to denote idol food that is eaten outside the temple (1993: 240). However, evidence shows that ἱερόθυτος would also be used by *pagans* to describe food that has been offered to gods in sacrificial worship.²⁸ This could suggest that the informant is a pagan, as other scholars argue (Fee 1987: 484; Garland 2003: 496; Büchsel 1964: 378; Soden 1964: 531, and also Witherington in a later work, 1995: 227).

Nevertheless, in recognizing that ἱερόθυτον is a pagan word, some scholars then propose that the informant could still be a weak believer who is using this term out of politeness (e.g. Barrett 1971: 242; Robertson and Plummer 1911: 221). However, considering the effort Paul is going to in the rest of his letter to encourage the believers to show consideration to others before themselves (which suggests that this is a particularly urgent challenge to change the culture of the believers in their thinking and behaviour), it would be quite remarkable that a 'weak' believer would have the maturity, sensitivity and self-awareness to use a pagan term in order to be polite to an unbeliever.

There are, however, a few more points to consider in trying to discern the identity of the informant. The first is that if Paul had envisaged the informant to have been a fellow believer, then he might have been more likely not only to have used τις but also ἀδελφός (ἐὰν δέ ἀδελφός τις; see 10.1). It is also possible that Paul is intentionally using the indefinite pronoun in v. 28a (ἐὰν δέ τις) to link it to that used in v. 27a when he refers to unbelievers: 'if anyone ... from the unbelievers' (εἴ τις ... τῶν ἀπίστων). The choice of τις could indicate that Paul was imagining the informant to be a pagan *guest*, for it would have been more appropriate to use the personal pronoun αὐτός to refer back to the pagan host of v. 27. Secondly, it must be remembered that Paul begins this scenario with a focus on the interaction between an unbeliever and a believer. There are no explicit references to weak believers in this scenario and, given the wider context of this passage and Paul's eye on the outsider in later verses (vv. 32-33), this could also suggest that the informant is envisaged as an unbeliever. Hence, considering all the arguments above, I would propose that the evidence indicates that Paul is thinking about an unbeliever revealing this piece of news to the believer.

This is important because Paul continues to write that if believers are informed that the food has been sacrificed, then they should not eat it in this situation, the reason being 'because of the one who revealed it and [because of] conscience' (v. 28b). He then quickly clarifies that he is not talking about their own conscience, but about that of 'the other' (συνείδησιν δὲ λέγω οὐχὶ τὴν ἑαυτοῦ ἀλλὰ τὴν τοῦ ἑτέρου, v. 29a). The issue is not eating the food in itself but eating it in front of others when it has been revealed as idol meat; thus, if the issue is not what is entering the mouth of the believer, then it is to do with how others might interpret the believer's actions, with how they perceive the believers and with the opinion that they might therefore make of believers and their faith. As such, Paul identifies that what is at stake here is the conscience, and specifically that of the other person (v. 29a). For some scholars, it is inconceivable that Paul might be concerned with the conscience of an unbeliever. Barrett writes, 'it is not easy to see how a non-Christian's conscience could enter into the matter, and it is therefore best to suppose that we have to do with a second Christian guest' (1971: 242; also Collins 1999: 384), and Fee exclaims, 'how can it have anything to do with a *pagan*'s conscience? Probably very little at all' (1987: 485).

However, what is uncontested is that the conscience refers back to the informant, ὁ μηνύσας in v. 28, so that the believers should not eat the food 'because of the informer and because of their (the informer's) conscience'. I have also argued that this person is most likely to be an unbeliever, and therefore it follows that the believers should not eat the food because of a concern for the *unbeliever*'s conscience. Paul's concern for unbelievers, and for their emotional, economic and spiritual well-being, is not unprecedented (e.g. 1 Cor. 7.12-16; 1 Thess. 5.15; Rom. 12.14, 17-20). Additionally, Paul continues to instruct the believers to follow his own example as someone who seeks to please others, who seeks the advantage not for himself but for the many, 'so that they may be saved' (1 Cor. 10.32–11.1). Thus, it would not be unusual for Paul to show (and encourage the believers to show) a concern for the unbeliever in their midst. This then leaves us to address the question as to how the believers' decision regarding eating idol meat might have an impact upon the unbeliever's conscience. In order to do this, it is important to turn briefly to Paul's understanding of conscience.

4.3.2a Paul's understanding of conscience

It was found in our previous chapter on Romans (Section 3.3.4) that Paul often uses the idea of conscience as that which witnesses to the outside world the internal morality of a person (Rom. 2.15; 9.1; 13.5; 2 Cor. 1.12; see also 1 Pet. 3.16; 1 Tim. 3.9; 2 Tim. 1.3). The conscience reveals and testifies to the moral and spiritual health of a person to an onlooker. However, Paul can also refer to the conscience as that which has the power to discern the goodness in something or someone else. As such, Paul writes of his hope that he and the other apostles can 'commend' themselves 'to every conscience of all people before God' (2 Cor. 4.2) and his hope that they are well known to their consciences (5.11). It is as if the conscience is the moral arbiter that sits on the inner throne of judgement and weighs and discerns the goodness in something external; as such, Paul and his other apostles want to be trusted and found to be morally and spiritually good. But he also sees that the conscience is something that can be harmed, as revealed by his argument in 1 Corinthians 8. The context here is that Paul is concerned about those 'weak' believers (possibly newly converted) who lack knowledge and understanding about their new freedom and their new faith, and as such, when eating idol food they consider themselves still to be partaking in this idolatrous ritual (8.7). This results in their 'weak' consciences being 'defiled': καὶ ἡ συνείδησις αὐτῶν ἀσθενὴς οὖσα μολύνεται (8.7c).

Paul is clearly vexed about this situation, and so counsels those believers who have a greater knowledge about the reality of this food (see vv. 4-6) to make sure that the 'weak' believers do not misinterpret their freedom so that they conclude that it is permissible to partake in idolatrous rituals in addition to following Christ (8.9-13). Paul exclaims that these thoughtless actions of the knowledgeable believers are 'destroying' the weaker believers and 'wounding their weak consciences' (8.11-12). He therefore calls the 'knowledgeable' believers to consider how others perceive them and thus change their actions if they are causing others to stumble (v. 9). Additionally, he describes how he himself, in a similar situation, would refrain from eating meat if that would mean some are prevented from stumbling (v. 13); he clearly intends that the 'knowledgeable' believers should follow his example.

Paul's use of συνείδησις in chapter 8 thus reveals another dimension to how Paul understands 'the conscience', for here it refers to that part of the self which is vulnerable, which can be harmed, and which is intricately connected to the decisions and actions of a person. The danger in this scenario is that the weak believer may witness something that they do not fully understand, that this misunderstanding then shapes their discernment of what is right and wrong, and finally leads them to act in a way that is born from a corrupted conscience. Paul refers to the conscience here as the inner method of *interpreting* a particular action or event. This interpretation then helps to form that person's bank of knowledge, and this then shapes how the person will act in the future. Thus, a weak believer, seeing a knowledgeable believer eating idol food, will interpret this by saying that it must be acceptable to eat food that has been sacrificed to other idols *and* believe in one God and in one Lord (8.6). This interpretation gives the (misguided) knowledge that it is customary to be able to be a follower of Jesus and still participate in other pagan religious practices, and this knowledge or belief will in turn lead them to act in a way that syncretizes Christianity with other pagan religions. Therefore, the conscience has a complex role in *determining* one's moral compass.

Paul does not use 'conscience' in a singular way, but it appears to have different yet connected roles: it is both that which helps to form the moral framework that lies behind a person's character and actions, and it is that which acts as a witness to this moral framework, revealing itself and the inner workings of the person to an onlooker. The conscience is dynamic and can be weak and dysfunctional, the corollary being that Paul believes it can also be strong and correct. These different usages signal that these are not wholly discrete meanings; what they have in common is a sense of an inner self-awareness that has interpretative and evaluative dimensions that could form one's moral compass and in turn shape one's actions.

4.3.2b *The meaning of conscience in 1 Corinthians 10*

It is possible that Paul, in using the two scenarios in chapter 10 to demonstrate the group norm laid out in 10.23-24, is deliberately using ones that pick up on his previous conversation in chapter 8, where relations between believers are in view. In this case, the reasoning behind refraining from asking questions in 10.25 and v. 27 ('because of conscience') might additionally include the concern from chapter 8 that if the 'weak' believers find out it is idol food and eat of it, then their consciences would again be 'wounded' because of their false understanding that they are being permitted to partake in idol worship.²⁹ As such, this demonstrates the group norm in v. 24, of seeking the advantage of 'the other'.

However, we have also argued that Paul is concerned about the conscience of the unbeliever, who in this situation is the one who declares the food as ἱερόθυτον. For if they then see believers knowingly and willingly eating of this food, then they might naturally interpret this act as the believers' endorsement of the unbeliever's idolatrous convictions and rituals (also Garland 2003: 497). They would not see the believer's stance against idols, or their freedom to eat all things on the understanding that there are no other gods. They would only see the believer affirming their perception of the world and their understanding of who they are and what they do as a worshipper of another god, and might perhaps conclude that 'Christianity was syncretistic' (Willis 1985: 241). They are then placed further from the truth of the gospel, and as such, further from salvation. Thus, if food is revealed as having been part of idol sacrifices, then 'By knowingly partaking of idol food, the Christian is tacitly condoning idolatry and thus lending a hand to the transgressors' (Cheung 1999: 157). For Conzelmann the action goes further than this, for the believer 'would objectify the power of the gods, and thereby "preach" faith in them' (1975: 178). Hence, Paul's references to conscience in verses 28 and 29a can be understood to be a concern for the conscience of the unbeliever, specifically a concern for how their conscience could misunderstand the believer's action, and how this misunderstanding would then inform their moral compass, which would then have been calibrated incorrectly.

Therefore, it is only when the meat has been revealed as being sacrificed that the believer's actions will be significant, for then the unbeliever is alerted to being aware of how the believer will respond. Up until the point when someone raises the issue about idol meat, it is acceptable for the believer to eat, for the unbeliever cannot form a misguided interpretation for they know that the believer is not aware if they are eating idol meat; but at the point when the issue is raised, then it would be catastrophic to eat of it. There is something significant here about the importance of the believer's freedom *and* the point at which this freedom would be damaging to the other person. When the conscience of the other person is not in danger of misinterpreting the believer's freedom, then there is no need to worry about one's freedom, how it will be interpreted and the conscience of the other person.

This may indicate that the rhetorical questions in verses 29b and 30 are connected more with these first two scenarios (vv. 25, 27).³⁰ In other words, as long as it does not damage another person's conscience, then the believer's freedom should guide their actions, and the believer does not have to direct attention to their freedom in a situation when it would then be incorrectly judged. The believer's freedom is always to be curtailed when another person's conscience is at stake; but on the other hand, when that other person's conscience is not at stake, why should the believer's freedom be curtailed? Thus, Paul asks, ἱνατί γὰρ ἡ ἐλευθερία μου κρίνεται ὑπὸ ἄλλης συνειδήσεως (v. 29b, 'for why is my freedom judged by another's conscience?'), and εἰ ἐγὼ χάριτι μετέχω, τί βλασφημοῦμαι ὑπὲρ οὗ ἐγὼ εὐχαριστῶ ('if I partake with thanksgiving, why should I be denounced for that which I give thanks?', v. 30).

However, the difficulty with this is that if the rhetorical questions in vv. 29b-30 are connected with vv. 25-27, then vv. 28-29a become an interruption in the flow of Paul's thought, rather than a significant turning point in introducing the concern for the conscience of 'the other', specifically that of the unbeliever. For vv. 28-29a are an important gear change in the flow of Paul's thought; they highlight the overlap between looking at the inward community and the outer one, and specifically point to the conscience of the other person as the outsider. If vv. 28-29a are not an interruption but an important development in Paul's argument, then the rhetorical questions must refer to this advice regarding the consideration of the unbeliever's conscience. The change from second to first person could indicate that Paul is presenting the opposing arguments he anticipates from disgruntled believers upon hearing his counsel (thus Gooch 1993: 92; Lietzmann 1949: 52; Witherington 1995: 228).[31] Wendland writes that Paul is putting forward this objection from the 'mindset of the strong ones' who 'refuse to recognise any other word as standing over their freedom' (1980: 83). This would link in with what we know of the wider attitude of the Corinthian believers, for they seem to believe they should be able to do whatever it is that feels right and edifying to them, regardless of (and perhaps even oblivious to) the impact this has on anyone else (see chapters 5, 6, 8, 10).

Furthermore, if Paul is posing potential arguments that might be used against his own, then it is possible to understand that the following verses (vv. 31–11.1) provide a counter-argument to these questions.[32] Watson provides a detailed analysis of the rhetorical function of these questions in vv. 29b-30, to firstly illustrate how they are connected to the preceding verses in 1 Cor. 10.23-29a since they function as questions of anticipation (1989: 312–13), 'predicting the negative response of the strong to the restrictions of 10:28-29a' (1989: 318), and secondly, to illustrate how they are connected to 10.31–11.1. He argues here that Paul is following a particular form of rhetorical question whereby he poses two questions that are 'aimed at' the weakest arguments of his opponents (namely 'their lack of respect for the conscience of others, and their justification of eating sacrificial meat in spite of others' conscience by appealing to their having blessed it'), in order to then put forward his own 'strong points in proposal of policy in 10:31–11:1' (Watson 1989: 311). It is to these final verses that we shall now turn.

4.3.3 The motivation: 'that they might be saved'

In the final verses of this passage, Paul declares an overarching goal for the believer: εἴτε οὖν ἐσθίετε εἴτε πίνετε εἴτε τι ποιεῖτε, πάντα εἰς δόξαν θεοῦ ποιεῖτε (v. 31). Wendland argues that Paul's immediate reference in v. 31 to the glory of God is reminding the believers (specifically the strong), that 'the glory of God must be the supreme measure of human activity', which means that it should not be possible for the believer to give thanks to God on the one hand, and yet in some way harm another person (1980: 84). Watson also rightly points out that 'living to the glory of God is to consider the needs of others in highest regard (Rom. 15.7; 1 Cor. 6.20; Phil. 1.11; 2.11)' (1989: 306). In the particular scenario pictured around the dining table, we have seen that the Corinthians must consider how the unbeliever might misinterpret their actions;

Paul now urges them in v. 31 to understand that their consideration of the other in every scenario is actually connected to how they are able to fulfil their duty to live 'to the glory of God'. But from other NT references we also see that the 'glory of God' is connected to knowledge of the gospel: in 2 Corinthians Paul writes that 'the god of this age has blinded the minds of the unbelievers, to keep them from seeing the light of the gospel of the glory of Christ, who is the image of God' (4.4), and in contrast God has shone into the hearts of the believers 'the light of the knowledge of the glory of God in the face of Jesus Christ' (4.6). The glory of God is connected with knowledge and understanding. Thus, living to the glory of God is also about knowing, revealing and testifying to the true gospel. This also connects with our passage in 1 Corinthians 10, since we have already seen that Paul is concerned with how the knowledge of the gospel is revealed through the actions of the believers and interpreted and applied by the conscience of the unbeliever. He is particularly concerned about the fact that some actions of the believers may actually prevent others (and specifically, unbelievers) from understanding the gospel.

Paul's instruction in 1 Cor. 10.31 is not just a recapitulation of his earlier instructions in vv. 23-24, but a sharp response to the potential opposing arguments of some believers in vv. 29b-30. If someone should question why another person has the right to question or judge their freedom, or why their act of blessing is not enough to make their chosen action acceptable, then they should remember that they are called to do all things for the glory of God – which involves considering the needs of others and considering how they might reveal the true gospel, giving thought to how others might perceive and interpret their actions. For Paul, the glory of God is also connected with people acknowledging and proclaiming the Lordship of Christ (Phil. 2.11), and his confession in 1 Cor. 10.33 that he seeks for the salvation of others is an example of how to live 'to the glory of God'. The Corinthian believers are to consider the other in all their actions, specifically how they might be revealing (or veiling) the gospel of Christ, and as such, helping or preventing others from being saved.

Paul then develops his answer in verse 32: ἀπρόσκοποι καὶ Ἰουδαίοις γίνεσθε καὶ Ἕλλησιν καὶ τῇ ἐκκλησίᾳ τοῦ θεοῦ. The adjective ἀπρόσκοποι is used by Paul only on one other occasion in Phil. 1.10, to describe how the believers should appear before Christ in the eschaton, as 'blameless' (see also Acts 24.16). Paul does, however, use the noun πρόσκομμα in a previous chapter in 1 Cor. 8.9, where he warns the believers not to let their freedoms become a 'stumbling block' to those who lack knowledge and understanding. This would suggest that in the use of the adjective ἀπρόσκοποι (the negative form of the noun in 8.9), Paul is warning all believers (not just the 'strong') to make sure that they themselves do not become a 'stumbling block' to those around them (e.g. Barrett 1971: 243–4), and more specifically, that they do not prevent others from accessing, or from drawing closer to, the glory of God as revealed in Jesus Christ (see also Fee 1987: 489). In all matters of life, not just in matters of eating and drinking, but in everything (v. 31), they are to ensure that they do not inadvertently turn others away from God, and therefore, from the hope of salvation (v. 33). However, Paul's instruction is likely to have a stronger meaning than simply 'preventing' others from hearing the gospel, and Thiselton proposes that it is more likely a call to the believers not to behave in a way that would be destructive or damaging to another person (2000: 794). This would correspond with Paul's description in 8.12 of the knowledgeable believers 'wounding' the consciences of the weak believers. Paul is not simply concerned that the believers could, by their behaviour, put off others from the gospel of Christ, but that they could damage the ability of others in being able to perceive, interpret and accept the gospel.

Furthermore, he refers to Jews, Greeks and the church of God, so as to remind believers that this 'group norm' of not being destructive to (the conscience of) others includes insiders *and* outsiders. When Paul instructs other believers elsewhere in his letters not to act in such a way that puts a 'trap' before others or that would make others 'stumble', it is mostly with reference to ingroup relations (e.g. Rom. 14.13, 20-21 and 1 Cor. 8.13, using a mixture of πρόσκομμα, σκάνδαλον, προσκόπτει, σκανδαλίζει and σκανδαλίσω). Willis comments that in 1 Cor. 10.32 the 'emphasis clearly is upon the last named group, "the church of God"', since Paul has been focused on the 'weaker members' (1985: 255–6). However, this ignores the fact that Paul has been introducing in this passage the 'unbeliever' (10.27, 29a), and it also alienates this verse from the following verse where Paul widens the context from simply being about food and drink to 'all things' (πάντα), where he refers to 'all people' (πᾶσιν) and 'the many' (τῶν πολλῶν) and how he seeks for their salvation (v. 33). Its immediate context alone suggests that in 1 Cor. 10.32 Paul is urging the believers to think not only of ingroup relations, but of their relationships with different groups within the outside community.[33] Rather than emphasizing one particular group, Paul is emphasizing the universality of this group norm. For, in terms of SIT, this group norm invites the believers to view and treat other insiders and all outsiders in the same way; they are to make sure that they are not destroying the faith of other insiders, or the opportunity of outsiders to accept the true faith. This compels us to remember one of the opening verses in this passage, where Paul insists that not all actions are edifying (v. 23b). Believers are not to destroy, but to build up; this is true for how they live among fellow believers *and* among unbelievers.

Paul emphasizes this point by offering his own style of ministry and discipleship as an example: καθὼς κἀγὼ πάντα πᾶσιν ἀρέσκω μὴ ζητῶν τὸ ἐμαυτοῦ σύμφορον ἀλλὰ τὸ τῶν πολλῶν, ἵνα σωθῶσιν (10.33, 'even as I in all things please all people, not seeking my own advantage but that of the many, so that they may be saved'). The repetition of 'all things' and 'all people' and 'the many' emphasizes the fact that for Paul, how the believer behaves and responds to other people is not just restricted to eating, but is relevant for the whole of life's encounters and events. The statement about 'pleasing' everyone in all things is used by Paul to expand on what it means not to be a destructive influence in the life and faith of another person; if the believers are not to damage an unbeliever's opportunity of perceiving and receiving the true gospel of Christ, then this means that they should go out of their way to 'please' them and seek for their advantage.[34] Thus Collins proposes that the two ideals of not being a 'stumbling block' (or cause for damage) and of pleasing others are 'virtually synonymous' (1999: 389). Clearly, what it means to please others must have its limitations, and, anticipating the many responses asking for clarity on this, Paul immediately sets out that the objective of pleasing and seeking the advantage of others is precisely so that they might reach salvation. It must also be taken as an illustration of what it means to 'do everything for the glory of God' (10.31), rather than as a contradiction to this.

In other letters Paul seems to suggest that the believers cannot seek to please both God *and* other people, speaking negatively about seeking to please others and emphasizing that the duty of the believer is to seek to please God (e.g. Gal. 1.10; 1 Thess. 2.4; 4.1; 1 Cor. 7.32; cf. 2 Tim. 2.4). In contrast, those of the flesh (Rom. 8.8) and those who put Christ to death (1 Thess. 2.15) cannot, and do not please God. Nevertheless, Paul does not rule out pleasing others: in Romans 15 he instructs the 'strong' believers not to please themselves (v. 1) but rather to please their neighbour so as to edify them (v. 2, ἕκαστος ἡμῶν τῷ πλησίον ἀρεσκέτω εἰς τὸ ἀγαθὸν πρὸς οἰκοδομήν). Their neighbour here is their fellow believer who is 'injured' by what the 'strong' believers eat (14.15). Thus, Paul counsels the strong believers to behave in a way that would 'please' the weaker believers by not injuring them such as to 'destroy the work of God' (14.20); clearly the pleasing of weaker believers is intricately connected to their edification in their faith. So too in 1 Cor. 10.33, Paul's advocacy of aiming to please unbelievers is intricately connected to their salvation.

For Paul, therefore, pleasing others here is to do with being in a position where the believer can help the unbeliever to see and accept the gospel of Christ, which will lead to their salvation. Their spiritual well-being is driving Paul's motivations, and he recognizes that in order to 'please' others, he needs to be in a certain relationship with that other person. This relationship is marked with the believer prioritizing the unbeliever over their own desires and freedoms, and also presumes a certain amount of friendship, if the relationship is one that imagines the believer being invited into the home of an unbeliever.[35] Pleasing the other person takes into consideration how the unbeliever would view the believer's behaviour and form an opinion of it and of the gospel. As Garland writes, Paul's 'overriding concern as an apostle is how to gain followers for Christ. Consequently, he pays heed to how others perceive the faith and actions of Christians' (2003: 501). Gaining followers for Christ is deeply connected to how these potential followers view and form an opinion of the believers and the gospel they present. Thus, pleasing others here is about being able to present accurately and attractively the gospel of Christ; it is not about putting '*truth* second to *please* people' (Thiselton 2000: 795). It is not about 'the kind of conduct that often characterized the itinerant philosopher or religious charlatan, those who curried the favour of others in order to gain their approval' (Fee 1987: 490). Rather, it is about introducing truth to the other in a way that is unmistakable, inoffensive and compelling; this is what it means to please others, for this then also may lead to their salvation.

Furthermore, Paul makes it clear that seeking the advantage of the other in evangelistic discipleship should be a mark of *all* believers (1 Cor. 11.1). The Corinthian believers should adopt Paul's own pattern for evangelistic ministry and his own desire for outsiders to become full members of the believing community, by giving thought and importance to how outsiders view and interpret the gospel of Christ. They are not to shy away from changing their own behaviour in response to this; in fact, how others perceive them and the gospel should shape how they live out the gospel before others. In this way, they will not only bring glory to God, but will also see the salvation of many and the growth of the believing community.

4.3.4 Summary

Paul wishes the Corinthian believers to recognize that what is at stake in all of their decisions is the salvation of the unbeliever: if an unbeliever misinterprets the actions of the believer, then their conscience is fed the wrong information about the gospel of Christ, and they are further from the knowledge of the glory of God. The opinion of the unbeliever is vitally important; how they perceive and interpret the believer and their actions will in turn form their knowledge of and response to the gospel, and as such, their conversion from outsider to insider. An important group norm of believers is that they should always, in everything, make sure that they are not damaging the faith of other believers, or the potential for an outsider to become an insider; rather, they are to seek not to please themselves in exercising their own freedoms, but to please others in the sense of causing them to know the God of salvation. In essence, a group norm of believers is to constantly recognize what outsiders think, to understand the importance of what they think with regard to their possible salvation, and to appreciate how what others think informs their own vocation as missional disciples.

4.4 1 Corinthians 14.13-25

4.4.1 Introduction: worship and edification

After chapter 10, Paul turns his attention in several places to the context of worship. He addresses the role of men and women in worship, the divisions that are apparent when they come to eat the Lord's supper (chapter 11), the different gifts of the Spirit given to different members of the body of Christ and the value of each member (chapter 12). It becomes clear that Paul is focused upon two specific gifts: prophecy and tongues. Thus, having already mentioned the different expectations for men and women praying and prophesying (11.4-5, 13), he writes that some believers will receive the spiritual gift of prophecy, some the gift of tongues and others the interpretation of tongues (12.10), and that it is God himself who has appointed some to be prophets and some to speak in tongues (12.28). In a discourse on the nature and significance of love, Paul refers only to the gifts of speaking in tongues and prophetic gifts to illustrate that having love is an important criterion for the use of such gifts (13.1-3). Paul concludes that the believers should 'pursue love' but also 'eagerly desire the spiritual gifts', and furthermore, that they should especially desire the gift of prophecy (μᾶλλον δὲ ἵνα προφητεύητε, 14.1). His reasoning is based on what gift he believes will be capable of building up the whole community: whereas prophecy leads to the building up, encouragement and consolation of others (14.3), tongues only edify the one speaking them (14.4).[36]

Paul is not prohibiting speaking in tongues (see 14.39); he is, however, emphasizing the concern we have seen throughout this letter, that of the importance of acting in a way that will benefit others, and worship is not an exception to this group norm (14.5, 12). He details at length why speaking in tongues does not edify others (14.6-12) and concludes that the one who does have this gift should also pray that they might be given the gift to interpret it (v. 13) for the spirit and the mind must both be engaged in worship (vv. 14-15). It is at this point that Paul brings into the discussion another person, the ἰδιώτης (v. 16), normally translated as 'unlearned', which could possibly refer to unbelievers.[37] Paul writes that unless the one speaking in tongues (praying with the spirit) is also able to provide an interpretation (praying with the mind), then this ἰδιώτης is unable to say 'Amen' at the end of the thanksgiving, since they do not understand what has been said (14.15-16). There is a clear link between knowledge and edification. This believer may well be doing a good thing in giving thanks to God, but this is not edifying the other person (ὁ ἕτερος, v. 17) because it is denying them understanding. Thus, Paul argues that even if the believer justifies their behaviour by or because of their giving thanks to God, if their actions do not also edify the other person, then they are in vain. Paul then specifically refers to 'unbelievers' (οἱ ἄπιστοι), but states that tongues are a 'sign' (σημεῖον) for unbelievers, whereas prophecy is for the believers (v. 22). However, he then continues with an illustration that seems to oppose v. 22: if the ἰδιῶται ἢ ἄπιστοι enter the worship space when believers are speaking in tongues, they will say that the believers are 'out of their minds' (v. 23). A lack of opportunity to deepen understanding not only has a negative impact upon edification but also upon the perceived health and state of the believers' minds from the view of the 'outsider'. However, if τις ἄπιστος ἢ ἰδιώτης enters when all the believers are prophesying, this leads to a most remarkable conversion experience in the 'unlearned' one or 'unbeliever' (v. 24). For, according to Paul, they will be 'convicted by all' and 'judged by all' (v. 24), 'the hidden things' of their hearts will be revealed, and they will respond in worship, declaring, 'God is really among you' (v. 25). Clearly for Paul, prophecy enables 'all to learn and all to be encouraged' (v. 31), which includes outsiders.

Once more, as in chapters 7 and 10, we see that, whereas Paul begins a topic of instruction that focuses at first on the believing community, he then widens the frame of reference to include outsiders and how they are impacted upon by the believers' behaviour, and how hopefully they are to be included within the believing community. This last point, however, hinges on the outsiders' view and opinion of the believer and their practices. Thus, Paul encourages the believers to acknowledge this and, if necessary, change their behaviour in order for the outsider to be edified and to respond positively to their experience of worship in the faith community.

4.4.2 The unlearned and the unbeliever

As has been seen, Paul refers a couple of times in this passage to 'the unlearned' (v. 16, 23, 24) and to 'the unbeliever' (v. 23, 24). In exploring Paul's concern for the outsider, it is firstly important to identify who Paul is referring to in these descriptions. A clear point of difficulty is to do with the identification of the person described as 'the one occupying the place of the uninstructed' (v. 16, ὁ ἀναπληρῶν τὸν τόπον τοῦ ἰδιώτου). Some scholars argue that this person is a believer who is lacking spiritual gifts, although within this line of thought some argue for Paul referring to such people as taking a metaphorical place, and some propose that there was an actual physical place for such believers. Thus, for Moffatt the ἰδιώτης represents those believers who are 'the ordinary worshipper' but who are also metaphorically 'outside this region of spiritual ecstasy, uninitiated into such mysteries' (1938: 220). Garland and Barrett argue that 'in the place of' refers not to a physical place but rather metaphorically to those believers who 'fill the role' of 'the novice' (Garland 2003: 641; also Robertson and Plummer 1911: 313) and 'the simple listener' (Barrett 1971: 321). Thiselton also proposes that 'the uninitiated person' is a good way to translate ἰδιώτης for they are believers who are 'embarrassed and excluded' from participating fully in the worship (2000: 1114–15; also Fee 1987: 673).

In contrast, Héring is persuaded that these people do 'occupy a definite place in the assembly', and as such are not 'pagans' who have wandered in by chance, but are either 'ordinary' believers who do not possess the spiritual gifts, or unbelievers who are 'sympathetic' to the faith but not fully baptized (1949: 127). In a similar vein, for Schrage the ἰδιώτης is the '*Nicht-Fachmann*' (non-specialist) or '*Nicht-Eingeweihte*' (non-initiated, 2012: 401), and for Morris they represent a person somewhere between a believer and an unbeliever, an 'inquirer' (1988: 191). It is also possible that the phrase, ὁ ἀναπληρῶν τὸν τόπον (v. 16) could indicate that the 'unlearned one' is used to denote *anyone* who lacks spiritual gifts, regardless of whether or not they are a believer.

The opinion that the ἰδιώτης is a believer lacking spiritual gifts concords with how this word is used elsewhere in the New Testament, albeit only on two other occasions. Paul uses it to describe himself as being 'unskilled in speech' (ἰδιώτης τῷ λόγῳ, 2 Cor. 11.6) and in Acts 4.13 Peter and John are described as 'uneducated' (ἀγράμματοί) and 'unskilled' (ἰδιῶται). These two references show that ἰδιώτης is used to highlight a particular lack of skills in these believers. However, having found that this word is used outside the NT to denote both a member of a community who lacks skills, and to identify 'the outsider', Schlier concludes that 'the term ἰδιώτης takes on its concrete sense from the context' (1965: 216). Accordingly, in order to understand the identity of the ἰδιώτης in v. 16, one must also consider its use and context in vv. 23-24, where it is combined with ἄπιστος. For Schlier, this shows that the ἰδιώτης 'are those who do not belong to the community … they are not members … the context demands a reference to non-Christians' (1965: 217). Indeed, the response these 'unlearned' ones would have towards experiencing believers prophesying suggests that they are unbelievers. For Paul writes that they would be moved to worship God, declaring, 'God is really among you' (v. 25). Such 'unlearned ones' have the same cynical and unbelieving response to hearing tongues as the unbelievers; this suggests that Paul is referring to the same person, the one who is the unbeliever is also the one who is the unlearned, the unknowing.

It is possible, however, that the 'unlearned one' in v. 16 is the believer who lacks knowledge of spiritual gifts, whereas in vv. 23-24 the 'unlearned one' is the unbeliever who lacks knowledge of the Christian faith.[38] It has previously been seen how Paul can begin a discussion by focusing on believers and then shift this focus to outsiders, sometimes with a slight degree of overlap (e.g. 7.1-11 and vv. 12-16; 10.1-27 and 27-33). Perhaps Paul includes ἢ ἄπιστοι in v. 23 (and in v. 24) to add further definition to this term here and indicate that now he is focusing upon the unlearned one who is the unbeliever. Hence, it would not be unusual for Paul to show concern for the believers who are unable to participate in the worship and be edified (1 Cor. 14.16-17) and then to widen this concern to encompass unbelievers who are unable to participate because of their misunderstanding and perception of speaking in tongues (v. 23), and therefore show his concern for their potential conversion (vv. 24-25). The two responses of the 'unlearned' may also reveal that two different groups of people are being referred to: for it is reported that the first unlearned person (v. 16) reacts to hearing tongues simply with an acknowledgement that they cannot participate in the prayer; the reaction of the second unlearned person (v. 23-24), however, is one of scepticism and contempt for the believers displaying this gift.

Additionally, the concern for Paul regarding the first 'unlearned one' is that they are not able to be edified (v. 17), whereas for the second 'unlearned one' it is that they would not have a conversion experience and would acquire a negative opinion of the believer (v. 23, vv. 24-25).[39] The meaning of ἰδιώτης does not primarily define faith or lack of it; what it does, however, define is a person's lack of skill, leading to their inability to fully understand or participate. This is why, for Paul, uninterpreted tongues are a problem because both the person of faith and of no faith, if they have no skill in understanding tongues, will be unable to participate in the worship and will be pushed further away from full participation in the faith community. It seems likely therefore that Paul is particularly concerned about anyone who lacks the knowledge to participate fully in worship, and in verse 16 he is referring to believers, and in the latter part of the passage, he is referring to unbelievers (vv. 23-25).

4.4.3 The importance of what unbelievers think

Significant for our study is the fact that this reveals Paul's concern about what unbelievers *think* when they observe something in the life of the believer that they do not understand; but he is also concerned about a believer's action that closes off any opportunity for the unbeliever to gain understanding. Hence, it was seen in chapter 10 that the believers' decision to eat or refuse meat can potentially either enhance or confuse an unbeliever's understanding of the Christian faith. Similarly, Paul is concerned about how speaking in tongues might be misinterpreted by the unbelievers. He exclaims in v. 23, 'will they not say that you are out of your minds?'[40] Paul's concern about uninterpreted tongues is not just that some believers won't be able to understand but also that unbelievers will react so negatively to them that they then build up a negative stereotype of believers as being 'crazy'. This experience neither provides an understanding of the gospel to unbelievers (and as such prevents a possible conversion experience), nor does it provide a positive view of the believers in the eyes of the unbelievers. In other words, tongues push an unbeliever further away from knowing the gospel; they are hardened in their unbelief because they are hardened in their 'unknowing' and therefore repelled further from participating in the body of Christ. For Paul, uninterpreted tongues present an obstacle in the way of increasing knowledge and in edifying the church. Indeed, the church may also be scorned and receive a negative stereotype in the minds of the unbelievers.

Paul, however, explains that prophecy will have the opposite impact upon unbelievers. He writes that if an unbeliever enters into a worshipping space and they encounter prophecy, a sixfold process of conversion will ensue: the unbeliever will be convicted, judged and shown the 'hidden things of his heart' (see also 1 Cor. 4.5; 2 Cor. 4.2; Rom. 2.16); this will then lead to the unbeliever falling down, worshipping God and declaring God's real presence among the believing community (1 Cor. 14.24-25).[41] Fitzmyer succinctly describes the effects of prophecy on the unbeliever as, 'conviction, scrutiny, and exposure of his or her heart', which then leads to 'conversion, submission and adoration' (2008: 522). For Paul, prophecy opens up a vat of knowledge to the unbeliever, firstly because they are convicted (ἐλέγχω) of their sin and secondly because they are convicted of the truth.[42] This newly found knowledge leads the unbeliever to be judged, in other words, to 'stand under the verdict of the cross' (Thiselton 2000: 1128) where this person sees his or her own life, even the hidden things, in a new way. As such, in humility and awe they adopt an attitude of worship that conveys a sense of unworthiness (see Gen. 17.3; Rev. 7.11; 11.16). Now, having been able to access truth and knowledge of themselves and of God, they can fully participate in the worship of the faithful community, being able to lift up their own voices in an act of worship, declaring God's presence (1 Cor. 14.25).

Whereas uninterpreted tongues are only going to edify the speaker and those who can interpret them, prophecy offers the opportunity for all to learn and to be encouraged, including the newly converted (v. 31). Hence, Paul calls for the believers to acknowledge this and to adapt their worship accordingly, not just to take account of other believers, but specifically to take account of unbelievers. They, too, are to be concerned for how the unbelievers, the outsiders, may view them in their worship and thus form a potentially negative and damaging stereotype of the insiders, but they should also be concerned to worship in a way that will open up knowledge for the unbeliever, and lead to their salvation.

4.4.4 Deepening unbelief or building up belief

It is in appreciating the function and impact of uninterpreted tongues and of prophecy upon unbelievers that we can begin to understand our final point of difficulty in this passage to do with unbelievers, which is found earlier in verse 22.[43] For, after the edited quote from Isa. 28.11-12 in v. 21, Paul writes, ὥστε αἱ γλῶσσαι εἰς σημεῖόν εἰσιν οὐ τοῖς πιστεύουσιν ἀλλὰ τοῖς ἀπίστοις, ἡ δὲ προφητεία οὐ τοῖς ἀπίστοις ἀλλὰ τοῖς πιστεύουσιν (v. 22). As can be seen from the Greek, a literal translation of verse 22 simply ties the translator and interpreter in knots, since a literal translation is not only fraught with its own difficulties (such as how to translate σημεῖον, and how to fill in the apparent blanks in the second half of the verse), but it also seems to say the exact opposite of what Paul then explains in the following verses, which we have explored above.[44] For if tongues add to the lack of knowledge and therefore unbelief of unbelievers (v. 23), it is at first unclear as to how Paul can then describe them as a 'sign' to unbelievers; and if prophecy leads to a deepening of knowledge and their conversion (vv. 24-25), it is similarly mystifying as to how they can be called a 'sign' not for unbelievers, but for believers. As such, Thiselton writes that these are some of the 'most difficult verses in our epistle' (2000: 1122), Fee states that we find here a 'notorious crux' (1987: 681) and Hays finds 'great confusion' and describes Paul's argument as 'garbled' (1997: 239-40).

Many commentators conclude that tongues are a sign of judgement for unbelievers; however, they then differ on how they understand prophecy as a sign for believers.

Barrett, for example, argues that tongues function to deepen the unbelievers' unbelief and thus condemn the unbeliever (1971: 323; also Hays 1997: 240; Robertson and Plummer 1911: 316), and that prophecy is a sign of judgement on believers, since the Corinthian believers tend 'to shut their ears to prophecy because they gain more satisfaction from listening to tongues than from hearing their faults exposed and their duties pointed out in plain rational language. Thus they incur judgment' (1971: 324). Given the Corinthian believers were happy to ignore the sexual immorality happening within their congregation (chapter 5), the above proposal is to some extent quite possible. However, the difficulty is that whenever Paul has previously encouraged the use of prophecy, he has not indicated that the believers are hesitant to use it for this reason. Collins also understands that tongues are a sign of judgement but that prophecy is a sign for believers because 'it is an instrument of conversion of the nonbeliever' (1999: 508). However, he fails to explain how the positive impact of prophecy on the *unbeliever* is then considered a sign to the *believer*, and also what kind of sign prophecy becomes. Fee, however, adds flesh to this suggestion as he writes that, since tongues are a sign of God's disapproval (for as v. 23 explains, they are unintelligible and therefore unbelievers 'receive no revelation from God' and 'they cannot be brought to faith', 1987: 682), prophecy then becomes a sign of God's approval for the believers. This is because the conversion experience of the unbeliever (vv. 24-25) shows that 'God's favour' is upon the believers (1987, 682–3). Garland also understands tongues as a sign of judgement for unbelievers since 'it hardens them in their unbelief' (2003: 650) and prophecy for believers as a 'sign of God's presence among them' because of the conversion of unbelievers (2003: 651). The difficulty with this interpretation regarding prophecy is that the idea of finding God's approval is not raised in the rest of the passage, and it is quite unusual for Paul to write that the conversion of unbelievers reveals God's approval on the *believers*.

However, it might be possible to re-examine these verses if we take σημεῖον to refer not to a sign of something present, but as a signal for something future: tongues or prophecy then signal the impact they will have upon unbelief (for the unbeliever) or belief (for the believer). As such, tongues signal further unbelief in the unbeliever, and prophecy signals further belief in the believer. Regarding the use of tongues, it is apparent that Paul's use of an (edited) quote from Isa. 28.11-12 functions to illustrate that even so-called 'believers' do not recognize or understand the voice of their own God when unknown speech is used (v. 21). These verses in Isaiah also refer to 'other tongues' (ἑτερογλώσσις) and to the inability to give heed to God (καὶ οὐδ᾽ οὕτως εἰσακούσονταί μου).[45] The prophet is declaring that God will use the people of Assyria to communicate with his own people, and in so doing has chosen to communicate in a way that they will not be able to hear or understand as a punishment for their behaviour. Paul apparently refers to this to support his argument that when an unknown language is heard without translation, it is as if it is not heard, for it is not understood; consequently, people are prevented from communicating with God. As such, if believers cannot hear God (whom they should already know) through the unknown tongues of other people, how much more will unbelievers be unable to hear God (of whom they do not know) through the unknown tongues of believers?

Unbelievers are at a double disadvantage: they lack both knowledge of God and of tongues. Thus, for unbelievers, tongues are a sign of the furthering of unbelief, of the increasing chasm between God and the unbeliever because of the ability of unknown tongues to increase confusion, to deepen ignorance, to prevent a maturity of understanding.[46] In this case, they are perhaps not so much a 'sign *of*' but a signal pointing *to* the effect of tongues on those who have no means of understanding them.[47] For Paul, if unbelievers hear believers speaking in tongues, it is for them akin to hearing a foreign language and, possessing no knowledge to be able to interpret them, they remain ignorant about God and therefore continue in their position as 'outsiders'. On the other hand, Paul has made it clear that believers should have the ability to understand tongues in worship, for they are to pray for the gift of interpretation, or at least know someone who can provide an interpretation for them. This opportunity for understanding tongues is not available to unbelievers.

In the same way then, prophecy signals a furthering of belief for believers, not a furthering of unbelief for unbelievers. Paul writes, 'prophecy is not for the unbelievers, but for those believing' (v. 22b). In all other comparisons between tongues and prophecy, the point Paul makes is that prophecy can impart knowledge and therefore build up the whole community of faith. It would make sense for Paul to be reiterating this statement here in v. 22, that prophecy builds up faith (or the community of faith), and in verses 24-25 he shows that prophecy can build up this community also by increasing the number of its members. As such, verse 22b is more likely to mean: 'and prophecy is not for the unbelievers a building up of their unbelief, but to the believers a building up of belief'. Unlike tongues, prophecy does not lead to the 'building up' or strengthening of unbelief, but rather to the building up of belief. Paul's illustrations in vv. 23-25 show how tongues are a sign of further disbelief for unbelievers, and how prophecy is for the building up of believers.[48] In order to interpret verse 22, it is therefore vital to recognize Paul's wider comparison of tongues and prophecy which functions to illustrate his concerns about knowledge and edification of all. This means that there is no need to introduce new ideas or themes, and this interpretation inserts into the sentence only what is said elsewhere in the passage.

4.4.5 Summary

As much as Paul is concerned about the whole worshipping community, he is also concerned for those outside it, for what they might think of the worshipping community, and ultimately, for how they might join it. The importance of what outsiders think of the worshipping community goes beyond a concern for the kind of stereotype the believers might be given, and is rooted in the potential for outsiders to be saved. Thus, Gladstone writes, 'Although Paul is certainly concerned with the impression the worshipping body makes on its visitors, he is ultimately concerned with the active result that impression makes' (1999: 183). If Paul was only concerned about reputation, he would either advise the believers to make sure that no one was present who might misinterpret their worship, or simply prohibit the use of tongues. However, the fact that he goes on to encourage the use of prophecy in order to present opportunities for the conversion of outsiders, shows that he is also concerned about the spiritual welfare, and the salvation, of unbelievers. Trebilco correctly observes that the reaction or opinion of the outsiders to the worship of the believers is a key factor in 'deciding what actually takes place in the assembly' (2014: 192). There is no doubt that for Paul, 'the opinions of outsiders are important' (MacDonald 1988: 42). However, the importance of what others think is also rooted in the fact that this will directly influence their reception of the gospel. Once more believers are to take note of what outsiders think of them – and this time in the context of worship – in order to recognize how their impact upon outsiders is influencing the potential salvation of outsiders. This recognition in turn may require, and indeed does require, a change in the believers' behaviour for the advantage of the outsider.

4.5 Conclusion

This chapter has demonstrated the juxtaposition set forth in Chapter 1, namely that Paul can describe the unbelievers in negative terms but also show great concern for them and even allow the unbelievers to influence important decisions concerning the ingroup. As Trebilco notes:

> What is in fact said about unbelievers, then, belies the negativity that seems to be inherent in the designation. They are spoken of negatively in that they lack an essential feature that is salient within the group – πίστις. But what is said about unbelievers is not negative in such a way as to vilify or demean outsiders, nor are they spoken of in such a way as to encourage social exclusion, and 'other-regard' for these unbelievers should direct some key features of worship.
>
> (2014: 193)

However, this 'other-regard' goes beyond simply causing the believers to make some changes to worship: for Paul, this 'other-regard' seems to be both a core principle for how believers should behave (and thus an important part of how believers understand their own discipleship and identity) and also the mechanism by which other parts of their group's norms are controlled or shaped. Believers by their nature should always consider the opinions of others; but in so doing, they should also be willing to allow (with discernment) how these opinions should shape other aspects of their group's norms. What others think is a key factor in determining some of the norms and patterns of the ingroup.

It is this response to the opinions of outsiders that Chapter 1 also indicated was missing in the work of SIT, which neither recognizes nor appreciates the importance of outgroups in forming the social identity (or aspects of it) of the ingroup. Unsurprisingly then, in Brian Tucker's recent book, *Reading 1 Corinthians*, in which he uses the lens of SIT to explore this letter, not only is his treatment of 1 Corinthians 7, 10 and 14 extremely brief, he completely fails to notice the importance of the role of outsiders in the shaping and modifying of the social identity of believers (2017: 82, 102–4, 120). However, it is clear upon reading 1 Corinthians that Paul fully understands the decisive impact outsiders have upon the social identity of the believers. Paul reveals the importance of what outsiders think and demonstrates the role this plays in the lives of the believers, including personal and social relationships and their worship. The opinions of outsiders might not perhaps alter or shape important ethical norms of the insiders, but this does not mean that the impact of their opinions is insignificant in regulating certain decisions of a believer.

Additionally, what others think plays a significant role in reminding believers of one of their core understandings of their social identity: that they are missional disciples. Paul makes it very clear that understanding what others think is vital in their missionary vocation of enabling others to find salvation in Christ. The motivation for the believers acknowledging the opinions of others is unashamedly connected with a missional hope; whereas this *might* be part of the motivation in 1 Thessalonians and Romans, it is only explicitly identified here in 1 Corinthians. Hence, Paul is keen for the believing spouse to remain with their unbelieving spouse (if that is the desire of the latter) since not only does the unbeliever become sanctified through the marriage, but there is also the hope that they might find salvation (7.14, 16). In chapter 10, after asking the believers to consider how their decisions regarding food presented at a meal might negatively impact upon (and mislead) the conscience of an unbeliever, Paul sums up these instructions with a final plea to the believers to imitate him in his desire to seek the advantage of the other person, 'that they may be saved' (10.33; 11.1). One major factor that should shape how believers live their lives is a concern to seek the spiritual advantage of the other person, to please others rather than to frustrate them with regard to enabling their reconciliation to the God of salvation. And finally, in chapter 14, Paul's overriding concern is for all who are present at worship (believer and unbeliever) to be edified, which, for the unbeliever, ultimately means that they should encounter God in a way they can understand and in a way that leads them to a personal declaration of faith (14.25). Paul is motivated by a strong hope and desire for many more people to be saved, and this in turn influences his instructions to the believers in how they should respond to outsiders and be sensitive to their opinions and their experiences of the ingroup. The opinion of the outsider in each of these scenarios plays an important role in how the insider discerns how to behave, and this discernment is anchored in missional hope, which is revealed to be a core aspect or norm of a believer's identity.

Finally, whereas Paul refers to his own missionary strategy of 'becoming like' the other person in order to create the 'contact points' needed for positive acquaintanceship with outsiders (1 Cor. 9.19-23), in his instructions to the Corinthian believers he urges them to recognize the contact points that already exist. These are largely founded on sharing social connections rather than sharing value-based connections as we have seen in 1 Thessalonians and Romans (although the former does not exclude the latter). Thus, he points to a marriage between a believer and an unbeliever (1 Corinthians 7), to social relationships and even friendships between believers and unbelievers (1 Corinthians 10). It is unclear whether the unbeliever who walks into worship has been invited, already has social connections with someone present or is simply genuinely interested in exploring another religion; but that this is likely to happen reveals the fact that the believers do not have to work hard to create opportunities to encounter unbelievers in positive ways.

Paul is very aware that in Corinth the believers are visible and sociable, and he seeks not to curb this, but to use this for the growth of the ingroup. But this missional hope is reliant on the believers taking note of how the outsiders view them, and in turn, of how the believers consequently respond. Interestingly, we find here what Jenkins terms as an 'internal–external dialectic' which shapes some of the ingroup's norms (2008: 40, 42), but which also has the potential to completely transform the social identity of the outsider into that of an insider.

Notes

1 Fitzmyer points out that although ἄδικος in 6.1 'has a predominantly legal sense', it is used in 6.9 in 'a clearly moral sense, "evildoers"' (2008: 251). Hays remarks that a closer translation of τοὺς ἐξουθενημένους is 'those who are despised' (1997: 94), and, given the context, it is clear that these 'despised' people are those who are unbelievers, οἱ ἄπιστοι (6.6; also Horrell 1996: 139).

2 Paul's reference to τὰ ἔθνη in 5.1 reveals his nervousness around how this behaviour is going to be seen in wider society. That Paul returns to sexual ethics at several points in the letter also reveals his frustration with the believers' behaviour in this area. Hence, he writes that since their bodies are members of Christ (6.15), they should not take part in fornication (6.16-18), uniting their body with that of a πόρνη (v. 16). It is precisely because of 'the acts of fornication' (7.2) that Paul recommends the believers to marry, and although it is good for the unmarried and the widows to remain as they are, if they do not have self-control then they should also marry (7.8-9; see also 7.5, 36).

3 1 Cor. 6.6; 7.12, 13, 14 (twice), 15; 10.27; 14.22 (twice), 23, 24. This term is only used three more times in the undisputed epistles (2 Cor. 4.4; 6.14, 15) and then in 1 Tim. 5.8 and Tit. 1.15.

4 And thus, as Trebilco notes (2014), Paul sometimes uses terms to designate believers and unbelievers in the same passage, e.g. 1 Cor. 7.12 (οἱ ἀδελφοί) and 14.22 (οἱ πιστεύοντες).

5 E.g. Witherington 1995: 173; Garland 2003: 278-97; Trebilco 2014: 187; Horrell 2016: 195, 286-7; Tucker 2017, e.g. 31-2; 76-7.

6 See also Trebilco 2017: 50.

7 However, with regard to SIT, one's social identity is not simply about who one relates to or with, but it also must involve a sharing of core beliefs and values, not just a sharing of space.

8 Lang, in exploring this passage, ignores the mention of οἱ ἄδικοι but writes that οἱ ἄπιστοι in 6.6 are those who share the same social space as the believers because of the phrase ἐν τῇ ἐκκλησίᾳ (6.4, and which, he argues, Paul always uses 'locatively' 2018: 995), and that the verb ἐξουθενέω is elsewhere used by Paul in relation to believers (2018: 995-6). They are thus part of this special category of 'insiders'. Crucially, however, even though he recognizes Paul's 'recommendation that the ἄπιστοι [should] not arbitrate internal ecclesial disputes' (2018, 996), he fails to link this to 6.1 where Paul first articulates his frustration that the believers are taking

their disputes to οἱ ἄδικοι. It is highly likely that οἱ ἄδικοι and οἱ ἄπιστοι are the same people, but Lang fails to engage with this or propose a reason why they should be understood as two separate groups. As Trebilco writes, Paul 'uses ἄπιστοι in v6 because it is a key designation in 1 Corinthians that underlines the outsider status of these judges – they do not share the key feature of πίστις, which is a strong part of the family likeness that ἀδελφοί (v5–6, 8) have in common' (2017: 30).

9   In correcting a misinterpretation from an earlier letter, Paul writes that the Corinthian believers are not to dissociate themselves from οἱ πόρνοι τοῦ κόσμου τούτου, in addition to οἱ πλεονέκται, ἅρπαγες and εἰδωλολάτραι, for he reasons that the believers would then have to leave the world (5.10). This conveys a generalized image where most outsiders are unethical and immoral, to the extent that there is no escape from them: 'such offenders were too numerous to avoid in Corinth' (Barrett 1971: 131).

10 Fee suggests that Paul, in 'becoming like a Jew', adopted once more some of the 'religious peculiarities' such as certain food laws and 'special observances' (1987: 428). The reference to 'those under the law' could be another reference to Jews (Fee 1987: 428; Thiselton 2000: 702) or perhaps simply to 'God-fearers and prosleytes [sic]' (Witherington 1995: 212), and those 'without law' are probably Gentiles (Witherington 1995: 212). The reference to 'the weak' is probably not to 'weak believers' (e.g. Barrett 1971: 215; Hays 1997: 154–5), but to unbelievers (since Paul hopes to gain these outsiders also for their hope of salvation) from a low social background (e.g. Collins 1999: 351; Thiselton 2000: 705).

11 See also Acts 16.1-3; 21.17-26.

12 For Luke's image of Pauline adaptability, we may note the scenario in Acts 17.16-34, where Paul first establishes 'points of contact' or 'common territory' with his audience (e.g. quoting from pagan poets, v. 28) in order to create 'bridges' and build 'credibility' with his audience (Flemming 2002: 202–3). He neither sanctions every aspect of their beliefs, nor syncretizes the gospel with them, but opens up the possibility to engage constructively to reveal the differences and challenge their beliefs. In other words, Paul 'establishes rapport with his audience, and then through a series of contact points, he builds conceptual bridges that they can cross', but this engagement with this culture is in order to transform it (Flemming 2002: 207).

13 As such, Paul's criticism of Peter in Gal. 2.11–14 is because Peter is, in the words of Witherington, 'reacting to pressure' (1995: 211, footnote 30). Peter seems to be caught up in the tensions between Gentile and Jewish Christians but in trying to resolve this he excludes Gentile believers and gives the impression that they have to 'judaize' in order to be welcome at the common table. As Paul sees it, Peter's accommodation is not 'within Christ's law' (1 Cor. 9.21).

14 Thiselton 2000: 527; Barrett 1971: 164; Hays 1997: 121; Fee 1987: 299; Conzelmann 1975: 121.

15 Lang also argues that it is implausible for the head of the household, whether pagan or Christian, not to have imposed their respective devotion(s) upon the rest of the household (2018: 988). However, by this logic, then surely it would also be impossible to find a situation where a fully converted head of the household (a believer) would not impose exclusive Christ-devotion on their spouse if they were, as Lang claims, a 'deviant insider'.

16 Paul, however, advises virgins not to marry 'because of the present calamity' (1 Cor. 7.26). Garland (2003: 323–5) persuasively argues that this does not refer to persecution (due to the lack of evidence for this in the rest of the letter) but to some

form of present crisis (e.g. a famine) which has been interpreted as a sign of the end times, which ties in with the 'apocalyptic tenor' of the passage (e.g. 7.29, 31).

17 For more on this, see Portefaix 2003: 147–58.

18 Thus Tucker also comments, 'the Corinthians' openness to a new religious movement was quite different from the response to Paul's gospel in other parts of the empire. The situation therefore allowed for more interaction with those who had not yet become convinced of the gospel message' (2017: 36).

19 Conzelmann, however, remarks that 'it looks as if holiness is crassly regarded as a thing; it is transferable, without faith (and even baptism) being necessary' (1975: 121).

20 Some texts instead read ἡμᾶς (e.g. B, D, F, G, including Chrysostom and Jerome) which would give this appeal a wider audience, reminding all readers that they are all called to peace. However, it is more likely that it should be 'you', for this would fit with the context of vv. 12–16 where Paul is instructing specific spouses within the wider faith community, and it also corresponds 'to the direct appeal of the following verse, the final argument in Paul's arsenal of arguments on behalf of marital stability within a mixed marriage' (Collins 1999: 272).

21 Thus Grosheide states, 'Marriage is no missionary institution' (1953: 167; see also Lockwood 2000: 244; Conzelmann 1975: 124).

22 As argued by Fee 1987: 303–4; Barrett 1971: 166; Garland 2003: 292.

23 See also Collins 1999: 272; Barrett 1971: 167; Hays 1997: 119–20.

24 Such as what type of food is being bought at the market (most scholars highlight that the μάκελλον especially sold meat and fish; Garland 2003: 491) and whether the unbeliever is inviting the believer to a private meal or to a meal at a temple. Given Paul's earlier instructions in 10.14-22 about not participating in the 'table of demons', it is likely that the scenario envisaged is that of an unbeliever inviting a believer into their home for a private meal (Garland 2003: 492; Fee 1987: 478, 482–3; Cheung 1999: 156), although Horrell notes that 'invitations to various kinds of social and celebratory occasions in a variety of settings are included' (2016: 196). Furthermore, as Garland writes, 'An inquiry about the nature of the food would be superfluous at a meal in an idol's temple' (2003: 493). Some scholars highlight the fact that *any* food in the market or at the house of an unbeliever could be associated with idol sacrifice (Garland 2003: 489), whereas others argue that this would not apply to everything (Cheung 1999: 154–5, 156, footnote 230; Barrett 1971: 240).

25 It is worth noting, albeit briefly, the slight difficulty at first glance in reconciling 8.10 (where some believers are 'reclining in an idol's temple', ἐν εἰδωλείῳ κατακείμενον) with 10.20-21 (where Paul forbids believers partaking 'of the table of demons') and the permission to eat food whose cultic origins are unknown (10.25-27). Fee concludes that the two references in 8.10 and 10.20-21 are concerned with 'eating of sacrificial food at the cultic meals in the pagan temples', whereas 10.23-33 is concerned with eating idol food from the market and consumed in private homes (1987: 359–60; also Smit 2000: 135, 140). It is likely therefore that the second scenario pictured in 10.27 is of a believer being invited to a meal in a private home. As such, the location of the food and the extent of the participation in the sacrifice is an important factor in Paul's discussion, together with how different believers (and outsiders) will interpret these scenarios in different ways. See also Cheung (1999: 82–112) and Witherington (1993: 237–54).

26 See Gooch (1993: 38–46) and Cheung (1999: 35–8) for the social importance of meals in Greco-Roman culture. Willis comments that 'dining invitations were a common feature of Hellenistic life, held for all major occasions of life … taking part in such meals was simply a part of family and community life for the early Christians' (1985: 236).

27 It is possible that v. 28 is also connected to the marketplace scenario, and indeed, Paul's answer would still apply. However, v. 28 more naturally reads as an extension to the scenario in the home of an unbeliever, and Paul does not indicate otherwise. Thus, most scholars take v. 28 to refer to v. 27 (e.g. Garland 2003: 494; Collins 1999: 387; Thiselton 2000: 787), although Cheung (1999: 160) and Willis (1985: 243) both highlight that Paul's instructions in v. 28 are applicable anyway to v. 27, and other similar occasions.

28 Both Aristotle and Plutarch use ἱερόθυτον to refer to idol offerings (Aristotle, 'On Marvellous Things Heard', 842b, p. 298, and Plutarch, 'Moralia: Table Talk' VIII. 8, 729c, p. 178 in which he refers twice to animals that have been sacrificed to the gods). See Schrenk for more examples (1965: 252–3).

29 Contrary to Fee (1987: 481), this does not necessarily mean that Paul is writing to the weak believers here (as in chapter 8); Paul consistently reminds all believers throughout his letters of aspects of faith that they should already be aware of or need to be reminded of, and there is no reason to suppose that in chapter 10 Paul is specifically addressing either weak or knowledgeable believers (see also Garland 2003: 490). Furthermore, the use of μηδείς ('no one' among the believers) in setting out the group norm in v. 24 indicates that he is addressing *all* believers.

30 See Fitzmyer 2008: 402; Collins 1999: 388; Garland 2003: 499. There is no reason to presume that this is a later addition to the text, and although Paul suddenly uses the first person here, it is unnecessary to see it as a reference back to chapter 9 and therefore another defence of his own freedoms (Fee 1987: 486–7). Indeed, Paul often switches to talking about himself when he wants to emphasize an attitude that should govern the whole believing community, as we see in 10.33–11.1 (see Garland 2003: 497–8 and Thiselton 2000: 788–93 for an analysis of these and other positions).

31 An obvious problem with this interpretation is that one would have expected Paul to begin the first rhetorical question not with the connective γάρ but with δε or ἀλλά, which would indicate a contrast to what has just been advocated. However, given the overall complexity of understanding these verses in their context, and taking into consideration my arguments above, I still believe that this is a better reading of these verses (also Soden 1964: 353–4).

32 Some scholars, however, simply state that Paul does not provide an answer (e.g. Willis 1985: 247; Barrett 1971: 243; Fee 1987: 486; Garland 2003: 498; Thiselton 2000: 789).

33 When Paul describes his own attempt at not putting an obstacle in the way of others receiving the gospel of Christ (see 1 Cor. 9.12, ἐγκοπή, and 2 Cor. 6.3, προσκοπή), this 'policy' clearly includes outsiders and insiders.

34 The word ἀρέσκω appears 17 times throughout the New Testament, and all references apart from three (Mt. 14.6; Mk 6.22; Acts 6.5) occur in the Pauline corpus.

35 Cheung notes that meals shared together were important 'expressions of friendship' (1999: 35), referring to Plutarch's assertion of the 'friend-making character of the dining table' ('Table Talk', 612D).

36   Paul is concerned throughout this passage to emphasize the importance of *all* those present in worship having the opportunity to be edified by being built up in faith, by drawing closer to God, and by encouraging one another (14.3-5, 6, 12, 17, 26, 31).
37   We will explore this term in detail below in Section 4.4.2.
38   See also: Fee 1987: 685; Barrett 1971: 324; Garland 2003: 651; Trebilco 2017: 108–11; Finney 2013: 194.
39   The majority of Paul's uses of οἰκοδομέω refer to the building up of either the individual believer or the whole church (e.g. 1 Cor. 8.1, 10; 14.3, 4, 5, 12, 26; 2 Cor. 10.8; 12.19; 13.10).
40   It might be possible that the unbelievers could associate what they saw the believers doing with the uncontrolled and frenzied behaviour they saw in some of the mystery cults (Conzelmann 1975: 423 footnote 26; Hays 1997: 238). However, the use of μαίνομαι in the NT is always in response to hearing the words of another (e.g. Jn 10.20; Acts 12.15; 26.24, 25). As such, it is more probable that Paul uses μαίνομαι here to indicate that their reaction is not concerned with emotional or hysterical behaviour, but to hearing what they do not and cannot understand, which causes them to conclude that the believers are unintelligible, irrational, even crazy (see also Garland 2003: 652).
41   Garland notes the similarity of such a confession in 1 Cor. 14.24-25 as with that found in Isa. 45.14, and comments that 'It is the confession of the vanquished in Isa. 45.14 (see also 1 Kgs 18.39; Dan. 2:47; Zech. 8.23), but in this case they are vanquished by the word' (2003: 653).
42   As Thiselton (2000) notes, this Greek word is often used in John's gospel to denote the exposure or revelation of sin or the truth by Jesus (Jn 8.9, 46; 16.8; see Acts 6.10). Refer to Thiselton (2000: 1128) for other examples outside the NT.
43   Fee also comments that 'contrary to many interpretations, this text (v.22) needs to be understood in the light of what follows, not the other way around' (1987: 681).
44   Paul does not use σημεῖον very often in his letters, and when he does it is often used in a positive sense to refer to the supernatural powers that point to God (Rom. 15.19; 1 Cor. 1.22; 2 Cor. 12.12) or to refer to the 'sign of circumcision' (Rom. 4.11). Clearly, the use of σημεῖον in our text in 1 Cor. 14.22 cannot be referring to 'signs and powers' from God, or pointing to God, since these signs would also be for believers as well as unbelievers, and it would stand in awkward contradiction to v. 23. Furthermore, unlike the other references to σημεῖον, in 1 Cor. 14.22 there is little explanation within the verse itself as to what Paul intends by its use. Garland also, after looking at Paul's use of σημεῖον in the rest of his letters, concludes that this does not help in ascertaining what it means here in 1 Corinthians 14 (2003: 649–50).
45   Garland (2003: 646) and Thiselton (2000: 1120) provide a thorough exploration of the differences between Isa. 28.11-12 (in both the LXX and Hebrew texts) and 1 Cor. 14.21.
46   Thiselton similarly briefly states that tongues are a sign of unbelief for unbelievers. However, he then writes that tongues should not be used in worship because of their association with being a negative sign of judgement coming from unbelief. This is inappropriate for a context where believers are present as the feeling of alienation and 'wrongness' potentially experienced by believers should be those that are experienced by unbelievers (Thiselton 2000: 1123). This surely reads too much into the text, and also ignores the fact that Paul is actually more concerned about the effect of tongues on unbelievers than on believers, in verse 23.

47 The word σημεῖον is used elsewhere in the NT in this sense of a signal or a potent, usually in connection with the eschaton (Mt. 24.3, 30; Lk. 21.11, 25; Acts 2.19) but also of the destruction of the temple (Mk 13.4; Lk. 21.7).

48 See Gladstone's translation: 'Therefore tongues are a sign, not resulting in believers, but in unbelievers. But prophecy [is a sign], not resulting in unbelievers, but resulting in believers' (1999: 185). Gladstone therefore translates the dative phrases in v. 22 not as referring to *existing* unbelievers or believers, but to the potential visitors of v. 23 who might become the unbelievers or believers (1999: 189).

5

Reputation and Relationship:
1 Timothy and Titus

5.1 Introduction

Thus far we have explored Paul's sensitivity to outsiders and his concern for how they view, interpret and form an opinion of the believers. We have also seen how this concern guides Paul in how he instructs the different believing communities to behave among their particular outsiders, and how this concern sometimes grows from a deep missional desire in Paul for outsiders to become insiders, but also, on occasion, from a grave anxiety about the viability and safety of the believing community in areas where conflict and tension mark the relationship between outsiders and insiders. However, whether Paul is coming from a concern about safety or salvation (or even a mixture of both), what is apparent is his conviction that the believers must recognize the points of similarity that exist between the two groups, which include those values, norms and social experiences that both groups hold as important or significant to the well-being of the whole community. These points of similarity hold the possibility for the type of acquaintance that would generate peace, stability, and even growth, for they create the potential for outsiders to view believers in more positive terms. As such, they are more likely to be able to encounter and respond positively to the gospel of Christ. For Paul, what outsiders think has the power to shape how the believers are to interact with them, and therefore how they are to understand their group norms and the underlying reasons for these norms.

We have concentrated our studies on 1 Thessalonians, Romans and 1 Corinthians because, whilst this concern for outsiders is found in other disputed and undisputed letters (e.g. Gal. 6.10; Phil. 4.5, 8; Col. 4.5-6), we do not find elsewhere the same conglomeration of verses or depth of thought around this area. However, the exception to this is 1 Timothy and Titus, where we find a repeated concern for the outsider: a concern for their opinion of the believing community, a concern for how they experience the presence of the believers, and a concern for their salvation.[1] At the centre of these concerns we find a focus on the reputation of the believing community and the importance of the quality of relationship between insider and outsider.

These letters, however, are not without their complexities, including discerning their authorship and dating. Most scholars contend that these letters are pseudonymous works likely to have been written at the beginning of the second century.[2] For others they are genuine Pauline letters written in the second half of the first century.³ Marshall argues that they are based on authentic Pauline material, but composed perhaps by a group of authors which may have included Timothy and Titus (1999: 57–92). There is no need to rehearse these arguments further, for important to our study is not necessarily knowing the exact historical identity of the outsiders referred to in the letters, but the fact that outsiders are recognized in these writings and that there exists a significant degree of concern over them. Similarly, what is important is not knowing the true author of each letter, but discovering that the author of 1 Timothy and of Titus also has a concern for the outsider, and particularly for how they view the insiders. Hence, for simplicity I will refer to 'the Author' throughout this chapter. If the letters are pseudonymous then this functions to show that Paul's concern for the opinion of outsiders has successfully filtered down to some of the other disciples, instructors or apostles in the Pauline tradition; if they are not, then it serves to show that this concern of Paul's never waned and his teaching in this area was never considered unimportant, irrespective of the other challenges further churches were facing. We will now turn to explore 1 Timothy and Titus, considering first how the Author builds up an understanding of the identity of the believers and of the outsiders, before highlighting those verses and passages that reveal a sensitivity towards and a concern for the outsider and their opinion of the church.

5.2 The Pastoral Epistles: Insiders and Outsiders

The Pastorals consist of two letters addressed to the disciple Timothy and one letter to Titus. Thus, it is not unexpected to find some instructions to these disciples of a more personal nature regarding their own physical, ministerial or spiritual well-being (e.g. 1 Tim. 4.12, 16; 5.23; 2 Tim. 4.5; Tit. 2.15), and also with regard to their relationship with the Author (2 Tim. 4.9-15, 21; Tit. 3.12-13). Whereas Paul opens some of his letters with a declaration of his gratefulness for the faith of those particular readers or his affection for them (1 Thess. 1.2-10; Rom. 1.8-15; 1 Cor. 1.4-9), in the Pastorals we see the Author opening his letters with personal and affectionate descriptions of Timothy and Titus (e.g. 1 Tim. 1.2; 2 Tim. 1.2; 2.1; Tit. 1.4). For the Author, these two disciples have an important task in combatting the false teachers by directly instructing them not to teach a different doctrine (1 Tim. 1.3; see also 2 Tim. 2.25; Tit. 1.13; 3.10).⁴ However, it seems that the major way Timothy and Titus are to face the false teachers is simply by devoting their time to their own teaching (e.g. 1 Tim. 4.6, 11, 13, 16; 6.2b; 2 Tim. 2.14; 4.2; Tit. 2.1, 15), and making sure that it is 'beyond reproach' in order that 'the one of the opposing side' (ὁ ἐξ ἐναντίας) 'may be shamed, having nothing bad to say about us' (Tit. 2.8).⁵ Their own teaching should not bring slander and division, but rather salvation to them and to those listening to them (1 Tim. 4.16).

However, they are also tasked with securing the organization of these faith communities and their internal cohesion. The Author tells Titus that he was left behind in 'Crete' for the very reason that he should 'put in order what remained to be done' by 'appointing elders in every city' (Tit. 1.5). To Timothy, the Author writes that if he is delayed in visiting him soon, then these instructions will equip him to 'know how one ought to behave in the household of God, which is the church of the living God, the pillar and bulwark of the truth' (1 Tim. 3.14-15). Hence, Timothy and Titus are given instructions concerning men (1 Tim. 2.8; 5.1-2; Tit. 2.2, 6), women (1 Tim. 2.9-15; 3.11; 5.3-16; Tit. 2.3-5), the rich (1 Tim. 6.17-19) and slaves (1 Tim. 6.1-2; Tit. 2.9-10). As for church leadership, Timothy and Titus are given careful guidelines as to the qualities that should be demonstrated in such leaders and the criteria that should be used in discerning whether or not they should be appointed. This includes the positions of overseers (1 Tim. 3.1-7; Tit. 1.7-9, ἐπίσκοπος), deacons (1 Tim. 3.8-10, 12-13, διάκονος), and elders (1 Tim. 5.17-22 and Tit. 1.5-6, πρεσβύτερος).

As such, the thrust of the letters seems to be very inward-looking, focusing on how Timothy and Titus should operate and organize the believing community, strengthening their norms so as to distinguish the true believers from the false teachers. It is perhaps therefore not unsurprising that these letters lack the kind of comparisons between the believers and the unbelievers that we have become accustomed to when exploring 1 Thessalonians, Romans and 1 Corinthians. When we do find a list of verbs and adjectives describing the kind of people who love pleasure rather than God (2 Tim. 3.2-4), rather than using this description to compare outsider and insider and thus give the believers a positive evaluation, the Author uses this list to demonstrate that these are the people who appear to be godly on the surface, but who are inwardly corrupt; in other words, the false teachers (2 Tim. 3.5-9). On another occasion, when the Author points out that the law exists not for the righteous but for those who are 'lawless and rebellious', this does not function to draw a boundary between believers and unbelievers, but between those who live in a way that opposes 'the healthy teaching according to the good news of the glory of the blessed God', and those who live according to it (1 Tim. 1.10-11). The boundary here is not about who believes in Jesus Christ, but who adheres to the divinely ordained way of life.

There is one other place where we come closer to reading a description of the unbelieving outsider in comparison to the believer. For, after urging the believers to behave in a certain way towards rulers, authorities and all people (Tit. 3.1-2), the Author continues, 'for once we also were foolish, disobedient, led astray, slaves to lust and various pleasures, living our lives in malice and envy, hated and hating one another' (3.3). However, the believers have now been saved through the 'washing of regeneration and renewing of the Holy Spirit' (3.5). He is quick to point out that they passed over the boundary between believer and unbeliever not by their own works in righteousness, but simply because of the appearing of the kindness and love of 'our Saviour God' (3.4-5; see also 2.11; 1 Tim. 1.12-16). In the eyes of the Author, these rulers, authorities, and all people mentioned in verses 1-2 are still on the other side of the boundary, and so must share that same description given to the believers before they converted to Christ.

In terms of SIT, the only evaluative component that is used in describing believers and outsiders appears in 1 Tim. 5.8. Earlier in this passage, the Author has outlined the anticipation that children (τέκνα) and grandchildren (ἔκγονα) should care for and financially support the widows in their family because they should show 'piety' (εὐσεβεῖν) to their own household and 'exchange benefits' (Barclay 2020: 272; ἀμοιβὰς ἀποδιδόναι) with their parents (5.4). In other words, they are to 'repay' their parents for the earlier care and financial support they received. The Author grounds this in a divine expectation for the importance and role of families ('for this is pleasing in the sight of God', 5.4; cf. 1 Tim. 2.3) but it also appears to be grounded in a wider social expectation. For the Author declares that if a believer fails in their duty to do this, then they have denied the faith and are worse than an unbeliever (τὴν πίστιν ἤρνηται καὶ ἔστιν ἀπίστου χείρων, 5.8). There is an underlying presumption that even an unbeliever would carry out this duty of care and financial support, and as such, that this is a universal code of household reciprocity that is to be upheld by all in society. Since children receive benefits from their parents then it is right that they should return these benefits in caring for their parent(s) in their need. Barclay also draws attention to Philo, who conceives this expectation to be so basic and obvious that it is even found in animals ('Decalogue', 106–20; Barclay 2020: 272). And in his study on the Latin *pietas*, Saller argues that 'before death *pietas* obliged parents and children to provide maintenance for one another in case of need, a reciprocal duty sanctioned by law at least as early as the reign of Antonius Pius' (1994: 111). Believers therefore have a twofold motivation to care for the widows in their family: this moral standard does not just originate from a natural ordering of the world, but from a divine one (1 Tim. 5.4). They should have no excuse in not realizing the importance of this duty, and the neglect of such is tantamount to a denial of their faith. The implication is that they are displeasing not only in the sight of all others (including unbelievers) who care for their families but also in the sight of God.

In summary, within these letters there is a focus upon inward-looking matters, concerning the false teachers and the consequent need for good teaching to be delivered by Timothy and Titus, and concerning the need to order and build up the 'household'. Secondly, there appears to be a lack of concern to describe the unbelieving outsiders and so the same level of boundary-building using cognitive and evaluative components is not as apparent in these letters compared to our other Pauline letters. In fact, the boundaries being constructed here are primarily between the believing community and those (who presumably claim to be believers) who are here denounced as deceitful and sick 'false teachers'. Furthermore, there is little evidence in 1 Timothy and Titus of any external situations, crises or events that might put pressure on, or cause a threat to the existence of the ingroup. When an ingroup is faced with persecution, like the believers in Rome and Thessalonica, then it becomes vital that the ingroup has a strategy in place for engaging with the outgroup and their persecutors. In the absence of such a threat, however, the ingroup is not forced to acknowledge, face and relate with the outgroup in the same way. Therefore, it would be reasonable to assume that there would not be too much concern for the opinion of the outsider and how this might impact on the daily existence of the believer.

However, contrary to this, there is a collection of passages that reveal a significant concern for the opinion outsiders have of believers, and this shapes the vision for how the believers are to conduct themselves with each other and in wider society. The question therefore arises: if this concern is not for the purpose of self-protection, why does this motif appear, and why is it so emphasized? As we will see, the Author desires for believers to be mixing and engaging effectively with outsiders, where outsiders are looking in on the believers, and where believers deliberately reveal their lives shaped by their faith. In these letters, we discover a collection of verses and passages regarding insider–outsider interaction which fall into two categories. The first category still focuses on insiders and their conduct, but these passages also reveal a concern for the *reputation* of the ingroup and therefore the outsiders' opinion of the believers. The second category focuses more on outward action, on how believers should be viewing outsiders and relating to them (1 Tim. 2.1-7 and Tit. 3.1-8), and there is evidence to suggest that the underlying motivation is missional. Whilst this chapter will attend to the second category of verses more than the first (since these are more overtly concerned with intergroup relationships), it is nevertheless important to explore the verses concerned with reputation, since they also highlight the Author's sensitivity to what others think.

5.3 The Importance of Reputation

The concern for reputation is something that appears to underpin the letters, repeatedly being referred to, but nowhere explicitly explained or explored. It seems that the Author presumed he did not need to clarify the importance of reputation, simply often stating that the reason he is advocating certain behaviour or policies is to do with reputation. We will now turn to the Author's concern regarding the reputation being created by church leaders, slaves and women.

5.3.1 Overseers, slaves and women

The Author writes that 'it is necessary' for overseers to have 'a good testimony' from 'outsiders' (δεῖ δὲ καὶ μαρτυρίαν καλὴν ἔχειν ἀπὸ τῶν ἔξωθεν, 1 Tim. 3.7). It is not enough for other believers to approve of them; outsiders must also approve of and commend believers in order for them to be overseers (see Rom. 13.3). Clearly, the believer must demonstrate a type of life or set of behaviours that outsiders would admire, which points to the existence of an overlap area in group norms between these two groups, where outsiders and insiders agree on what exactly is commendable and good. Furthermore, the implication is that if an overseer maintains their good opinion in the eyes of the outsider, then whatever leads them to achieve this good testimony means that they will also not 'fall into reproach' and 'a trap of the devil' (ἵνα μὴ εἰς ὀνειδισμὸν ἐμπέσῃ καὶ παγίδα τοῦ διαβόλου, 1 Tim. 3.7).[6] The Author has full confidence in the fact that whatever is considered good and unreproachable is the same for outsider and insider. These similarities are important to notice for they help with the acquisition of a good opinion and reputation in the eyes of the outsider.

The Author is also concerned to make sure that the leaders and teachers of the churches only speak and act in a way that is faultless, giving nothing to the person who seeks to accuse and slander them (see Tit. 2.8).[7] The hope is that the church leaders can, and should, protect themselves from shame and slander, by firstly having a good relationship with outsiders (1 Tim. 3.7) and secondly through their blameless lifestyles and ministry (Tit. 2.7-8; see also 1 Tim. 3.2-7). The overseer or church leader should be well thought of among outsiders, otherwise their reputation becomes even more vulnerable to the powers (whether earthly or spiritual) that seek their demise. It is likely that the Author is concerned that if the overseer is not respected among outsiders, and if he becomes a target for slander and reproach, then this will tar the whole believing community, and in terms of stereotyping, give the whole community a negative identity. As MacDonald notes, 'A bishop is apparently viewed by the author as being in a position to improve or damage the church's image in the eyes of the general public, based on his personal standing' (1988: 167).

These letters, however, are not simply concerned with how church leaders are viewed by outsiders but also with how slaves and women are perceived. In 1 Tim. 6.1 slaves are expected to give honour to their masters to protect the 'name of God and the teaching' from being 'slandered' or 'blasphemed' (ἵνα μὴ τὸ ὄνομα τοῦ θεοῦ καὶ ἡ διδασκαλία βλασφημῆται, 6.1b). The way that unbelieving masters experience and perceive their slaves has an impact on how they form an opinion of God and of the believing community.[8] In Tit. 2.9-10 the Author instructs Titus to ensure that in their relationships with their masters, slaves are 'to be submissive in everything' (ὑποτάσσεσθαι ἐν πᾶσιν; see also Tit. 3.1) and 'to be well-pleasing' (εὐαρέστους εἶναι). The following three instructions may be apologetic in nature to show that the believing slave contradicts any vices that they are popularly stereotyped as having: they should not talk back or pilfer but should 'show complete and good fidelity' (ἀλλὰ πᾶσιν πίστιν ἐνδεικνυμένους ἀγαθήν).[9] As such, instead of pilfering things of little value from their masters, slaves are to realize that they themselves become the valuable things which adorn or make beautiful (κοσμέω) 'the teaching of God our Saviour' (Tit. 2.10). Taken together, these instructions in 1 Timothy and Titus show the importance of a slave's conduct in both *defending* the gospel and the faith community and in revealing its *attractiveness*. Slaves were an important part of the Greco-Roman household, but, as Parker highlights, within this household 'slaves and wives stand out as the discordant and therefore dangerous elements' (1998: 158–9).

Interestingly for this work, Parker attributes this 'dangerous element' to the fact that both slaves and wives were 'outsiders' brought into a home, and they were therefore 'simultaneously the Same and the Other' (1998: 159) making them both to be 'intimate strangers' (1998: 175). Slaves were outsiders because they were thought of as being 'outside the fully human citizen community' (Wiedemann 1987: 25), and as such their disloyalty was greatly feared by some (Parker 1998: 160). However, Wiedemann even suggests that masters would beat their slaves to show them that 'they do not belong to that community' (1987: 25) and to perpetuate the idea that they are continually an 'outsider'. If this was the case, then it is conceivable to imagine the euphoria believing slaves might have experienced upon realizing that they were now considered an 'insider' within this new faith community, but also a rise in resentment for having previously been denied this social identity of 'insider' in their household. As such, the Author reminds them to honour their masters (1 Tim. 6.1) and be submissive to them (Tit. 2.9-10). Indeed, if as Patterson argues, a slave 'had no social existence outside of his master' (1982: 38), then for a master to realize that through this new faith community the slave *did* now have social existence and a new social identity, then this could be perceived as a threat to their own status and power, and so the Author may know that the master needs the reassurance that the slave's new faith would not have a negative impact on his role in the household, but only a positive one.

Although instructions to slaves do not form a major part of the PEs, the fact that the Author each time links these instructions with how the gospel may be viewed is not insignificant. Firstly, it gives these instructions a theological basis, but secondly, it signals the awareness of the vulnerable yet important position of slaves in the household and in the state, and therefore the importance of their testimony regarding the gospel. For, the master–slave relationship formed one of the fundamental partnerships of the Greco-Roman household (the other two being husband–wife; father–children), and maintaining this relationship was vital 'in regard to the purpose of the constitution and the happiness of the state' (Balch 1981: 61).[10] This is because the household and the state were seen as models of each other, albeit on different scales, so that the 'household is a microcosm of the state'; this means that 'subversion in one means inevitably subversion in the other' and thus harmony in the household creates harmony in the state (Osiek 1992: 82).[11] Furthermore, maintenance of the household not only preserved the order of authority and power which favoured free men (and therefore preserved the submission and dependence of women and slaves), but also since slaves accounted for around one-quarter of the population of the Roman Empire, 'their role was significant to socioeconomic stability' (Jobes 2005: 186).

Similarly, there are many verses in these letters that are dedicated to outlining how women should behave, precisely because how believing women are viewed will have a direct bearing on how the rest of the community is viewed. As such, young widows are to 'marry, bear children and manage the household' (γαμεῖν, τεκνογονεῖν, οἰκοδεσποτεῖν) so that they give to 'the adversary' (τῷ ἀντικειμένῳ) no reason for reproach (λοιδορίας, 1 Tim. 5.14; also 5.7).[12] Titus is to instruct both the older and younger women to behave in ways that would prevent the 'word of God' from being blasphemed (ἵνα μὴ ὁ λόγος τοῦ θεοῦ βλασφημῆται, Tit. 2.5). Older women are to make sure that their behaviour is holy, that they do not engage in slander, nor in excessive drinking of wine, and that they should be 'teachers of good' (καλοδιδασκάλους, Tit. 2.3), precisely so that they can encourage the young women to, among other virtues, love and be subject to their husbands, and to love their children (2.4). The Author hopes that by women committing themselves to this lifestyle, they will be able to prevent ὁ λόγος τοῦ θεοῦ from being slandered (2.5).

Much more could be said regarding the Author's instructions to women throughout the rest of the letters (e.g. 1 Tim. 2.9-15), but what is important to note is how this teaching overlaps with the ideological representation of women found in contemporary society. The behaviour the Author endorses for believing women is in line with the picture of respectable women in wider society, found in a range of other literature from around the time, including philosophical treatises, poetry and imperial legislation.[13] In fact, the depiction of the ideal and pious woman was taught, reinforced and promulgated via many different 'intersecting cultural domains' (Hoklotubbe 2017: 84), including monumental inscriptions and gravestones. There are, for example, many epitaphs that give praise to women who were faithful wives and dutiful mothers.[14] Epitaphs written around the time of the Pastoral Epistles (PEs) show that the aim of a woman's life was to please her husband and, as one epitaph comments, this is 'enough praise for a woman after death'.[15] Another epitaph comments that the deceased woman, Claudia, 'loved her husband in her heart' (Lefkowitz and Fant 2005: 16). Besides pleasing and loving one's husband, women were praised for bearing and raising children, and one epitaph notes that 'earth took this young mother and keeps her, though the children need her milk'.[16] Turia is also praised for her attendance to household duties as well as her affection for the family, including even the tombs of her parents.[17] This picture of the praiseworthy woman is reflected throughout the PEs (1 Tim. 2.15; 5.4, 9-10, 14, 16; Tit. 2.4-5).

Furthermore, in addition to such responsibilities, women were also expected to busy themselves with doing 'good deeds'. In a eulogy given by a son for his mother Murdia, we read: 'praise for all good women is simple and similar ... Sufficient is the fact that they have all done the same good deeds that deserve fine reputation'.[18] Likewise, the Author reports that women should decorate themselves with good deeds (1 Tim. 2.10). It is therefore clear that, whereas the instructions to women are often accompanied and explained by the desire to prevent the gospel from being slandered, the epitaphs would suggest that these instructions are also to show believing women as praiseworthy. In the same way that slaves are both to defend the gospel *and* to reveal its attractiveness to outsiders, we find that this expectation is also extended to the women in the believing community.

5.3.2 The underlying concern

From this brief overview, it is clear that there is an anxiety for 'the congregation to stand well with the outside world and to escape the scandal which slanderous talk will produce' (Kelly 1963: 119). The way in which believers were able to 'stand well' was procured by the believers behaving in ways that would have been considered worthy and respectable in the eyes of the outsiders. In Verner's study of the 'household of God', in exploring the different roles and expectations attached to various members of the household, he concludes that 'the prevailing social values of the church of the Pastorals in this area directly and uncritically reflect the dominant social values of the larger society' (1983: 145). And the 'explicit motivation' for all of these instructions to the different members of the believing community 'is the concern for the opinion of outsiders' (Bassler 1984: 32; also Verner 1983: 182).[19] Any concern or motivation the Author might have had for challenging hierarchical structures, or radically transforming society to promote equality rather than inequality, was simply not a priority here. Rather, in directing the believers to behave in socially respectable ways and by repeatedly justifying such instructions by appealing to how the outsiders might perceive them, the Author clearly shows a different priority of demonstrating the 'legitimacy of the faith' to outsiders (Hoklotubbe 2017: 100). It is also possible that the believers likewise share this concern over how others may perceive and experience them, since, as Trebilco notices, although the Author repeatedly mentions not giving any offence to others, he 'never argues at length that this should be a key motivation for action, but simply assumes that it is' (2004: 370).

Nevertheless, whilst the Author is motivated by a concern for outsider opinion, it is not always clear what is in turn motivating *this* concern. It is plausible that the

Author desires for the believers to have the type of reputation in society that would create good relationships with outsiders to enable them to live well and at peace in society, free from conflict and the threat of persecution. Dibelius and Conzelmann (1972) for example propose that the Author has come to a realization that the believers may need to wait longer for the return of Christ, and so they need a clear indication of how they are to live for a longer time in their community. As such, the believers are encouraged to behave in ways that accommodate the outside world, and that would limit any friction between believer and outsider. For Dibelius and Conzelmann, this results in a type of 'bourgeois Christianity' (1972: 37–40). Thus, the need to create stability for the believing community by protecting them from conflict motivated the desire for a good opinion in the eyes of outsiders. Whilst others have robustly criticized the 'delayed Parousia' proposal (e.g. Trebilco 2004: 383; Towner 1989: 61–74; Ho 2000: 6–10), Dibelius and Conzelmann do make a valid contribution to this discussion by pointing to the reasonable desire for peace and preservation of the church. It appears that the believers are facing a significant amount of conflict from false teachers, and it is not impossible that the false teachers will be creating friction with outsiders. Furthermore, the Author does refer to the hope that believers will be able to 'lead a quiet and peaceable life' (1 Tim. 2.2).

However, it is also plausible that another underlying motivation for good reputation is to do with mission, and certainly, motivations for preservation and for mission are not mutually exclusive. A mission motivation is the conclusion of Towner's study on the passages which call for a good reputation. Writing about the motivation behind the instructions to slaves in 1 Tim. 6.1-2, although he admits that there is no specific reference here to 'winning' the unbelieving master, Towner argues that in the letters as a whole, there is 'far more evidence of a mission motive than of an apologetic, self-preservationist motive as an end in itself' (1989: 178). Retaining certain social expectations and preserving or creating a good reputation meant that the gospel message 'might be advanced' (1989: 172). Again, in looking at the instructions to the widows in 1 Tim. 5.3-16, Towner concludes that although the 'salvation' of the outsider is not mentioned, there is nevertheless an underlying concern for 'the widow's testimony' and reputation which should 'extend beyond the believing community' (e.g. vv. 7b, 10, 14) and a 'sensitivity to the outsider's eye' (e.g. v. 8b). He draws attention to the fact that it 'is because the wanton behaviour of v. 11 and the foolish behaviour of v. 13 occur where the church has interface with the world that the outside critic is a concern. Correct behaviour in the case of the Christian must be able to withstand the scrutiny of this examiner' (1989: 189). This testimony of the widows to the outside critic is connected to their hope for salvation, for he argues that proclamation of the gospel, which includes witnessing to the gospel, leads to salvation (1989: 189), and once again, that the Author's 'consistent theology' is that the believers have an important role to play in 'mediating' salvation to the rest of the world (1989: 189).

Although Davies criticizes Towner's emphasis on a mission motivation in the Pastorals, and argues rather that 'the teaching is defensive rather than actively missionary' (1996: 34), we have seen in this section that, whereas some of the teaching is defensive, it is also about actively presenting the gospel as attractive. At this point, it would be wise to turn now to our second category of passages, which focus more on the interrelationship between insider and outsider, but which are also connected to the Author's proclamation of God as the Saviour of all (1 Tim. 2.1-7 and Tit. 3.1-8). These passages take us beyond the concern for reputation and any need to protect the faith community from slander, to a concern for positive and fruitful relationships between outsider and insider. After looking at these passages, we will be in a better position to assess whether there is indeed a significant concern for mission in the letters, and how, if at all, this is connected to the concern for reputation.

5.4 Building on Reputation: The Importance of Relationship

5.4.1 Introduction: 1 Timothy 2.1-7

In just a few verses at the beginning of 1 Timothy 2, we traverse very quickly from an instruction to pray for all people, including kings and those in authority (vv. 1-2), to a credal statement of the will and design of God for all to be saved (vv. 3-6). It becomes clear that the command to pray for others is to be practised with thoughtfulness and seriousness, because it requires a certain attitude of believers towards unbelievers, and because God has a concern for all to be saved. This is evidenced in Christ's giving of himself as a 'ransom for all' (v. 6), who is the one mediator between God and all of humanity (v. 5), and who is proclaimed by the Author (v. 7). Within these few verses there is frequent reference to 'all' people: prayers should be offered on behalf of πάντων ἀνθρώπων (v. 1), including πάντων τῶν ἐν ὑπεροχῇ ὄντων (v. 2), for God wants the salvation of πάντας ἀνθρώπους (v. 4), and Christ died as a ransom ὑπὲρ πάντων (v. 6). The Author is keen to emphasize that his frame of reference is not just the believing community, but *all* people, regardless of whether they are an insider or an outsider. As such, the repetition of πᾶς emphasizes the universal scope of this passage as well as the universality of the gospel and is certainly striking and significant when it is associated, as it is here, with the prayers of the believers for their unbelieving neighbours (see also Marshall 1999: 416).

5.4.1a Praying for all (1 Timothy 2.1-2a)

The Author is clear in his expectation that Timothy and the whole believing community should be engaged in prayer, not simply for themselves, but for others.[20] In fact, he urges (παρακαλέω) the entire community to 'first of all' (πρῶτον πάντων) turn to prayer for all (v. 1).[21] Schlatter writes that above all the other expectations or functions of the believing community (e.g. teaching, baptizing, caring for others) stands prayer, for believers own a 'priestly profession' ('Allein über all dem steht das Gebet, weil die Gemeinde den priesterlichen Beruf besitzt', 1958: 70). And here the Author is explicit in that the believing community should pray for 'all people' (πάντων ἀνθρώπων), which includes kings and all those in positions of authority (1 Tim. 2.1-2; see also Rom. 13.1-7). The fact that the Author uses the same phrase 'all people' in verse 4 where he is describing the desire of God to save 'all people' (πάντας ἀνθρώπους, also 4.10) indicates that his use of this phrase in v. 1 is not simply restricted to believers.

As Johnson notes, this is 'the first of several remarkable universalizing statements in 2.1–7' (2001: 189).[22]

It is also striking that the Author uses four different terms to refer to the prayers of the believers: δεήσεις (supplications, e.g. Rom. 10.1; 2 Cor. 1.11; 9.14; Phil. 1.4, 19; 4.6), προσευχάς (prayers, e.g. Rom. 12.12; 15.30; 1 Cor. 7.5; 1 Thess. 1.2; Phil. 4.6; Phlm. 4; Col. 4.12), ἐντεύξεις (intercessions, e.g. 1 Tim. 4.5; see also Rom. 8.26, 34) and εὐχαριστίας (thanksgivings, e.g. 1 Cor. 14.16; 2 Cor. 4.15; 9.11-12; Phil. 4.6; 1 Thess. 3.9). This not only emphasizes the fact that praying for all people deserves and necessitates commitment, but also that prayers for others should not be a quick automatic offering, but thoughtful and thorough. As Bassler comments, 'All forms of prayer made in, and by, the community are to be used to pray for those outside the community of faith' (1996: 50). Whereas it might be true that the Author did not intend for this list of different modes of prayer to form a 'liturgical menu' in a rigid way (Johnson 2001: 189), it does, however, illustrate that there is no type of prayer that cannot be used for 'all people' (Roloff 1988: 113) and it prevents the believers from simply praying a generic prayer for others that requires little thought or understanding of the other person. Contrary to Dibelius and Conzelmann, who suggest that the different terms 'do not invite a systematic differentiation' (1972: 36; also Towner 1989: 201), I would argue that they are so listed precisely to distinguish between the different forms of prayer to ensure that the believers are in fact ready and willing to *intercede* on behalf of the outsiders, to give *thanks* for them, and to *petition* God to act on behalf of these people. Praying in these different ways is important because it gives the believers no excuse to ignore the attitude and relationships that are needed to do so. For, if they are to intercede, petition, pray and give thanks, then this presupposes or indeed necessitates that they should know their neighbours well enough to know how to intercede for them, and why they should offer thanks for them. More than the believers simply being conscious of the outsiders, the Author clearly envisages a scenario whereby they should interact with, converse with, and observe enough of those around them to be able to understand where members of the outgroup might need God's help and how they might appreciate divine assistance or sustenance.

Furthermore, to pray in such a way requires the believers to look upon their unbelieving neighbours with kindness, generosity and thankfulness. In terms of SIT, the Author appeals to the 'emotional' component in describing the attitude the insiders should have regarding the outsiders. For, petitioning and interceding requires the one praying to desire the flourishing and safety of those for whom they are praying. As Knight writes, 'Prayers must manifest concern for others and perhaps particularly for their plight or difficulty' (1992: 115; also Schlatter 1958: 72). Additionally, that the believers should also offer thanks for these outsiders, including kings and those in authority, suggests that they should have an attitude of gratefulness for them. The theme of giving thanks in prayer for others is usually found in the opening sentences of Paul's letters (Rom. 1.8; 1 Cor. 1.4; Phil. 1.3-4; 1 Thess. 1.2; 2.13; Phlm. 4; with the exception of 2 Corinthians and Galatians) and the disputed epistles (Eph. 1.16; Col. 1.3; 2 Thess. 1.3; 2.13). In these references, the believing congregation is the object of this thanksgiving. However, it is not used in this way in 1 Timothy and Titus, but instead it is used to thank God for *outsiders*. Giving thanks for others suggests a recognition that God has been working outside the faith community, and a recognition that, even though a person might belong to an outgroup, they are nevertheless still within the sphere of God's will and activity. The theological basis for this is found later in 1 Tim. 4.4-5, where the Author writes that all of God's creation is good and therefore nothing should be cast aside but received with thanks; this reveals the root for the command in chapter 2 to pray giving thanks for all people, regardless of their religious or social identity. By asking the believers to thank God for their unbelieving neighbours, the Author is asking them to recognize that such unbelievers are also the work of God, and they have the capacity to contribute to the well-being of society. Thus, whereas Knight attributes this request to offer prayers of thanksgiving to an unspoken acknowledgement regarding politeness in prayer (1992: 115), it is more probable that this request is connected with the Author's desire for the believers to adopt or maintain a particular attitude and response towards the outsiders: namely, that the believers look upon their unbelieving neighbours with a generous nature – seeking to find qualities in their neighbours that lead them to give thanks to God.

This short instruction to pray is therefore more complex than Towner's proposal that the believers are simply called to pray for the salvation of all people (1989: 202). To do this does not demand the level of relationship that the Author is advocating in the believers interceding, petitioning and giving thanks for the outsiders. One can pray for the salvation of another person without even knowing them, and the motivation could also be self-serving, in the believer desiring to be part of a larger, more popular and therefore more influential group. The Author is indicating that an awareness of those outside the faith community is important, and not just an awareness, but also a recognition that they themselves are important. The mere presence of those outside the believing community must influence the believers in their behaviour and way of life – and here, the Author specifies that the presence of outsiders should shape the prayer life of the believer.

Additionally, the type of relationship that underpins these types of prayers would suggest at the very least that the outsiders *know* about the believers praying for them, which would also reveal the positive and benevolent attitude the believers have towards them. Although it is not an assumption explicitly made by the text itself in 1 Timothy 2, it is a safe one to make that this would have the potential to positively influence how the outsiders themselves view the insiders. And, whilst it is apparent that the practice of praying for those outside the faith community was often rooted in the hope that this would provide such a community with peace and protection, there is evidence to suggest that, for the Author, the trajectory of hope went beyond peace and protection, to the hope of approval and salvation.[23] For, although the Author continues to explain that such prayers might enable the believers to 'lead a tranquil and quiet life in all piety and respectability (ἵνα ἤρεμον καὶ ἡσύχιον βίον διάγωμεν ἐν πάσῃ εὐσεβείᾳ καὶ σεμνότητι, v. 2b; see 1 Thess. 4.11), which on the surface does appear to present a hope for peace and protection, his specific choice of words of εὐσέβεια and σεμνότης suggests less of a picture of living peaceably simply by not aggravating others, and more of a scenario where believers can interact with their neighbours with confidence that they will attract approval and their positive opinion. It is to this that we shall now turn.

5.4.1b In all piety and respectability

When the Author signals that these prayers of the believers may enable them to live in 'all piety and respectability' (ἐν πάσῃ εὐσεβείᾳ καὶ σεμνότητι, v. 2b), he is linking these prayers with a major theme in the letters. Firstly, the word εὐσέβεια and its cognates are used highly frequently in the Pastorals, revealing its importance to the Author.[24] It is often translated as 'piety' (largely referring simply to an inner *attitude* regarding God), but this translation conveys a narrower meaning of the word than how it is used in the Pastorals and in the Greco-Roman world, where it carries a sense of devotion leading to associated *action*. For the Author, a life of piety is firstly in response to, and flows from, knowledge of and belief in the God who redeems (Tit. 2.11-12). There is a strong correlation between sound teaching and piety (1 Tim. 6.3; Tit. 1.1), so that true piety is the visible, outward expression of a true faith.[25] But piety comes from a true faith *and* leads to selfless action or service. Thus, women who profess 'godly reverence' (θεοσέβεια, 1 Tim. 2.10) are not to turn to expensive or elaborate clothes, hairstyles or jewellery but to good works as their apparel. Even children and grandchildren of widows are to demonstrate their devotion by supporting their parents or grandparents (μανθανέτωσαν πρῶτον τὸν ἴδιον οἶκον εὐσεβεῖν καὶ ἀμοιβὰς ἀποδιδόναι τοῖς προγόνοις, 1 Tim. 5.4). Piety is an attitude of reverence and loyalty that sparks a life dedicated to acts of goodwill and a commitment to religious, familial or societal obligations. Thus, Roloff observes that in the Pauline corpus εὐσέβεια is about 'life in all its relationships that has been visibly shaped by the grace of God' (1988: 118).

However, in a similar fashion, it is widely noted that the εὐσέβεια word group was used in Greco-Roman society to refer to an attitude of reverence towards various gods and to the emperor, as well as to the orders or laws that were attributed to these gods or imperial dominion.[26] Piety was 'a combination of internal reverence or piety combined with right behaviour'; it was both 'belief and behaviour' (Witherington 2006b: 99, 100). Furthermore, piety was a 'highly regarded virtue and a duty' in Greco-Roman society (Marshall 1999: 137) for it was 'an essential element for social prosperity and peace within both the microcosm of the household and the macrocosm of the empire' (Hoklotubbe 2017: 102). In this way, piety 'sustained reciprocal relationships between kin, neighbours, allies' because it was the way in which one fulfilled 'religious, civic and imperial obligations' and also illustrated 'loyalty toward country, divinity, and ruler' (Hoklotubbe 2017: 6). Moreover, Saller, when exploring how the Latin *pietas* was used in various types of literature, argues that this virtue is not simply about duty to others but that 'its essence lay in devotion' (1994: 106). He illustrates how it was a key virtue in family relations and was used to describe actions that were 'selfless' flowing from a 'loving attachment' (1994: 108), but also that it had a reciprocal nature. The notion of 'piety' was brought about by ties of love and affection, and therefore contributed to the well-being of the family.

Given all of this, and remembering the Author's concern for reputation and the presence of the outsider, it is feasible to suggest that the frequency with which the Author uses εὐσέβεια and its cognates reveals a desire for the outsiders to see that piety is also a highly held virtue among believers.[27] The process of becoming a believer does not involve abandoning piety and some of its associated outward acts of goodwill or obligation (whether by duty or devotion), and as such, the believer is still able to maintain the reciprocal beneficial relationships with all in society. The affirmation of some of these societal norms for behaviour is not an act of submission to outside pressure, but a reminder by the Author that the believers *already* share some of these norms and virtues. However, perhaps because the false teachers appear to be contradicting some of these norms (e.g. marriage, 1 Tim. 4.3) the Author calls for the believing community to show their adherence to piety and the type of behaviour that flows from this virtue. As Hoklotubbe writes, 'One of the strategic aims of the Pastoral Epistles' use of language like εὐσέβεια is for outsiders who encounter Christians using such terminology to recognize something familiar and respectable about the Christian way of life and so have their prejudices disrupted' (2017: 216).

Therefore, the Author's frequent use of the εὐσέβεια word group highlights a 'contact point with pagan society' (Marshall 1999: 144), and thus provides the point of 'similarity or community of culture' that Barth argued was necessary for different social groups to interact (1969: 15). This area of similarity has the potential to generate the type of positive acquaintanceship between insiders and outsiders that can result in a positive opinion. However, if Hoklotubbe is correct in that 'Claims to piety in the ancient world carried a significant amount of cultural prestige' (2017: 7), then by revealing their piety the believers are also revealing the kind of attractiveness that might persuade the outsider not only to praise them but also to join them. This point of similarity is therefore not only a contact point but an *attraction* point. It demonstrates to outsiders the attractiveness of being an insider.

However, this *attraction point* of piety reveals a deeper truth to outsiders. The Author's encouragement for the believers to behave with piety is not simply demonstrating a 'Christianisation' of secular morality (Dibelius and Conzelmann 1972: 39–41), for as we have seen, piety in the PEs is a way of life that is grounded in, and an expression of, a knowledge of the truth of God and Jesus Christ: 'it is rooted in the Christ event' (Foerster 1959: 182). The Author illustrates that some of the cultural and ideological conventions and assumptions underpinning prescribed behaviour for certain members of society, and which encapsulate the virtue of piety, can be traced back to God (e.g. 1 Tim. 2.9-15; 5.4, 8; see also 4.4). Thus, referring to 1 Tim. 2.10, Hoklotubbe notes that 'By describing these feminine qualities as befitting piety toward God (θεοσέβεια), social conventions are given divine legitimation within Christian theology' (2017: 87). The Author's use of this word group therefore functions to present 'contemporary culture with the challenge that this highly prized Hellenistic cardinal virtue is truly attainable only in Christ' (Towner 2006: 174).

Thus, returning to our passage in 1 Timothy 2, it is important to note that when the Author refers to εὐσέβεια in verse 2, it is within the wider context of the believers' relationship with those in authority. It is a reminder that although living a life of piety and devotion is ultimately connected to their relationship with God, it is not *unconnected* to how one is found in relationship with others, and with those in imperial power. It is a claim that believers can live in true devotion to God whilst also showing deference to those earthly figures of authority. And, just as the Author details what 'devotion' should look like in their households (1 Tim. 5.4), it is possible that in 1 Tim.

2.2 he has already described what 'devotion' should look like among outsiders. For, although in v. 2 the Author uses ἵνα with the subjunctive of διάγω to form a purpose clause, whereby it is suggested that the prayers of the believers for others will *enable* them to live 'in all piety and respect' (1 Tim. 2.2), it is striking that the act of prayer for others is in itself an act of piety.[28] It is not simply that the believers are to pray 'in order that' they might be able to live in 'all piety', but rather the believers are to pray as an expression of their *existing* lives of piety, whilst hoping for more opportunities to live peacefully where they can continue to live according to this virtue. The type of positive intergroup relationships needed for the prayers of the believers has the potential to achieve peace, which in turn creates the right environment for believers to focus on piety rather than be distracted with negotiating conflict. However, the act of praying for others is also an *expression* of living according to the virtue of εὐσέβεια.

Secondly, the Author also hopes that the believers should live in all 'respectability' or 'dignity', using the word σεμνότης. This word (and its cognates) is also used frequently throughout the Pastorals to remind believers (and their families) to be aware of how they are observed and perceived in public (Towner 2006: 175). For example, it must be seen that the children of an overseer are 'respectful in every way' (1 Tim. 3.4), and deacons and women must also be known to be respectable (3.8, 11). Titus is instructed to make sure that the older men are respectable (Tit. 2.2), and Titus himself is to show in his teaching respectability, so that 'the opposing one may be shamed having nothing bad to say about us' (Tit. 2.7-8). In other words, respectability should be a group norm for every member of the believing community (see Phil. 4.8). It should be something that guides their actions regardless of who they are or what role they play in the community, but it should also have the effect of protecting the group from accusations and from gaining a negative reputation, as we saw earlier in this chapter.

In living in a way that was 'respectable' (1 Tim. 2.2), the believer had to take thought for what was deemed respectable in the eyes of the other. As Towner illustrates through a brief survey of how the σεμνότης word group is used in secular Greek, Hellenistic Jewish writers and the OT, the use of this term functions to describe either 'the measurable/observable virtue (that produces "dignity," etc.)' or to consider 'the end result of behaviour to be "deserving respect"' (2006: 175). The use of the adjective σεμνός in the Pastorals shows the importance for all believers to witness through the whole of their lives that which wider society would find dignified and respectable, and hence afford believers a measure of protection from those who would wish to speak ill of them (see Tit. 2.8). As Towner highlights, 'The focus of the term on outward, observable conduct is especially clear from the purpose statement given in Tit. 2.8, and consistently implicit elsewhere' (2006: 175).

Thus, whereas the outward behaviour denoted by the word εὐσέβεια has its genesis in a right belief in God, the outward behaviour denoted by σεμνός has its genesis in how a member relates with other members in the society, a relationship that is not restricted by any boundaries between different social or religious groups. The former is concerned ultimately with the believer's relationship with God (which impacts upon their observable lifestyle), and the latter is concerned with the believer's relationship with others, with correct conduct or 'dignified behaviour toward one another' (Witherington 2006b: 213). Hoklotubbe points out that the use of σεμνός together with εὐσέβεια shows the Author is concerned with using 'recognizable terminology' which 'functioned to build "linguistic bridges" between the *ekklesia* and the broader society' (2017: 73-4).[29] Clearly, these 'linguistic bridges' lead the way for more positive intergroup relations (hopefully by also countering the division, damaged relationships and bad reputation that the false teachers are creating), which would benefit not only the ingroup but also the outgroup. For, in some way the prayers of the believers make it possible for the believers to enjoy tranquillity and peace, which would offer them the 'opportune conditions' (Hoklotubbe 2017: 77) to demonstrate their pious and respectable lifestyles, and in turn, win the approval of others and reveal the attractiveness of the gospel. In the following verses, the Author links this outsider-approval with the approval of God, who is Saviour of all.

5.4.1c *The Saviour God of all*

In 1 Tim. 2.3-4 the Author declares: τοῦτο καλὸν καὶ ἀπόδεκτον ἐνώπιον τοῦ σωτῆρος ἡμῶν θεοῦ, ὃς πάντας ἀνθρώπους θέλει σωθῆναι καὶ εἰς ἐπίγνωσιν ἀληθείας ἐλθεῖν. In so doing, the Author is giving divine weight and authority to his command for believers to pray for all people, including outsiders. What is 'good and acceptable in the sight of God our Saviour' is for the believers to engage in a dedicated lifestyle of prayer for all.[30] It is a reminder that the worship of God's people must 'radiate into all areas of everyday life' because salvation is at the heart of the faith community (Roloff 1988: 199); it is not a group concerned only for its own well-being, for God's concern is for 'all people' (v. 4), and as such, he is delighted when believers pray for 'all people' (v. 1). However, given our argument above, that both praying for others (v. 1, which is in itself an act of piety) and a life of piety and respectability (v. 2) are intended to have a positive impact on all people, then it is possible that the Author is referring to verses 1 *and* 2 when he declares that 'this is good and acceptable in the sight of God our Saviour' (v. 3). The piety and respectability of the believers are held intrinsically together with the attitude of prayer and the quality of relationship they require.

The reason given for this is that God is not only *their* Saviour (τοῦ σωτῆρος ἡμῶν θεοῦ, v. 3), but the Saviour of *all*, for God 'wants all to be saved' (ὃς πάντας ἀνθρώπους θέλει σωθῆναι, v. 4a). It is important to note the word order here, with 'all people' coming first in the Greek, for emphasis. Salvation is a significant theme in these letters, introduced in the first few verses in both 1 Timothy and Titus where God is described as our 'Saviour' (1 Tim. 1.1; Tit. 1.3). God as 'our Saviour' is an important and frequent title for God or Jesus (1 Tim. 1.1; 2.3; 4.10; 2 Tim. 1.10; Tit. 1.3, 4; 2.10, 13; 3.4, 6), and this is combined with a belief that salvation is offered by God to all, to save sinners across the world, irrespective of ethnicity, economic status, or geography (1 Tim. 1.15; 4.10, 16; Tit. 2.11). There is an emphasis in these letters that God's salvation expands not only into the non-Jewish world, but that the number of those belonging to the believing community has not been exhausted. Clearly, this declaration in 1 Tim. 2.4 is not simply a statement that all people will be saved regardless of whether they are a believer or not, for the Author adds that God also wants all to 'come to a knowledge of the truth' (1 Tim. 2.4). Salvation and truth are held together and remind the reader of the importance of belief or faith in being able to accept the salvation that God offers to all people (1 Tim. 1.16; 3.16; 4.10; 2 Tim. 1.5).[31] As Marshall writes, 'The emphasis is thus on universal accessibility to God's salvation on the basis of a faith open to all and a gospel preached to all' (1999: 427).

However, the emphasis is also on the definition and character of God as Saviour, as the God who alone can save people. This is the narrative throughout the whole of the OT and NT which tells of how God repeatedly saves his people (whether as a group or as individuals, physically or spiritually, in the past, present or future realm; e.g. Exod. 14.13-31; 1 Kgs 19.3-9; Dan. 6.19-22; Zeph. 3.17; Ezek. 36.29; Mt. 1.21; Gal. 1.4; Col. 1.13), and God's saving power became the song of praise for many, including 'outsiders' (Exod. 15.2; Ps. 116.8; Isa. 12.2; Dan. 6.26-27; Lk. 1.46-55). Unsurprisingly, God is given the name 'God our/my Saviour' which is often used in the Psalms (e.g. Pss. 25.5; 27.9; 68.19; 79.9; see also 1 Chron. 16.35; Mic. 7.7; Hab. 3.18) and it is a name God gives to himself (e.g. Isa. 43.3, 11; Hos. 13.4). However, although the title for God as Saviour is found frequently in the PEs, in the rest of the NT it is only found in Lk. 1.47 and Jude 25 (Davies 1996: 42), and only for Jesus in Phil. 3.20 and Eph. 5.23.

Conversely, this description of a 'saviour god' was widely used in the contemporary Hellenistic world for other deities as well as for emperors, who were often thought of as deified rulers.[32] Trebilco argues that the 'more pronounced usage of σωτήρ in the Pastorals compared with other books of the NT' is a sign of 'acculturation of both the author and the readers', whereby the language of another group becomes more widely or frequently used in and by the ingroup (2004: 361). However, given the fact that this is also used in a passage where 'kings and all those in authority' are part of the focus, it could be that the Author uses the language of 'God our Saviour' to remind readers that whilst they are to be respectful and mindful of these other rulers, God nevertheless is the only Saviour of all. It is doubtful that the Author was intending to be deliberately polemical here (considering his present endeavours to encourage the believers to build peaceful and fruitful relationships with outsiders), but it would be surprising if his use of this vocabulary was unintentional. It creates an acknowledgement of the difficult path his readers need to negotiate when living amongst earthly rulers who may make claims of divinity, whilst worshipping the Saviour God of all heaven and earth. For this reason, Hoklotubbe also uses the term 'negotiate' to describe the efforts of this passage, which can account for 'the author's explicit compliance with imperial authority and, on the other hand, his application of titles associated with the emperor to both God and Jesus, however slight a polemic it might represent' (2017: 77). For Hoklotubbe, the term 'negotiation' describes more appropriately how the Author is attempting to hold together these two postures of loyalty and deference to the imperial cult and of 'offering its own counternarrative about the true location of piety and global mission of "God our Saviour" and Jesus the one mediator' (2017: 77).

As such, this passage is not about 'accommodation or resistance' (Hoklotubbe 2017: 77), but about the Author pressing this community into deeper and holier lifestyles amongst and with the outsiders, acknowledging their presence (and being thankful for it), but also making sure that their perspective is framed (or reframed) by God's sovereignty and mercy over all people. It is God's *character* and *will* that frames how they are to engage with outsiders, and the Author is so convinced of this that right at the beginning of this letter he reminds the believing community that 'our Saviour God'

(1 Tim. 2.3) is also 'their' Saviour God (v. 4), who 'wants' all to be saved. The use of θέλω (v. 4) most probably indicates more than a simple desire of God for all people to be saved, and rather a 'determination' or a 'will' for all to be saved (Witherington 2006b: 214; Marshall 1999: 427; Towner 2006: 177). God's 'salvific intentions fully include the non-Jewish world' (Towner 2006: 178), and the Author reminds the believers that God is, after all, the only God and there is only 'one mediator of God and of people' (εἷς γὰρ θεός, εἷς καὶ μεσίτης θεοῦ καὶ ἀνθρώπων, ἄνθρωπος Χριστὸς Ἰησοῦς, v. 5). In which case, the only hope outsiders have of accessing salvation and truth is through knowing and encountering this God who is the only God and therefore the Saviour of all. The declaration of God as the only God is seen elsewhere in these letters and is often connected also with the cosmic authority of God (e.g. 1 Tim. 1.17; 6.15-16; 2 Tim. 4.18). The Author concludes by stating that Christ Jesus gave himself as 'a ransom for all' (v. 6), which affirms not just God's desire, but testifies to his 'will' for all to be saved. As further evidence of this, the Author offers his own appointment as herald, apostle, and teacher of the Gentiles (v. 7). As such, the Author 'anchors universal access to God's salvation in the one act of redemption and the one message about it' (Towner 2006: 181). This all works together to show that salvation is the important and the controlling factor in this passage, specifically that salvation is a hope for all people, not just for the elite.[33]

5.4.1d Summary: relationships linking prayers and salvation

What is significant and often overlooked is the finding that the Author joins together the quality of intergroup relationships and the potential of salvation for all. This passage is not just about God's desire and will for all to be saved. Nor is it only about how the believers should pray for others. This passage rather brings both of these concerns together so that it connects the believers' attitude and behaviour towards unbelievers with God's will for the salvation of all people. The prayers act as a catalyst to create opportunities to raise up a positive opinion in the eyes of the outsiders as they look on the believers, for they see piety in action, which they hold dear, and respectable lifestyles, which they argue strengthen and protect society. This area of overlap cannot be downplayed. If the believers are known to be praying for unbelievers, if they are observed as good citizens who work for the welfare of all in the community, then they are clearly not misanthropes but are committed and valuable members of wider society. If outsiders are not then persuaded to become insiders, at the very least they must be persuaded to desire to interact with believers and continue being a neighbour with them in order to enjoy the benefits and blessings that these believers bring to the wider community.

This passage also reveals a significant role for the believer in the wider will of God for all to be saved. For the Author relates this inclusive hope for the salvation of all with the quality of relationship between believer and unbeliever. The prayers in v. 1 are therefore connected to the mission of God, and the prayers act to link the believers with this divine work. Towner writes that because 'salvation is the dominant thought of the passage, prayer for the state and the resultant peaceful conditions would seem to bear some relation to the missionary motive' (1989: 202). The potential for salvation is unlimited, by design (2.6) and will (2.4), and so all Christian life is played out on a stage where one is conscious of the effect one has, or could have, on others. The affirmation that God is Saviour of all undergirds theologically the sense that the church's horizon is wide and that their interest in others is not just as a reflex of their concern for self-preservation, but is to do with their concern for others, which is not simply limited to their physical or social welfare but also to their spiritual welfare.

Thus, although there are few (if any) direct instructions on evangelism in the Pastoral Epistles, the believers should look on others as part of the sphere of God's will and activity. Just as everything created by God is good (1 Tim. 4.4), so the world of humanity is to be embraced as a potentially positive sphere, where good can and should happen, and where salvation is, and should be, available to all. Furthermore, whilst believers are to recognize their part in witnessing to this gospel for the salvation of all, they are also to acknowledge that how the unbelievers view their attitude, practice and lifestyle, impacts upon the potential for the outsider to become an insider. In a way, the Author envisages in this passage both the outsiders looking in, and the insiders going out to convert the outsiders (although this is not explicitly stated). For there is a double dimension here of mission, which includes both witness (making sure that what the outsiders see when looking in is good: piety and respectability) and action (believers proactively engaging in the type of relationships with outsiders which would enable these different types of prayers to be said, and thus building relationships that could potentially lead to conversion).

As such, the importance of the outsiders to the faith community is simply the fact that they are currently *outsiders*: the very existence of the faith community is orientated around the Saviour God of *all*, and one of the reasons for existence is to enable others to take hold of this salvation. Believers are to be concerned enough about the lives of the outsiders so as to be able to pray genuinely for them, and they are to live in ways that would generate a positive opinion in the eyes of outsiders. This kind of discipleship forms a certain quality of relationship with the outsiders, which is held together and motivated by the Saviour God of all. In Titus 3 we also find the Author combining God's saving activity with the way in which believers are to behave among, and be experienced by, outsiders, and we shall now turn to this passage.

5.4.2 Introduction: Titus 3.1-8

Whereas the instructions regarding prayer in 1 Tim. 2.1-2 begin with the universal 'all people' (v. 1) and then clarify that this should also include kings and those in authority (v. 2), the instructions given in Tit. 3.1-2 begin with a specific instruction concerning behaviour and attitude towards rulers and authorities (ἀρχαῖς ἐξουσίαις, v. 1), followed by instructions concerning behaviour and character towards 'all people' (πρὸς πάντας ἀνθρώπους, v. 2, see also v. 8).[34] That the Author has an eye on outsiders is not only evidenced in the reference to rulers and authorities in verse 1 but also with the use of μηδείς ('no one') and πᾶς ἄνθρωπος ('all people') in verse 2, together with the use of καί ('also') in verse 3 to describe how believers once were *also* 'foolish' before they were saved by God (v. 5). The Author comments, 'We ourselves were also foolish' (v. 3) and continues to list a series of vices that describe the life of those outside the saved community and which therefore *also* belonged to the believers before they encountered God's mercy (see Fee 1988: 202). This verse therefore appears to be a supplementary comment on the previous verses, where the Author is now describing the group of people who should be in receipt of the believers' actions as instructed in verses 1-2, and as such, suggests that the reference to 'all people' in verse 2 must not only include outsiders, but perhaps even refers to outsiders alone. In verse 3 the Author appears to be explaining *why* it is necessary for the believers to be engaged in 'every good work' and not to be slanderous or quarrelsome but gentle and meek (vv. 1-2), because the people they are envisioned to be interacting with are those who are the opposite, who are not only foolish but who are consumed by hatred (v. 3), for this depicts those before they are transformed by God's Spirit (v. 5). As such, by the time we arrive at the simple reference to 'man' (ἄνθρωπος, v. 8), although it now lacks πᾶς, it carries with it the force of 'everyone'.

This passage demonstrates not only a sensitivity towards outsiders but also a concern for how the believers should interact with them. They should, for example, show an attitude of submissiveness to rulers and authorities, a readiness and devotion to do every good work, gentleness and meekness (vv. 1-2, 8). These attitudes should then feed into more specific actions, such as being obedient to the rulers and authorities, not speaking evil of others or being quarrelsome, and acting in ways that benefit all people (vv. 1-2, 8). It is not difficult to see how these attitudes, character traits and behavioural patterns would not only potentially create a positive opinion of believers in the eyes of the outsiders but also work to build a strong and trustworthy foundation for relationships between insider and outsider.

However, as with 1 Timothy 2, we find that these instructions and expectations are firmly embedded in the Author's emphasis on God as Saviour. For, in verses 3-7, the Author writes that although the believers were once like the unbelievers (v. 3), God demonstrated his love and kindness (v. 4) by saving them because of his mercy and 'through the washing of regeneration and renewing of the Holy Spirit' (v. 5). This Spirit was poured out through Jesus Christ, 'our Saviour' (v. 6), resulting in the believers' justification and salvation (v. 7). Hence, the instructions regarding how believers are to behave among unbelievers (which, as we will explore, are all concerned with benefitting the outsider and thus with increasing the believers' positive image in the eyes of the unbeliever) are made possible and indeed explained by the believers' own need for kindness, love and mercy pre-conversion, and their encounter with the saving God. Once again, the Author, although not explicitly, connects the concern for how the unbelievers observe and experience the believers, with the salvific intentions and nature of God through Jesus Christ (and this time also the Holy Spirit). Towner summarizes this short passage, saying, 'the purpose of the whole section is summed up in missiological terms: when believers devote themselves to "doing what is good" ... the benefit is spread to people in general' (2006: 769). We will now turn to explore in more detail the parenesis here in Titus 3, and the apparent link with salvation.

5.4.2a Foundations for relating to rulers and authorities

The Author begins this section using the present imperative of the verb ὑπομιμνήσκω to emphasize to Titus the importance of ensuring that the believers are wholeheartedly following the instructions on how to behave with outsiders, whether those in authority or those in the general public. They are firstly to make sure that they are 'subject' (ὑποτάσσω) and 'obedient' (πειθαρχέω) to rulers and authorities (v. 1a). This is clearly not the first time these believers have heard of this instruction (hence the verb, 'remind'), and indeed we find this teaching repeated elsewhere in Rom. 13.1-7 and 1 Pet. 2.13-17. We explored these two passages earlier in Chapter 3, but it is worth highlighting once more the fact that, whereas the same verb for submit is used (ὑποτάσσω, Rom. 13.1, 5; 1 Pet. 2.13), only the additional command to 'obey' (πειθαρχέω) is found in Tit. 3.1.[35] In fact, this is the only place in the NT where πειθαρχέω is used for obeying unbelievers, for in Acts it is used to describe obedience to God and to Paul (Acts 5.29, 32; 27.21). It is possible that the Author in Titus uses both 'subject' and 'obey' to emphasize the fact that the believers must have a certain attitude of submission towards rulers and authorities, but also a certain response towards them which stems from this attitude: that of obeying their laws. Not only is a right attitude needed towards these particular outsiders but also a behaviour.

As in Romans, there appears to be an absence of any critical description of rulers and authorities, but unlike Romans, there is also an absence of any other specific description of such people. Paul in Romans is quite determined to explain the divine origin of the authority that these rulers own, and therefore of how such rulers are part of God's wider work of judgement and of rewarding good with praise, and evil with wrath (Rom. 13.1-5). The Author in Titus, however, does not explain why the believers should give their submission and obedience to rulers and authorities, and they are neither encouraged that they will win the praise of these outsiders, nor threatened with fear that they could incur wrath (cf. Rom. 13.3-4). Perhaps this is indicative of the difference between the two situations or contexts. It appears that in Rome, Paul needs to emphasize the importance of this behaviour by appealing to God's overall omnipotence in this area, and in so doing, convince the believers to submit to these earthly rulers (and in fact there is evidence that some have been resisting these rules, Rom. 13.2). Conversely, the lack of reasoning given to the believers in Titus and the lack of a description of these rulers and authorities could suggest that there is neither a resistance to submission and obedience from this community, nor a specific need to convince the believers to embody such an attitude and behave in such a way.[36] But this in turn raises the question of why the Author then feels the need to include this among his instructions.

However, considering the wider passage, it appears that there may well be both a description of these rulers and authorities, and an underlying motivation for the believers' submission and obedience. As indicated above in Section 5.4.2, the use of καί in Tit. 3.3 introduces into the conversation a comparison between the recipients of the believers' actions and attitudes in verses 1-2, with the believers themselves prior to their conversion – the implication is that whilst 'we were once ... ', the people pictured in verses 1-2 are still like this.[37] In so doing, the Author suggests that the outsiders referred to in verses 1-2 (which therefore includes the rulers and authorities) are, because they are in a state of pre-conversion, 'foolish, disobedient, being led astray, slaves to various lusts and pleasures, passing lives in malice and envy, hated, hating one another' (v. 3). But the fact that the Author then proceeds to explain that the believers themselves needed God's kindness, love and mercy to be transformed and saved, strongly suggests that this critical description of outsiders is not a call for believers or for God to stand in judgement upon them (cf. Rom. 12.19), but to recognize in these outsiders the same desperate need they themselves had for kindness, love and God's transforming mercy. This description also acts as a reminder that members of this faith community were not awarded their membership based on their own superiority. As Schlatter observes, 'the community is not gathered from those who sin less than the others, as if the reason for their calling were to be found in their smaller share in human reprehensibility. They are in debt like others for what they were and did, and what brought them into communion with God is very different from their own work' (1958: 201).

Hence, it is possible that the reason Titus needs to remind believers to submit and obey rulers and authorities (and the rest of the instructions in verse 2), is not connected to their own needs (e.g. to win praise, Rom. 13.3), but to the needs of the outsiders. The driving need is for the outsiders to encounter the same kindness, love and mercy that the believers received, and these transformational characteristics are now to be revealed and channelled through the believers to the outsiders. It is also possible that, although there is no specific promise of reward for the believers for their behaviour to outsiders as in Rom. 13.3, there is an indication that their behaviour will indeed be 'profitable' for all – for both believers and outsiders (Tit. 3.8c). This verse, however, is connected not just to the instruction to submit and obey rulers and authorities, but to the rest of this passage, and specifically the instruction that believers should always be ready and devoted to doing 'good works' (Tit. 3.1, 8). We will therefore move on to explore the rest of these instructions to the believers regarding their attitude towards, and relationship with, *all* outsiders.

5.4.2b Foundations for relating to every outsider: a commitment to good works

The Author identifies twice in this passage that the believers should be devoted to doing good works: believers must be 'ready for every good work' (πρὸς πᾶν ἔργον ἀγαθὸν ἑτοίμους εἶναι, v. 1b), and believers 'may be concerned to be engaged with good works' (ἵνα φροντίζωσιν καλῶν ἔργων προΐστασθαι οἱ πεπιστευκότες θεῷ, v. 8).[38] This clearly is an important group norm that should also be evident to those looking upon the faith community from the outside. In fact, this motif of good works/ doing good is used throughout these letters, and it appears more frequently in the PEs than anywhere else in the NT (Williams 2014: 149).

For the Author, good works are firstly the mark of a genuine believer who has been cleansed and sanctified and thus made ready 'for every good work' (εἰς πᾶν ἔργον ἀγαθόν, 2 Tim. 2.21; see also Tit. 2.14 and 2 Tim. 3.17). Being ready 'for every good work' is the divinely ordained function of the believer (see Phil. 1.6; Eph. 2.10), but it is also dependent upon (and hence flows out of) their state of holiness and knowledge of the truth as revealed in Scripture. As such, 'false' believers are those who, although they claim to know God, by their outward actions (their 'works', ἔργα) they deny him: there is a mismatch between their words and their works, and as such, they are 'unfit for every good work' (καὶ πρὸς πᾶν ἔργον ἀγαθὸν ἀδόκιμοι, Tit. 1.16). Thus, in correlating good works with a genuine believer, the Author is not simply taking a motif used in the Hellenistic world, but is combining it with 'a theological meaning and salvific outcome' (Williams 2014: 155; see also 1 Tim. 5.24-25; 6.17-19). Being committed to doing good works 'serve[s] a crucial purpose' in holding onto salvation (Williams 2014: 156).[39]

Secondly, good works are visible to all. Whereas sin is conspicuous, so too are 'good works', not being able to be hidden away (1 Tim. 5.25). Thus, women are not to adorn themselves with extravagant hairstyles or expensive jewellery or clothes (1 Tim. 2.9), but rather with 'good works' (δι' ἔργων ἀγαθῶν, 1 Tim. 2.10). Likewise, the criteria to discern which widows to support include the fact that they must be well known for their 'good deeds' (ἐν ἔργοις καλοῖς μαρτυρουμένη, 1 Tim. 5.10a, which include bringing up children, showing hospitality, washing the feet of saints and giving assistance to the oppressed), having devoted themselves 'to every good work' (εἰ παντὶ ἔργῳ ἀγαθῷ ἐπηκολούθησεν, 5.10c).[40] The Author also calls Titus to be 'a model of good works' (τύπον καλῶν ἔργων, Tit. 2.7) which, together with the quality of his teaching, will ensure that any opponent has nothing 'bad' to say of 'us' (2.7-8). Good works must correlate with teaching or with words that are spoken (see also Tit. 1.16), and this connection between words and deeds will also shape how outsiders view and respond to the wider believing community.[41] This connection is also seen in Titus 3, for, after the Author instructs Titus to remind the believers to be ready 'for every good work' (3.1), they are then commanded to take care regarding how they speak to others (3.2), and again, after the believers are urged to devote themselves to good works which are 'profitable' for all (3.8), they are then warned not to get involved with controversies, quarrels and fights, for these are 'unprofitable' (3.9). Good deeds must go hand in hand with correct teaching and careful conversation which is not characterized by quarrelling or slandering but by gentleness. Together, deeds and conversation present a very visible identification of the genuine believer, and the language of 'good works' depicts 'the visible dimension of Christian existence in terms of service for others inspired by faith' (Towner 2006: 792).

Thirdly, it is evident from these references that good works are such because they are good for the wider community – good works benefit others.[42] At times, the recipients belong to the faith community (e.g. Tit. 3.13-14), and in other places the recipients are not specified (e.g. 1 Tim. 2.10; 6.18). Although Davies argues that there is no evidence that the 'good works' referred to throughout these letters would 'extend beyond the believing community' (1996: 34), when the Author returns to this motif in Titus 3, it is in the context of instructing the believers on how to conduct themselves specifically with outsiders. This, together with the use of πᾶς in v. 1, would strongly suggest that outsiders are included as the recipients of the believers' devotion to good works. And, if this is the case, then there must be an acknowledgement that what is understood as good must be shared and received as such by both insiders and outsiders (Knight 1992: 333; Fee 1988: 201, 209; Bassler 1996: 205). Furthermore, by not dictating exactly what counts as a 'good work', the Author is indeed both presuming that the believers should have this knowledge, and expecting them to assume responsibility, both individually and as a community, to discern how others, namely outsiders, would see and receive their deeds as being good. As Williams concludes, 'the language of good works is meant to project a bridging of the gap between Christians and outsiders. The motif allows the author to stress the continuity between the virtues of his community and the values of non-believers, thereby creating a sense of solidarity' (2014: 149). As such, there is a recognition of an overlap area where both insider and outsider can agree on what is 'good' and on what is received as 'good'. Clearly, this point of similarity has the potential to become a point of attraction, creating the chance for outsiders to have a positive opinion of insiders.

5.4.2c Foundations for relating to every outsider: speech flowing from character

The Author moves in verse 2 to issue four other group norms that should shape how believers relate to all people. The use of μηδένα at the beginning of the second verse, and the phrase πρὸς πάντας ἀνθρώπους in the concluding instruction shows that whilst the frame of reference does not now exclude 'government officials', it goes beyond those in authority to include everyone, including all outsiders (Knight 1992: 333). As illustrated above, the move from urging believers to live a life shaped by good works, to urging them to take thought for how they use their speech, is a pattern found elsewhere (e.g. 1 Tim. 2.10-11; Tit. 2.7-8) and demonstrates the Author's understanding that the way an outsider perceives and experiences the words of a believer must correspond with the way they experience the believer's actions.

Therefore, with reference to speech, the Author firstly commands that believers should not 'blaspheme' or 'slander' others; in other words, they are to 'speak evil of no one' (μηδένα βλασφημεῖν, Tit. 3.2). This is the only time in the PEs when unbelievers are the potential recipients of slander from believers. Unbelievers are often *described* as blasphemers (e.g. 1 Tim. 1.13; 1.20; 6.4; 2 Tim. 3.2), and slaves and women are instructed to behave in certain ways to prevent τὸ ὄνομα τοῦ θεοῦ καὶ ἡ διδασκαλία (1 Tim. 6.1), and ὁ λόγος τοῦ θεοῦ (Tit. 2.5) from being blasphemed. In Tit. 3.2, however, it is the believer who is instructed not to speak slanderously or disrespectfully of anyone, with the connotation that they are not to speak of someone else in a way that would create a negative opinion about them (and perhaps the community they represent or identify with). Once again, the Author's instruction here could also be motivated by a desire for the genuine believers to distinguish themselves from the false teachers who are engaging in such a form of speech (see 1 Tim. 6.4). But it also corresponds with earlier Pauline teaching, especially that given to the Roman believers, who are to 'bless' rather than curse (Rom. 12.14), to refrain from returning evil for evil, and to consider and carry out whatever is good 'before all people' (12.17). Whereas, I have argued, the context for this is that of persecution and conflict, the Author of Titus 3 does not root this instruction in a concern for how a believer should respond when facing threats, insults or abuse, and in so doing, generalizes this instruction so that it is a key norm for how a believer should behave towards anyone in any circumstance.

The next command regarding speech follows on from this, stating that believers should 'not be quarrelsome' (ἄμαχος), and to help with this, they should be 'yielding' or 'tolerant' (ἐπιεικής). This latter word can be translated as 'gentle' but it carries more the sense of being courteous in 'not insisting on every right of letter or law or custom' (Bauer et al. 2000: 371), and therefore understandably is partnered by the Author with the believers' ability not to be argumentative.[43] Importantly, these two descriptions should also characterize the overseer and help them to gain a 'good testimony' from outsiders (1 Tim. 3.3, 7). It would be logical therefore to draw the same conclusion here, that the tolerant and non-argumentative nature of the believers would win for themselves a good testimony from outsiders. Clearly, the idea is that both characteristics should be visible to all people and both should be valued by all people.[44] This is in contrast to the false teachers, who are said to be involving themselves with controversies and 'disputes over words' (λογομαχία, 1 Tim. 6.4), and the believers are repeatedly instructed to avoid 'fights' (μάχη) since they are 'unprofitable' (ἀνωφελεῖς, Tit. 3.9) and to distance themselves from speculations, 'knowing that they produce fights' (εἰδὼς ὅτι γεννῶσιν μάχας, 2 Tim. 2.23; see also 2.24). Believers, however, need to let their courteous and tolerant character guide their words (or even halt their words) in situations when they would otherwise have corrected the other person (see also Mounce 2000: 445; Marshall 1999: 479). For the Author, character must not be underestimated in its ability to display and teach the true gospel, and to counter false opinions or stereotypes.

Although the Author does not specify the context, the instructions in Tit. 3.2 not to 'speak evil' of anyone and not to be drawn into quarrels by displaying great tolerance, may point to situations where believers might actually desire to retaliate or speak disrespectfully about others. However, the Author makes it clear in the next and final instruction in verse 2, that regardless of the situation or context, believers are to demonstrate that they are not driven by a sense of self-importance and as such, should 'display all humility to all people' (πᾶσιν ἐνδεικνυμένους πραΰτητα πρὸς πάντας ἀνθρώπους). He emphasizes that 'all humility' is needed when engaging with outsiders, and, given its place in the sequence of instructions in verses 1-2, the Author could be concluding that the underlying quality that enables the believer to submit and obey rulers and authorities, to be ready for every good work, and to be respectful, non-argumentative and tolerant, is humility. This is the quality used to describe Christ (2 Cor. 10.1), but it is also expected to be a character of all believers (Gal. 5.23; see also Eph. 4.2; Col. 3.12 and Jas 3.13). Although it is often used to describe the manner in which others should be corrected (1 Cor. 4.21; Gal. 6.1; 2 Tim. 2.25; 1 Pet. 3.15-16), the reference to 'all people' in Tit. 3.2 implies that this is a quality that all believers should fully use and demonstrate in all situations. As Marshall writes, 'the rule' of humility 'is unalterable in all circumstances' (1999: 304).

Furthermore, the word ἐνδείκνυμαι (see also Tit. 2.10; 2 Cor. 8.24) can often be used not just for someone 'showing' or 'displaying' something, but also in the sense of 'proving' something which might be surprising to others, of 'convincing' or 'persuading' others about something which might not otherwise be believed, or about a view that needs to be strengthened (e.g. Rom. 2.15; 2 Cor. 8.24; Eph. 2.7; 1 Tim. 1.16; Tit. 2.10). As such, the use of ἐνδείκνυμαι here in Tit. 3.2 is not so much about encouraging the believers to *reveal* their meekness, as if they need to be more intentional in showing it, but also that they need to *prove* it, to *convince* outsiders that in all things and in all ways they are people not full of self-importance, but that they look to the needs of others and act in humility in all ways. Given how the Author describes the nature of the false teachers, it is possible that the Author knows the true believers need to be intentional in proving that they are distinct from these false teachers and in proving that they are good, courteous and gentle, a non-threatening and positive presence in the wider community. It is not simply enough to demonstrate these good characteristics that are foundational for a good reputation and for good relationships; believers need to devote themselves in all areas of life to proving and convincing outsiders that they are a positive presence in society who collectively seek to serve the other, rather than themselves.

5.4.2d Underlying motivation

After the instructions in verses 1-2 the Author then turns to write a rich description of how the believers, before they became members of this faith community, were recipients of God's kindness and love not because they were entitled to this, but because of God's mercy, which led them to being saved (3.3-7). He is clear to emphasize that it was God's actions of goodness, even though they were devoid of it, that transitioned them from being outsiders to insiders. These verses then provide the theological basis for the instructions in verses 1-2, for the believers are to remember that God responded to their own vices not with that which they should have deserved, but with kindness, love and mercy. In the same manner, they too are now called to respond to unbelievers. God's mercy to the unpleasant (vv. 3-5) is to be matched by the believers in their kindness and humility to all (vv. 1-2). As such, the 'universal scope of Christian courtesy' links 'with the thought of God's universal love in vv.3f' (Marshall 1999: 304). But what is significant is that this love and mercy of God led to their salvation: ἀλλὰ κατὰ τὸ αὐτοῦ ἔλεος ἔσωσεν ἡμᾶς (3.5). This suggests therefore that this link is not just between 'Christian courtesy' and 'God's universal love' but rather that the way the believers behave towards outsiders is linked to God's continuing saving work through the Holy Spirit and Jesus Christ. The believers have already been reminded of the universal implication of God's grace in Tit. 2.11 which brings salvation to all: Ἐπεφάνη γὰρ ἡ χάρις τοῦ θεοῦ σωτήριος πᾶσιν ἀνθρώποις. But it also brings great transformation in redefining and reforming character and identity (2.12-14). It is within this conversation that the Author appears to change subject for a moment in considering how believers should behave towards outsiders (3.1-2), before continuing his wider conversation about the God of salvation and his transforming grace and mercy (3.3-7). However, rather than 3.1-2 being a brief change of subject, these instructions illustrate that the Author sees the believers' attitude to outsiders as being deeply and divinely connected to the ongoing work of salvation for all.

This is noticed also by Marshall, who comments that 'the unspoken implication would seem to be that this attitude may lead to the conversion of unbelievers, which, if correct, would move the thrust of the text beyond the level of *christliche Bürgerlichkeit*' (1999: 298–9). If the believers are successful in convincing outsiders of their gentleness and non-threatening behaviour, clearly the outsiders would view the believers with a more positive opinion, and verses 3-7 show that this, for the Author, is not simply to benefit the believers by giving them a more positive social identity but also to benefit the outsiders by opening up for them the possibility of knowing God's mercy and salvation. Behaving in a way that reflects God's goodness and mercy is therefore an important part of the believers' interaction with outsiders. It is clear for the Author that 'if the manifestation of God's love in Christ had the effect of transforming their [the believer's] lives (through conversion, as vv. 4-7 show), then their manifestation of the life of Christ should have similar results in the lives of others' (Towner 1989: 197). Thus, the outward-facing behaviour is optimistic: it reflects the hope of an expanding, potentially more inclusive community, even if it is not clear how this might come about.

Furthermore, after providing this theological rationale in verses 3-7 and confirming its trustworthiness (Πιστὸς ὁ λόγος, v. 8a), the Author then articulates his desire for Titus to 'strongly affirm these things' (καὶ περὶ τούτων βούλομαί σε διαβεβαιοῦσθαι, v. 8b). Most commentators agree that the Author is referring to the instructions regarding practice (vv. 1-2) *and* the teaching regarding God's saving nature (vv. 3-7), which together become that which is referred to by the Author as 'these things' (v. 8b).[45] These instructions and this teaching together are important to the Author; practice should not be isolated from theology, but nor should theology be isolated from practice. As such, the duty of Titus to 'remind' the believers of their response to outsiders and how this links to God as Saviour becomes more of an emphatic 'insist' after the Author explains how their practice is to be rooted in their theology. Their practice is not just about being 'good' but about their call to mirror the mercy and kindness of God in the world.

But the reason for insisting upon these things is that believers can devote themselves to good works (ἵνα φροντίζωσιν καλῶν ἔργων προΐστασθαι οἱ πεπιστευκότες θεῷ, v. 8c), and the Author then concludes that 'these things are good and profitable to all': ταῦτά ἐστιν καλὰ καὶ ὠφέλιμα τοῖς ἀνθρώποις (v. 8d); that the Author adds 'to all' links this verse textually and thematically to the rest of the wider passage in which the Author refers to all people, and this would suggest that that which is good and profitable are all the ways in which the believers are to conduct themselves with all people (vv. 1-2 and 8, motivated by vv. 3-7). Thus, irrespective of whether 'these things' refer to everything from verse 1 (e.g. Mounce 2000: 453) or simply to the good works mentioned in verse 8 (e.g. Towner 2006: 793), what is significant is that the Author identifies the value of the believer's outward behaviour (directed towards outsiders) as being 'profitable'. The Author believes that all people, and, specifically outsiders, should benefit from the believer's behaviour and theology.

Hence, the rationale for the particular way the believers are to behave is not solely to benefit themselves but also to benefit *all* people. The Author made it clear that the believers' own 'works in righteousness' could not benefit their own salvation (v. 5), but their good works now, however, can be 'excellent' for others and 'useful' (v. 8), perhaps even useful in the sense of others finding salvation, if they reflect the love and mercy of God. For, although the Author only uses ὠφέλιμος twice more in the PEs, from these two other occurrences we can see that something is 'profitable' if it encourages a person in the hope of salvation, or if it enables a person to deepen their divine vocation and purpose in the world. The term ὠφέλιμος is used in 1 Tim. 4.8 to describe the value of godliness being that which can hold onto the promise of salvation (see also 4.10), and it is used in 2 Tim. 3.16 to describe the value of Scripture as 'useful', which can enable the believer to be equipped 'for every good work' (3.17). It may be then that the 'good and beneficial' nature of the behaviour of the believers (Tit. 3.8d) is such because it has the potential to begin a soteriological and moral transformation in all people, including outsiders.[46] Good deeds then are acts of benevolence and kindness that make a positive contribution to mission.[47]

5.4.2e Summary

This passage in Titus 3 once again reveals a sensitivity to the presence of outsiders and an awareness of contact points of similarity, a concern for how the outsiders should view and experience the believers, and a concern that the outsiders should benefit from knowing and relating with the believers. The way in which the believers are to relate to and behave among their outsiders harnesses that which is found as 'good' by both insider and outsider and uses it to 'profit' all. In other words, the Author notices the points of similarity, the points at which both insider and outsider would meet in agreement, and he translates this into clear instructions to the believers, bringing to the fore specific group norms that would particularly promote a positive opinion in the mind of the outsider. Furthermore, these are rooted in the Author's teaching on God as Saviour, and as such, the character and practice of the believer is connected to the character and practice of the Saviour God. The importance of the outsiders lies in the fact that they are not only constant reminders of the transformation the believers themselves have experienced because of God's saving mercy, but that they motivate the faith community to act out of this transformation and bring good to all.

5.5 Conclusion: Reputation and Relationship

A major concern for the Author is the reputation of the believing community and the quality of relationship between believers and unbelievers. These two strands are woven through most of the teaching in 1 Timothy and Titus, but the tools used to weave in these strands consist firstly of a recognition of the importance of an area of similarity between ingroup and outgroup, and secondly of a belief that God is the Saviour of all. What others think is highly important to the Author; but this can be shaped by the revealing of an area of similarity, of a 'community of culture' between the groups, and it appears to be motivated by a universal horizon that the one God is Saviour of all, and as such, that there is universal potential for the gospel to be known and accepted. There is an appreciation of what Jenkins terms the 'internal–external dialectic' (2008: 40), whereby what outsiders think of the insiders is as significant as the ingroup's own image of themselves. As such, a concern for public image, a recognition of areas of intergroup similarity and a belief in God as Saviour converge in the Author's thoughts and writings. How the believers behave towards outsiders is almost always linked to God's nature as Saviour. In the words of Towner, 'the author's theology gives respectability a higher purpose; it is a necessary component of the Church's missionary operation in that it allows the Church to maintain a redemptive interface with the observing world' (1989: 189).

Thus, once more, we discover that, whilst differences between the two groups are not erased, certain similarities are brought to the fore in order to influence the outsiders' opinion of the insiders. Whereas differences are emphasized in SIT, the Author, like Paul, emphasizes similarities. However, as Hoklotubbe argues, this recognition of points of similarity is not a 'flat understanding of "accommodation" or "secularization"', but a careful navigation through the distinctive elements of both outgroup and ingroup, and the points of connection or similarity, in order to 'build bridges between the *ekklesia* and the outside world so that all might be saved' (2017: 78; also Trebilco 2004: 373-9). Given the fact that it appears the false teachers were encouraging a more revolutionary stance, especially perhaps for women in shunning marriage and embracing celibacy (1 Tim. 4.3; and as demonstrated in *The Acts of Paul and Thecla*), and since the crux of the Christian faith *was* radical and in opposition to some firmly held beliefs of the empire (that Jesus Christ alone is the Saviour of all), then perhaps 'there needed to be an emphasis, even an overemphasis, in the ethical sphere on Christians behaving as good citizens, and even modelling virtues that pagans admired' (Witherington 2006b: 149). However, even though on the surface the believers might be seen to present 'the ideal of good Christian citizenship' or 'christliche Bürgerlichkeit' (Dibelius & Conzelmann 1972: 40), the Author takes 'popular ethics' (1972: 40) and grounds them in a theology of God who is the Saviour of the world. As such, he identifies that these ethics are not necessarily a new construct of society, but that they are a part of modelling one's life on God the Creator and the Redeemer of all life (e.g. 1 Tim. 2.1-6; Tit. 3.1-8).

The Author therefore links together the area of similarity with God's saving work, which in itself, has no boundaries. It is possible that the area of similarity creates the type of impression of believers that encourages outsiders to change groups and become insiders belonging to the believing community. Indeed, Tajfel remarked that a member of one group might be persuaded to join another group that has a more positive social identity (see Tajfel 1981: 256). As MacDonald writes, 'For a community with a universal vision of salvation, not only was a certain amount of openness to outsiders inevitable, but the approval of outsiders was essential for its continued existence' (1988: 170).[48] As such, although these two groups are distinct, the Author clearly believes that they are found within one larger group where God is Saviour of all. Although the Author does not appear to be concerned with what Capozza and Brown (writing on SIT) describe as a 'redrawing' of group boundaries (because there is still a conversion experience that holds the believers apart from the unbelievers), he nevertheless understands that both groups belong to 'a larger superordinate category' (2000: xiv). For, the exploration of these passages has drawn our attention to the universal vision of 'God as Saviour of all', which places the ingroup within a wider entity of 'all people'. This larger category is theologically rather than socially based, and it provides a wider frame for the internal categorization between 'in' and 'out'. Thus, although there is an awareness of difference between the ingroup and outgroup, there is also an awareness of how this difference is not ultimately fixed, because the mercy of God can change this difference. As such, the Author is clear that the ingroup should not just ignore outsiders or disregard them because they are part of the larger divinely designed category. The ingroup of believers thus view the outsiders with a mixture of present anxiety (lest they slander them) and future hope (that they join them).

Furthermore, within this divinely ordained category, some similarities exist across the groups because they are part of the divinely ordained moral cosmos: both insider and outsider are aligning themselves to this moral cosmos – they are both assimilating to God (whether or not they realize this). This is demonstrated in 1 Tim. 2, where the Author states that the behaviour of the believers towards the outsiders is 'good before God' and not just before outsiders. The Author is placing this moral commonality on a theological canvas: this is good not just because insiders or outsiders think it is good, but because God thinks that it is good. There is an appeal to a universal cosmic sacred order. If we were to conclude that the believers simply had to live to fit in with outsiders, this would, for the Author, be reductionist: the claim of the text is that believers should do what is right because God judges it to be so, not because outsiders do. Hence, for the believers to pray for others and demonstrate their piety and respectability is more than a socially acceptable custom – it is a divinely ordained norm that belongs to the larger divine category where 'all' belong to God. Similarly, for believers to look after the widows in their family, it is not just because this is a socially acceptable norm but because 'this is acceptable in the sight of God' (1 Tim. 5.4, 8).

Consequently, when these verses and passages are read in their wider context, it is apparent that all of the Author's instructions are in one sense 'redemptive in orientation', for they aim 'at the accomplishment of the salvation already initiated in the individual and in the world' (Towner 1989: 178; see also MacDonald 1988: 170). The believers need to show sensitivity towards how outsiders will perceive them, and therefore should take note of what they think, as this helps to shape how the believers reveal their faith in ways that are attractive, and in ways that will reveal to them the Saviour God of all.

Notes

1. Whilst 2 Timothy shares some of the same concerns as seen in 1 Timothy and Titus (e.g. regarding the false teachers, 2.16-18; 3.6-9) there are striking differences in that it never mentions the need for a good reputation nor does it issue any instructions on how believers should behave among outsiders (both of which we will see are significant concerns in 1 Timothy and Titus). 2 Timothy also focuses more on the Author's own experiences of ministry, persecution and betrayal, and warns believers of the potential for such in their own lives (e.g. 1.12, 15-17; 2.3, 9-10; 3.10-12; 4.6-8, 14-18).
2. E.g. Dibelius and Conzelmann 1972: 1–10; Bassler 1996: 17–21; Davies 1996: 105–17; Aageson 2008: 5; Roloff 1988: 23–39; Quinn and Wacker 2000: 1–23; Collins 2002: 1–14; Williams 2014: 150.
3. E.g. Fee 1988: 1, 23–6; Knight 1992: 21–52; Mounce 2000: xlvi-cxxix; Johnson 2001: 98–9; Witherington 2006b: 49–75; Köstenberger 2019.
4. The false teachers form the backdrop to most of the Pastoral Epistles and are referred to frequently (e.g. 1 Tim. 1.3-7; 19b-20; 4.1-3; 6.3-5, 9-10, 20-21; 2 Tim. 2.17-18, 25-26; 3.1-9, 13; Tit. 1.10-11, 15-16). They oppose the 'sound' teaching and desire to be 'teachers of the law' (1 Tim. 1.7) but are instead vain and idle in their talking (1 Tim. 1.6; Tit. 1.10) and confuse others with their speculations and controversies

(1 Tim. 1.4). They deceive (1 Tim. 4.1-2) and divide (Tit. 1.10-11) and have corrupt minds (2 Tim. 3.8, 13). However, the Author does not disclose much information about their teaching, although we know that they have been forbidding marriage and some foods (1 Tim. 4.3), and that Hymenaeus and Philetus are teaching that the resurrection has already happened (2 Tim. 2.17-18). Timothy and Titus are simply to contradict their teaching by keeping to that which they themselves received from childhood (2 Tim. 3.14-15; also 1 Tim. 6.20 and 2 Tim. 1.14).

5   Since the Author is referring here to the quality of Titus' teaching, the reference to 'the one of the opposing side' is most likely referring to the false teachers rather than to any hostile members belonging to the unbelieving group.

6   Many commentators translate διάβολος as the 'devil' (e.g. Bassler 1996: 68; Witherington 2006b: 239; Fee 1988: 83; Dibelius and Conzelmann 1972: 54), whilst a few others translate it as 'slanderer' (MacDonald 1988: 167; Davies 1996: 78). Although the Author uses the plural of διάβολος on three other occasions to describe the potential behaviour of women and general sinful people as slanderers (1 Tim. 3.11; Tit. 2.3; 2 Tim. 3.3), on another three occasions he uses the singular of διάβολος to refer to 'the devil'. Hence, in 2 Tim. 2.26 the Author uses a similar description of 'the trap of the devil' (τῆς τοῦ διαβόλου παγίδος) to that found in 1 Tim. 3.7 (παγίδα τοῦ διαβόλου), in describing the place from which their opponents operate, since they have been 'captured' by him in order to do his will, and in 1 Tim. 3.6 he warns the overseer about falling into the 'judgment of the devil' (εἰς κρίμα ἐμπέσῃ τοῦ διαβόλου). Whereas the plural references appear to be referring to those who take part in a specific ungodly behaviour, the singular ones are used as a name for the 'devil'.

7   This surely suggests some concern with potential if not actual hostility. Perhaps the reality is not of the believers facing persecution, but more of a damaging loss of honour.

8   Since the Author specifically refers to believing masters in 6.2, it is likely that he is referring (although not exclusively) to unbelieving masters in 6.1. Knight comments that such slaves would also avert an unbelieving master from thinking that the gospel makes 'slaves less respectful and poorer workers' (1992: 245).

9   Parker comments that the vices commonly attributed to slaves were 'seen as endangering the master's goods and household', and that slaves were thought to be 'ignorant of *pietas* (devotion, duty), lacking in *fides* (faithfulness), and imbued with treachery' (1998: 160). Wiedemann writes that 'Ancient literature ascribes to slaves an assortment of vices … They are lazy, talkative, interested only in food, sex, and sleep, compulsive liars, and steal the wine' (1987: 25). If this is so, then it is easy to see how the Author's instructions to slaves are urging them to contradict this critical appraisal and demonstrate the benefits of having a Christian slave.

10 Balch's proposal is that the household code is rooted not just in Jewish teaching but as far back as Plato and Aristotle (1981).

11 This explains why, for the Author, the overseer must be able to manage his household if he is to manage God's church (1 Tim. 3.4-5).

12 The word λοιδορία is used throughout the NT for verbal abuse ('aggressive challenge', MacDonald 1996: 159) with the intention of causing distress to other people (also 1 Pet. 2.23; 3.9, Jn 9.28; Acts 23.4; 1 Cor. 4.12; also 1 Cor. 5.11; 6.10), and the word used for 'adversary' or 'opponent' (ἀντίκειμαι) is used throughout the NT normally for the one person who, as an enemy of the faith, would judge critically, or would persecute and harm believers (Lk. 13.17; 21.15; 1 Cor. 16.9; Phil. 1.28).

13 Compare for example 1 Tim. 2.9 with both Juvenal (*Satire 6*, 287–94; 457–9; 507) and Plutarch (*Moralia: Advice to Bride and Groom*, 142.C.30), and 1 Tim. 5.13 with Juvenal (*Satire 6*, 402–12). See also Winter, 2003. As Hoklotubbe notes, these guidelines in 1 Tim. 2.8-15 reflect the 'moral and social concerns associated with Augustan legislation and imperial self-representation, which carries forward into the celebration of the modesty ... concord ... and piety ... of women in Trajan's and Hadrian's households' (2017: 84).

14 One of the difficulties with referring to literary sources is that they offer and reflect the opinions of literary elite. On the other hand, epitaphs 'preserve ideals more faithfully than historical fact, but as such constitute a record of models of approved public and private behaviour in women's lives' (Lefkowitz and Fant 2005: 205). Tomb stone epitaphs would also use a standard formula composed to describe the deceased, and they would be visible to a wide audience; they can thus give us a good insight into the expectations of a good woman that were held by the general public.

15 From the tomb of the Statilii, Rome, 1st cent. AD (CIL VI.6593 – CLE 1030. L) in Lefkowitz and Fant 2005: 19.

16 Athenodora. Athens, Christian period (Kaibel 176. G) in Lefkowitz and Fant 2005: 20.

17 Portefaix 2003: 153.

18 First century BC *(CIL VI.10230 = ILS 8394. L)* in Lefkowitz and Fant 2005: 43.

19 Although Wagener argues that the instructions concerning women are rather to do with conflict within the ingroup whereby men and women are competing for leadership positions (and thus the Author endeavours to 'eliminate women' from such roles; 1994: 65), referring to 1 Tim. 2.9-10 he nevertheless recognizes that the Author is concerned the women should not give 'offense to the outside world' (1994: 87).

20 The lack of a second person pronoun (as in 1 Tim. 1.3) indicates that the Author is not just instructing Timothy, but that this instruction is an expectation set upon the whole believing community (also Marshall 1999: 418).

21 The addition of 'first of all' (πρῶτον πάντων, v. 1) might indicate that this instruction is simply to be the first in a sequence, but it could also imply that it is first in importance (see Rom. 3.22; 2 Cor. 8.5; 2 Pet. 1.20; 3.3). Given the apparent link between the instruction to pray and God's desire for the salvation of all, the use of the superlative πρῶτον probably implies its priority in terms of importance. See also Marshall 1999: 419; Knight 1992: 114; Schlatter 1958: 71.

22 Whereas many commentators note that the use of 'all people' is a universal statement (e.g. Johnson 2001: 189, 191; Dibelius and Conzelmann 1972: 35; Towner 1989: 202; Marshall 1999: 420), Knight argues that it means 'all *kinds* of people' (and therefore not necessarily individuals) because of the specification of civil rulers as a subgroup, rather than envisaging an absolute universalism (1992: 115). However, there is nothing to suggest either here or later in 2.4 and 4.10 that 'all people' actually means all kinds of people, and the emphasis on 'all' throughout this passage suggests that indeed it has a universal intention.

23 The link between praying for those outside the faith community in the hope to secure peace and protection was often a common feature within the Jewish community. E.g. Jer. 29.7; Baruch 1.10-13; Ezra 6.9-10 and 1 Maccabees 7.33. See also Marshall 1999: 421; Davies 1996: 62; Towner 2006: 168; Dibelius and Conzelmann 1972: 37–8; Johnson 2001: 195–6.

24 E.g. 1 Tim. 1.9; 2.2, 10; 3.16; 4.7-8; 5.4; 6.3, 5-6, 11; 2 Tim. 2.16; 3.5, 12; Tit. 1.1; 2.12. This word group is only found elsewhere in the NT in Acts (3.12; 10.2, 7; 17.23) and 2 Peter (1.3, 6-7; 2.9; 3.11).
25 Conversely, profane and empty talk leads people to ungodliness (ἀσέβεια, 2 Tim. 2.16), and since some of the false teachers have opposed the truth and have a false faith, they might appear to have 'a form of godliness' but they have 'denied its power' (2 Tim. 3.5, 8).
26 See: Hoklotubbe 2017: 5–6; Witherington 2006b: 99; Bassler 1996: 51; Foerster 1959: 175–8; Towner 2006: 172; Trebilco 2004: 361; Roloff 1988: 117.
27 As Foerster notes, the use of this term 'is also connected with the fact that the author always has in view the effect of the walk of Christians on those who are without [the Christian faith]' (1959: 183).
28 Similarly, we find in the writings of Philo an understanding that the duty to pray for earthly rulers was an expression of piety. Philo describes how the Jewish houses of prayer were essential for Jews in 'showing piety to their benefactors' (τὴν εἰς τοὺς εὐεργέτας εὐσέβειαν), which includes the emperor (*Against Flaccus*, 48).
29 It is notable that this picture of tranquillity and quietness, of piety and respectability, stands in complete contrast to the lives of the false teachers as represented by the Author (see 1 Tim. 4.3; 6.20-21; 2 Tim. 2.16, 23; 3.5; Tit. 1.11; 3.9).
30 Brown 1917: 16; Fee 1988: 64; Knight 1992: 113, 118; Marshall 1999: 424; Roloff 1988: 119.
31 The 'truth' is also an important thread running throughout the PEs: it is that which is taught by 'Paul', needed for conversion, owned by those who are genuine believers, and therefore that which stands in contrast to the myths taught by, or propagated by their opponents who have turned away from the truth (1 Tim. 2.4, twice in v. 7; 3.15; 4.3; 6.5; 2 Tim. 2.15, 18, 25; 3.7, 8; 4.4; Tit. 1.1, 13, 14).
32 For examples, see Trebilco 2004: 360.
33 It is possible that the false teachers did not believe in the potential for 'unlimited' salvation, believing only in the election of the elite (see Witherington 2006b: 215; see also Schlatter 1958: 75).
34 These two words for rulers and authorities are sometimes used to refer to angelic powers (e.g. Col. 1.16; 2.10; Eph. 1.21; 3.10; 6.12), but also for human authorities (e.g. Lk. 12.11; 20.20; Rom. 13.1-3). Given the similarity here in Tit. 3.1 with Rom. 13.1-7, and the wider context in Tit. 3 where outsiders are in view, it is more likely that the Author is referring to human rulers and authorities in Tit. 3.1 (see also Witherington 2006b: 155; Fee 1988: 201).
35 We also find in these two passages the theme of doing good (Tit. 3.1, 8), albeit expressed in slightly different ways (Rom. 13.3; 1 Pet. 2.14-15).
36 Contra Kelly who writes that this command was needed since Cretans had a reputation for rebelling against an outside authority (1963: 249).
37 The use of γάρ in verse 3 also connects the discussion back to vv. 1-2.
38 The verb φροντίζω is found only here in the NT but means 'to be intent on, be careful/concerned about' (Bauer et al. 2000: 1066). The word προΐστημι is mostly used to mean 'rule' or 'direct' (1 Tim. 3.4-5, 12; 5.17; 1 Thess. 5.12; Rom. 12.8) but in Titus the Author uses it to mean 'to be concerned about/engaged with' (Tit. 3.8, 14).
39 The Author, however, stresses that pre-conversion, God's gift of salvation is not conditional on seeing any works of righteousness in someone, since this salvation is offered solely because of his mercy (Tit. 3.5).

40 The use of both 'good works' and 'every good work' in this one verse shows that there is no significant difference between the use of the singular or plural, but that the reference to 'good works' might indicate a collection of specific acts (see Tit. 3.14 and possibly 1 Tim. 6.18) but not always (Tit. 2.7; 3.8). Additionally, 'every good work' might refer more generally to the type of lifestyle which is characterized by good deeds of any kind that aim to benefit the other person, in other words, actions unspecified by the Author, but which should be obvious to a believer in any specific context (Tit. 3.1; 2 Tim. 2.21; 3.17). Dibelius and Conzelmann write that the 'genuine Pauline epistles use only the singular, and consequently understand the expression in a different way' (1972: 47), although they do not elaborate upon or give evidence for this statement. It is true that whilst the undisputed letters use only ἔργον ἀγαθόν, there are only four occurrences (Rom. 2.7; 13.3; 2 Cor. 9.8 and Phil. 1.6; see also Col. 1.10; 2 Thess. 2.17), which besides being a small sample for comparison, do not appear to show any significant difference in use compared with the PEs. For example, Rom. 2.6-7 shows that Paul uses the singular and plural of ἔργον interchangeably and in the same context (see Schreiner 1998: 112), where those who are devoted to 'good work' are those who are genuine and who seek to follow the truth (Rom. 2.7). Additionally, the use of 'every good work' in 2 Cor. 9.8 is, like that in the PEs, referring to the expectation that true believers will be fruitful in 'every good work'.

41 Interestingly, after the women are instructed to 'dress' themselves with good deeds, the Author immediately moves on once again to language, but this time, specifically to the fact that women should be silent in learning and are not permitted to teach (1 Tim. 2.11-12).

42 Although the Author very rarely gives details regarding what exactly these good works consist of, Barclay argues (when commenting on 1 Tim. 5.10) that they refer 'to the low-level, everyday benefactions which form the support system of the poor: a gift of food, care of children, nursing the sick, sharing household items, a small loan in a crisis, hospitality, and so on' (2020: 277). See also 1 Tim. 6.2 where the Author uses εὐεργεσία to refer to the 'good service' of slaves which benefits or helps their masters.

43 Knight also notes that these two descriptions should go together, since there is only one infinitive governing them (1992: 334).

44 See also the reference to 'gentleness' in Phil. 4.5, where believers are to make sure that this is 'known to all people': τὸ ἐπιεικὲς ὑμῶν γνωσθήτω πᾶσιν ἀνθρώποις.

45 Mounce 2000: 452; Towner 2006: 789, 791; Knight 1992: 350; Fee 1988: 207; Marshall 1999: 330.

46 In contrast, arguments are 'unprofitable and futile' (ἀνωφελεῖς καὶ μάταιοι, 3.9) for they are divisive, and clearly would raise up a negative opinion of believers in the eyes of the outsiders.

47 See also Towner 2006: 794.

48 Also Witherington who writes of the need for the boundary to 'remain porous if evangelism was a primary commitment' (2006b: 149; see also Köstenberger 2019: 58).

6

Conclusion

6.1 Introduction

The opinion of outsiders is of remarkable importance to Paul. Despite his depiction that, in general, unbelievers are neither holy nor righteous, he is nevertheless convinced that they do play a vital role in how believers shape aspects of their lives around the warp and weft of their local context. What others think signals both the work that believers may need to do to protect themselves or to present the gospel in a more accessible and attractive way, and how well the believers are doing in their vocation as missional disciples. And so, how those outside the faith community look upon, interpret, and respond to the believers is a thread that weaves its way through the thoughts of Paul and the Author, and it surfaces explicitly in several areas of instruction. This book has analysed the main texts where this is evident: it has provided a thorough, textual exploration of the instructions within the Pauline corpus that reveal a sensitivity to the presence of outsiders and a concern for what they think, whilst also identifying the underlying motivations. In so doing, this book has revealed the importance of the outsider in the different Pauline communities, and how the presence *and* the opinion of the outsider influence some patterns of ingroup behaviour and understanding of their ingroup identity. This research has therefore drawn insights from SIT to trace boundary construction and maintenance of some of the faith communities as described in the Pauline corpus, but it has also suggested a way that SIT could be developed to include an appreciation of the importance and relevance of the outgroup for the social identity of the ingroup. This book has noted the role of similarity between groups in creating opportunities for positive intergroup relations, which in turn strengthens the viability of the ingroup and may even cause the expansion of its boundaries to accommodate the conversion of outsiders into insiders.

6.2 Overview

Chapter 1 began by highlighting the juxtaposition and apparent contradiction found within the Pauline corpus. For, unbelievers (the outgroup) and believers (the ingroup) are described in such polar terms that one could logically conclude that intergroup interaction should be prohibited or at least cautioned against. Furthermore, from these descriptions, the thought that outsiders could contribute to the ingroup's understanding of their own identity is unimaginable. However, it is also apparent that there is a significant number of instructions asking the believers not only to interact with outsiders but also to pay attention to what would be received by them as good or honourable; believers should recognize the 'contact points' where both groups find agreement on shared values and expectations regarding what is 'good'. Additionally, a brief survey of these passages noted occasions when the believers are asked to acknowledge the opinion of the unbelievers, and then to adapt their way of life in order to benefit the outsider.

At this point, concepts such as boundaries, groups and identity proved to be important in understanding these passages, and so Chapter 1 then turned to explore social identity theory (SIT). This theory brings together ideas as to how boundaries are formed and maintained, how and why ingroup members will behave in a certain way towards outgroup members, and the importance and role of difference in shaping and protecting group boundaries. Whereas contributors to SIT recognize that similarity will exist between groups, the driving force behind SIT is the power of, and need for, *difference*. Thus, similarity between groups is harnessed to provide the ingroup with the means to evaluate themselves positively against the outgroup, and so to provide themselves with an increased positive social identity, and ironically, in so doing, to use a point of similarity to enhance difference between the groups. The initial experiments by Tajfel and Turner were also used to argue that recognized difference leads to categorization, which in turn determines how an ingroup member might behave towards an outgroup member, and that this will likely be guided by a bias to discriminate against the outgroup members and to favour the ingroup members (see e.g. Tajfel and Turner 1979: 38–9).

As such, Chapter 1 found that when SIT has been used by NT scholars, it has often been used to explore passages that reveal significant internal crises or conflict – this means that the need to focus on ingroup cohesion and to increase a positive social identity by highlighting intergroup difference has been more salient than any other concern. NT scholars are also increasingly turning to other disciplines, theories and propositions in the field of social identity, to enhance how SIT can help to explore community formation, group belonging, and behaviour in the NT. This suggests that there are certain aspects of SIT that remain underdeveloped, particularly around the importance of the outgroup in developing the attitude and behaviour of the ingroup. I highlighted Jenkins, who, although not writing on SIT as such, argues that social identity is a combination of how the ingroup member defines their identity *and* how the outgroup defines it (2008: 40, 42). His proposal that 'what people think about us is no less significant than what we think about ourselves' (2008: 42) mirrors the finding that in the Pauline corpus there is a concern for what the outsider thinks of the insider. This suggests that there is the possibility for SIT to be developed to recognize the importance of the outgroup on the forming and shaping of the cognitive, emotional, and evaluative components of social identity (I will return to this in Section 6.3 below).

Chapter 2 focused on Paul's letter to the Thessalonians. At first glance, Paul does not appear to spend a great deal of time referring to the outsiders or how believers should be sensitive to their presence. In this short letter, there are only three brief occasions where Paul indicates an awareness of the outsider, and these could easily be overlooked. Nevertheless, through our exploration it became apparent that Paul is deeply concerned about the outsider and their relationship with the insider. Thus, he reminds the believers that the outsiders are not to be dismissed for they should feature in how the believers behave – outsiders should be recipients of their 'superabundant' love and of their pursuit of what is good (3.12; 5.15). The dimension of 'all' is an important group norm, for, despite the believers being recipients of hostility from outsiders, they are to make sure that 'all' are recipients of their love and of that which is considered by all to be 'good'. It is a risky move to make for it requires the believers to draw closer to those who have the power to harm them; but for Paul, there is no getting away from the fact that this dimension of 'all' is an essential part of what makes a believer an insider. One could perhaps even argue that this group norm of indiscriminately loving all and pursuing good for all is an essential part of the group boundary – if the Thessalonian believers were not to do this then they themselves will have dismantled their own faith community. Perhaps, for Paul, the greatest threat to the faith community is not the hostility from outside it, but from the potential abandonment from within it of the command to love all and pursue good for all.

However, Chapter 2 also found that, alongside this dimension of 'all', the believers need to acknowledge the influence of 'with': that they are to live with regard to how the outsiders view and experience them. Paul recognizes the profound impact that the negative opinion driving the hostility has upon the health of the believers' faith and upon the very existence of the faith community. Thus, contrary to SIT, Paul advocates an approach whereby believers neither deny their differences nor draw attention to them, lest they aggravate their outsiders even more. Paul would have them live quiet and independent lives, and paradoxically their invisibility in this area makes them more attractive to the outsider (4.11). As much as believers are to follow the rule of 'all' with regard to loving and pursuing good, they are, however, in all other areas to control their visibility among, and type of interaction with, outsiders (4.11). In this way they are to respect how others view them. Additionally, Paul recommends that the believers should recognize points of similarity between the two groups, and provides a concrete example of what this should look like: believers should 'walk honourably' with outsiders (4.12), which might even lead the outsiders to view the insiders with admiration. Outsiders hold a key position regarding the social identity of the believer, for what they think of believers has significant control over the growth or decline of the ingroup. However, Paul hopes that the believers still have the potential to transform their public image, even if it is via the art of sensitivity, by paying attention to intergroup difference and similarity and the impact this makes upon how others view and respond to them.

The book then moved on in Chapter 3 to explore two passages in Paul's letter to the believers in Rome. It was argued that, as for the Thessalonian believers, there is a serious element of hostility that characterizes intergroup relations, whereby some outsiders are persecuting insiders. However, contrary to the policy given to the Thessalonian believers, Paul urges the believers in Rome to make every effort to be seen, and to be seen in ways that will counter the narrative that is causing the current hostility. As such, by re-creating their public image it is hoped that believers can achieve peace in their society and even win praise. It would be purely speculative to propose a reason for the difference between Paul's course of action for the threatened believers in Thessalonica and that for those in Rome. Perhaps the hostility had reached such a level in Rome that the believers had no other choice but to adopt a more active response in the face of evil, or perhaps Paul had more confidence in the hope that the believer could achieve a transformation of public opinion. Either way, Paul once again is convinced that outsider opinion is of great importance to the formation and even existence of the ingroup. Not only this, but it is clear that negative opinions have the power to determine which of the ingroup norms need to be most salient.

This is because persecution urges the believers to understand themselves not just as the rightful recipients of God's blessing but also as the givers of God's blessings (Rom. 12.14). This is an important aspect of their identity, and, together with their identity as peacemakers and reconcilers (12.18), these aspects are those that, by their very nature, may only be truly or fully realized in the face of hostility. Furthermore, they are to concentrate on doing that which is seen and received as good by all (12.17), and are even to be ready and willing to care for the welfare of their enemies (12.20). Paul clearly appeals to a shared sense of what is good and right, and it is hoped that these actions will positively inform the outsiders' view of the insiders, and perhaps even lead to a complete reversal in the current public image of the believers.

This train of thought continues into Romans 13. Paul constructs a positive image of certain outsiders for the believers: the local authorities and rulers are working as God's agents in the world to praise what is good, and to punish what is evil. He indicates that both the insiders and these particular outsiders are working to uphold what is good, and that even outsiders have a divine commission (whether or not they recognize this as such). What these outsiders think of the insiders is important because, in theory at least, in some way it indicates what *God* thinks of the insiders. Paul therefore urges the believers to act accordingly to win public commendation (13.3). Praise rather than persecution is a realistic hope because of the existence of this contact point of what is known and experienced as 'good'.

As such, we find a reciprocal situation whereby the opinion held by outsiders of insiders has the power to shape and emphasize aspects of the ingroup's norms; but this in turn has the power to change public opinion of the insiders, which can then inform (and transform) the outgroup's behaviour towards the ingroup. Paul knows that a crucial element in this reciprocity of shaping opinions and behaviours of both groups (the cognitive and emotional aspects of social identity), is the recognition of a universal ethic, whether that is concerned with what is understood as καλός, or with social expectations in looking after those in need and in paying what is owed. These contact points of similarity create the potential for positive interaction and 'acquaintanceship' between groups (see Bar-Tal 1998: 111) leading to positive opinions of insiders. This in turn allows for the re-creation of public opinion, and therefore the pursuit of peace rather than the experience of persecution, and the gaining of praise, rather than of punishment. As such, whereas SIT proposes that difference between groups is important for the maintenance of group boundaries, Paul is aware that points of similarity between groups are important for the protection of group boundaries, owing to the importance of outsider opinion.

Chapter 4 explored 1 Corinthians and argued that in this letter, although Paul is clearly frustrated by the division and conflict that exists *within* the ingroup, he is keen to ensure that the believers are certain about one thing: that an important group norm is to show sensitivity and a concern for how others view them. Moreover, this letter demonstrates the juxtaposition outlined in Chapter 1: although Paul describes the outsiders in ways that are far from flattering, he is adamant that their opinion is so important that it should influence several dimensions of the life of the believer. As such, this group norm (of sensitivity to and concern for the opinions of others) is not simply about *noticing* but also about *responding* carefully to what others think: it therefore shapes other norms (e.g. their attitude towards being married to an unbeliever, 1 Corinthians 7; what they eat, 1 Corinthians 10, and how they worship, 1 Corinthians 14). It was found that in 1 Thessalonians and Romans there is an effort to identify and utilize 'contact points', those areas where there is a widespread acceptance of what is good and honourable. In 1 Corinthians, however, Paul points to the contact points that exist because of the types of interpersonal relationships and commitments that are already in operation across the group boundary. These relationships provide the arena for the believer to exercise this key norm and to discern how this in turn shapes other ingroup patterns and expectations.

However, the importance of this norm, and its influence on other ingroup norms, is not to do with self-preservation (cf. 1 Thessalonians and Romans); in fact, it was noted that there is a significant degree of social acceptance and a lack of intergroup conflict. Rather, the importance of this norm is rooted in Paul's missional hope for more to be saved: the motivation is to enlarge the boundaries of the ingroup to welcome more people who have converted to exclusive faith in Jesus Christ. The rights or freedoms of the ingroup take second place to the opinions of outsiders, and especially when these opinions would further alienate an outsider from the truth of the gospel. Although this missional motivation might be present in Paul's instructions to the believers in 1 Thessalonians and Romans, it is only explicitly announced in 1 Corinthians. It therefore becomes clear that a core understanding of the believers' identity is that they are missional disciples, and what others think of them indicates how well they are living out one of their purposes for existence, namely, to 'win' others for God. This all suggests that an important aspect in social identity is the presence and importance of the outgroup on the social identity of the ingroup, both in the daily application of practical aspects of life and worship, but also in the appreciation of a larger, soteriological framework in which the believers are to understand themselves as missional disciples. For Paul, writing to the believers in Corinth, the importance of what outsiders think is crucially connected to a major ingroup understanding of their goal and mission as disciples: to enlarge the boundaries to welcome more and more of those who were once 'outsiders' and who now find themselves declaring their own belief in Jesus Christ.

Finally, Chapter 5 turned to 1 Timothy and Titus and demonstrated how the Author reveals both an assumption and a recommendation that believers should have good relationships with those outside the faith community, or at the very least that they should show benevolence towards outsiders. Furthermore, the letters suggest that the concern over reputation and how outsiders view the church is not simply to do with the believing community having a positive or negative social identity among other outgroups, but also to do with the vocation of the believing community as being missional, as endeavouring to connect its behaviour among outsiders with the mission of God in the world, facilitated by gaining a positive reputation among outsiders. In 1 Timothy and Titus we find that there is indeed a recognition of the fact that the social identity of the believers cannot be formed in isolation: it is a combination of how they themselves understand their difference and their specific reason for existence, and also how others see and understand them, and ultimately, what they think of them. This resonates with the proposal in Jenkins that there is an 'internal–external dialectic' in the formation of the definition of an identity, so that it is a combination of internal self-definition and external definition by others (2008: 40, 42). The Author therefore encourages the believers to consider their reputation and the impact this has upon the outsiders' perception of the gospel. Women, slaves and Christian leaders in particular are to behave according to the standards and expectations of wider society, but the Author attaches to these shared values and expectations an understanding that these are divinely ordained and divinely evaluated: what others think is important, but this is contained within what God thinks. There is therefore not a denial or abandonment of a distinctive Christ-shaped lens with which to view life and to discern one's ethical behaviour, but rather a widening of this lens which includes how believers should view outsiders and vice versa.

Unsurprisingly, it was found that there is also a concern for the quality of intergroup relations, which in turn reveals a concern for the relationship between God and all people. The mere presence of outsiders should shape how believers pray and show their devotion, but the Author declares that they should engage in such worship with an attitude of thankfulness for outsiders, with a concern for their well-being and a desire for God to reveal his power and goodness among them (1 Tim. 2.1-7). Believers are to live their lives obediently and submissively to leaders, to watch how they conduct themselves in speech and in action, and to be focused on doing good works that will benefit all (Tit. 3.1-8). The attitude with which they are to conduct themselves among outsiders is to mirror that of God, especially the kindness and mercy they themselves received when they too were unbelievers, and which led to their conversion and salvation (3.3-7). And once more, integral to these instructions is the recognition of contact points, whereby the Author uses motifs and terminology (e.g. piety and good works) that would win approval for the believers from the outsiders. However, these verses are couched in a wider context that calls to mind the character of God as Saviour and the nature of God as one who desires and wills for all to be saved (1 Tim. 2.3-6; Tit. 3.3-7). For the Author, the attitude and behaviour of believers towards outsiders is intricately linked with the nature of God and the ongoing salvation work of the Holy Spirit: what others think is important because it is an indication of whether or not the believers are living out their vocation in revealing the true gospel where God is merciful and wants all to be saved.

Hence, we find that there is not such a great gap between the undisputed letter of 1 Corinthians, and the disputed epistles of 1 Timothy and Titus. These three letters are overtly concerned with how outsiders view and form an opinion of the believers, which is motivated by a concern for mission. And in 1 Timothy and Titus, we have seen that, whilst the Author does not diminish the importance of the differences between believers and unbelievers, he works to re-imagine these two groups belonging to a larger category that recognizes the sovereignty of God over all people, but also God's desire for all to be saved. It is important to notice the significance of this theological motif: the notion of the importance of outsiders is not simply for pragmatic reasons (to avoid conflict), but it is also hinting at a wider vision of the world as ordered by God. The importance of outsiders in the Author's thought reveals a vision of God's cosmic ordering, where, whilst there might be two categories of believers and unbelievers, these two groups are both part of a larger, all-encompassing cosmic group defined by God's desire for all to be saved. To understand the importance of outsiders is to have a deeper knowledge of the character and work of God in the world.

6.3 Social Identity Theory in Dialogue with the Pauline Corpus

Throughout this exploration, this book has additionally demonstrated that Social Identity Theory offers a theoretical vocabulary to enable insight into how group members understand their belonging. The insights of SIT provide us with the tools to explore how members belong to a social group and what binds them together with other members of that group (e.g. beliefs, expectations regarding behaviour and experiences), but also what distinguishes them from outgroup members and therefore where the boundary lies between who is 'in' and who is 'out'. SIT also recognizes the power that categorization and stereotyping has over how members should view themselves and those outside the group, and that normally this would be to discriminate against outgroup members and to show favouritism to ingroup members. However, whilst SIT is helpful in deepening an understanding of how Paul and the Author construct the difference between the believers and unbelievers and the boundary between the two, there are limitations in SIT. Since it is fixated on the creation and maintenance of difference, and because it tends to presume conflict with outgroups, it therefore ignores the importance and role of the outgroup in forming the social identity of the ingroup. As such, when applying SIT to the passages this book has explored, it has been found that it cannot explain the whole of these passages for it largely ignores the impact of the outsider on the insider. Perhaps this explains why, when scholars like Esler and Tucker (who have explicitly sought to understand different NT letters using SIT) have studied some of our passages, their exegesis and commentary is brief and lacking fresh insight: SIT is not equipped on its own to explore the importance of the outsider for the ingroup's social identity (see Section 3.4, note 53, for comments on Esler's very brief exploration of Romans 13, and Section 4.5 for comments on Tucker's work regarding 1 Corinthians 7, 10 and 14).

For, a significant finding in this study has been that, without undermining its difference or its identity, a group can remain highly conscious of the perspectives and opinions of outsiders and might even adjust its own (still different) identity accordingly, if there are good group reasons to do so (e.g. survival or growth). However, in practising sensitivity towards what others think, the ingroup recognizes areas of common opinion between the groups and makes use of these contact points to turn them into what I have termed 'attraction points'. Again, this does not need to diminish or destroy the group's own distinct identity. SIT focuses on differentiation where the bias is towards exploring difference and categorization; the work in this theory is helpful up to a point, but detailed study of the Pauline corpus shows that it is more complex than this. For, whilst Paul and the Author do work to highlight these differences, there are also occasions where the differences are muted and the similarities are highlighted and encouraged, to create a positive opinion in the eyes of the outsider. This finding in the Pauline corpus reveals an area where NT scholarship could aid in the development of social science theory, and not just deploy it as if it is fixed.

6.4 Conclusion and Implications for the Church

Undoubtedly, most teaching within the Pauline corpus is naturally inward-looking. Horrell writes, 'The ecclesial focus of Paul's ethics can hardly be missed', for Paul is concerned with the 'formation, relationships and behavioural norms of the assemblies of Christians' (2016: 271). But as Gaventa argues, 'For all his concern about building up the church's life, Paul is also concerned for the outsider ... For the church to understand itself as existing in isolation, set apart *from* the world rather than *for* it, is a gross misreading of Paul's letters' (2016: 98). Despite this, as Furnish also comments, there is a lack of 'extensive' studies exploring the importance of outsiders to Paul (2002: 106). This book has therefore aimed to reveal that for Paul and the Author, an understanding of the importance of the presence and the opinion of the outsider is integral to how the believers view themselves, God and their faith, discern which norms to prioritize in any given situation, decide how to change expectations for ingroup behaviour, and how to live out their vocation as missional disciples. At times the very existence of the faith community is in the hands of what others think and at the mercy of the public image of the ingroup; a negative opinion may lead to the ruthless persecution of believers. However, it is also true that the growth, development and maintenance of the faith community is also determined to some degree by what others think; for a positive opinion may lead to the salvation and conversion of outsiders into insiders, of unbelievers into believers.

Nevertheless, for Paul and the Author, the believers are not powerless in this; the key to gaining a positive opinion lies in the quality of relationship that the believers can create with their unbelieving neighbours. Sometimes these have already been formed because of social arrangements (as evident in 1 Corinthians) or because of political systems (Rom. 13.1-7; 1 Tim. 2.1-2; Tit. 3.1), and sometimes there needs to be an intentional desire for the believers to reconcile themselves with outsiders in the pursuit of peace (Rom. 12.18), or in the demonstration of respectability (1 Thess. 4.12). One aspect is certain, though: regardless of how these relationships are created or developed, an essential part involved in the gaining of a positive opinion is the revealing of areas of similarity between the two groups. These create contact points where positive relations may be formed between members of both groups, and which may lead to positive outsider opinions with the realistic hope that through this, God, who is the Saviour of all, may be praised.

Since this research concerns texts that have some normative roles for the contemporary church, its implications could be significant for faith communities today. For, this book raises serious questions around the level of impact outsiders should have on the decision-making of contemporary faith communities in different areas of faith and life. It calls the church to a greater awareness of the important place public opinion has in the faith, mission and vocation of the church, and it challenges the church to seek the voice and thoughts of the outsider when reviewing current norms and practices. The work of this book could be significant in the exploration of some of the ethical issues with which the church is wrestling today, including whether and how the opinion of the outgroup has been listened to in an attentive manner.

Moreover, this book raises the importance of the *specific* and *local* relationship between ingroup and outgroup. It was suggested in this book that local conditions in ingroup and outgroup relations may have played a role in the specific instructions given to the different faith communities, why there might be differences between them (e.g. around marriage and celibacy in the PEs and in 1 Corinthians) and how some norms are prioritized as being more visible to the outgroup over others. This might suggest that the church should consider the importance of the local level when making decisions, forming new norms, or amending existing ones that will be applied on a global level. This work has revealed that within the Pauline corpus there is an attentiveness to the specific dynamics in the relationship between the different faith communities and their different outgroups, and it is the specific and the local that often influences how faith communities are shaped. Clearly there are expectations and norms that are essential for any faith community despite its local and geographic location; however, this book has also found that there can be difference even between faith communities, on account of the importance of the different local outsiders. This book could therefore be extended to explore how the church can be attentive to the different specific local intergroup relations when making decisions regarding norms or vision that will be applied at a national or even global level.

As highlighted at the beginning of this research, the catalyst for this work was a remark made at a conference discussion regarding the role of women in the church. This remark criticized any anxiety for how the 'outside world' was viewing this debate, and even went so far as to say that 'outsiders should not influence our [the church's] decision-making'. Ironically, a few years ago I attended a national Church of England conference that was exploring a vision for the church, and a participant said that 'our priority' for this vision should not be in 'seeking human acceptance and approval'.

If, however, we take seriously the findings of this book, then the church needs to recognize and concede that any vision for mission and ministry must acknowledge and value the place that the outsider has, including their opinion (whether that is approval or condemnation), in the shaping, revealing and prioritizing of the patterns and norms of those who seek to live out the gospel of Christ. Furthermore, it is clear that for Paul and the Author, sometimes outsider opinion acts as a litmus test in discerning how successfully the faith community is revealing the attractiveness of living as disciples of Christ, but also that human approval can even signal divine approval (Romans 13). In the Pauline corpus, the ingroup's relationship with outsiders is more complex than one might automatically presume, and it is one that is intricately connected to the vocation and mission of the church. However, the importance of what others think is also deeply ingrained in how believers view and understand God. They are to know and believe that outsiders may be considered as such on one level (and justifiably so), but also that they are nevertheless part of a larger divine category where God sees them, incorporates them into his reign and plan for redemption, and expects for them to be loved, served, honoured, blessed and respected by the believers. The importance of what others think not only has a pragmatic impact upon the faith community, but the importance of outsiders is also deeply linked to the ingroup's own understanding of God, so that what others think is important because God thinks *they* are important. As such, seeking and responding to what others think should be at the heart of any vision of the church, regardless of location or generation, because it is at the heart of how God views and responds to the world.

References

Primary Sources

Aland, Barbara, Kurt Aland, Johannes Karavidopoulos, Carlo M. Martini and Bruce M. Metzger, eds. (1983), *The Greek New Testament*, 4th edn, Stuttgart: United Bible Societies.
Aristotle. (1936), *Minor Works: On Marvellous Things Heard*, trans. W.S. Hett, Loeb Classical Library, London: Heinemann.
Charlesworth, James H., ed. (1983), *Apocalyptic Literature and Testaments*. Vol. 1 of *The Old Testament Pseudepigrapha*, New York: Doubleday.
Josephus, Flavius. (2007), *Against Apion*, in *Flavius Josephus: Against Apion. A Translation and Commentary*, trans. J.M.G. Barclay, Leiden: Brill.
Juvenal. (1991), *Satires*, trans. Niall Rudd, Oxford: Clarendon.
Martinez, Florentino Garcia and Eibert J.C. Tigchelaar, eds, (1997-1998), *The Dead Sea Scrolls: Study Edition*, 2 vols, Grand Rapids, MI: Eerdmans.
Philo. (1929-1962), trans. by various authors, 10 vols, Loeb Classical Library, Cambridge, MA: Harvard University Press.
Plutarch. (1927-1976), *Moralia*, trans. by various authors, 15 vols, Loeb Classical Library, London: Heinemann.
Polycarp. (2003), *Letter to the Philippians*, in *The Apostolic Fathers*, ed. and trans. Bart D. Ehrman, 2 vols, Loeb Classical Library, Cambridge, MA: Harvard University Press.
Tacitus. (1937), *The Annals*, trans. C.H. Moore and J. Jackson, 4 vols, Loeb Classical Library, Cambridge, MA: Harvard University Press.

Secondary Sources

Aageson, James W. (2008), *Paul, the Pastoral Epistles, and the Early Church*, Peabody, MA: Hendrickson.
Adams, Edward. (2000), *Constructing the World: A Study in Paul's Cosmological Language*, Edinburgh: T&T Clark.
Balch, David L. (1981), *Let Wives be Submissive: The Domestic Code in 1 Peter*, Atlanta, GA: Scholars Press.
Barclay, John M.G. (1987), 'Mirror-Reading a Polemical Letter: Galatians as a Test Case', *Journal for the Study of the New Testament*, 10 (31): 73-93.
Barclay, John M.G. (1992), 'Thessalonica and Corinth: Social Contrasts in Pauline Christianity', *Journal for the Study of the New Testament*, 15 (47): 49-74.
Barclay, John M.G. (1993), 'Conflict in Thessalonica', *Catholic Biblical Quarterly*, 55 (3): 512-30.
Barclay, John M.G. (2020), 'Household Networks and Early Christian Economics: A Fresh Study of 1 Timothy 5.3-16', *New Testament Studies*, 66 (2): 268-87.

Barentsen, Jack. (2014), 'Stereotyping and Institutionalization as Indications of Leadership Maintenance in the Pastoral Epistles: 1 Timothy as a Test Case', in J. Brian Tucker and Coleman A. Baker (eds), *T&T Clark Handbook to Social Identity in the New Testament*, 389–406, London: Bloomsbury.

Bar-Tal, Daniel. (1990), *Group Beliefs: A Conception for Analyzing Group Structure, Processes and Behaviour*, New York: Springer-Verlag.

Bar-Tal, Daniel. (1998), 'Group Beliefs as an Expression of Social Identity', in Stephen Worchel, J. Francisco Morales, Darío Páez, and Jean-Claude Deschamps (eds), *Social Identity: International Perspectives*, 93–113, London: SAGE.

Bar-Tal, Daniel. (2000), *Shared Beliefs in a Society: Social Psychological Analysis*, London: SAGE.

Barrett, Charles Kingsley. (1957), *A Commentary on the Epistle to the Romans*, London: Black.

Barrett, Charles Kingsley. (1968), *A Commentary on the First Epistle to the Corinthians*, London: Black.

Barrett, Charles Kingsley. (1971), *The First Epistle to the Corinthians*, 2nd edn, London: Black.

Barrett, Charles Kingsley. (1991), *The Epistle to the Romans*, 2nd edn, London: Black.

Barth, Fredrik, ed. (1969), *Ethnic Groups and Boundaries: The Social Organization of Culture Difference*, Long Grove, IL: Waveland Press.

Barth, Karl. (1933), *The Epistle to the Romans*, trans. Edwyn C. Hoskyns, London: Oxford University Press.

Barth, Karl. (1959), *A Shorter Commentary on Romans*, trans. D.H. van Daalen, London: SCM.

Bassler, Jouette M. (1984), 'The Widows' Tale: A Fresh Look at 1 Tim 5:3–16', *Journal of Biblical Literature*, 103 (1): 23–41.

Bassler, Jouette M. (1996), *1 Timothy, 2 Timothy, Titus*, Nashville, TN: Abingdon.

Bauer, Walter, William F. Arndt, F. William Gingrich and Frederick W. Danker. (2000), *A Greek-English Lexicon of the New Testament and Other Early Christian Literature*, 3rd edn, Chicago, IL: University of Chicago Press.

Bergren, Theodore A. (1998), *Sixth Ezra: The Text and Origin*, Oxford: Oxford University Press.

Bertschmann, Dorothea H. (2014), 'The Good, the Bad and the State—Rom 13.1-7 and the Dynamics of Love', *New Testament Studies*, 60 (2): 232–49.

Best, Ernest. (1972), *A Commentary on the First and Second Epistles to the Thessalonians*, London: Black.

Betz, Hans Dieter. (1979), *Galatians: A Commentary on Paul's Letter to the Churches in Galatia*, Philadelphia: Fortress.

Beyer, H.W. (1964), 'εὐλογέω', in Gerhard Kittel and Gerhard Friedrich (eds), trans. Geoffrey W. Bromiley, *Theological Dictionary of the New Testament*, vol. 2, 754–65, Grand Rapids: Eerdmans.

Boyarin, Daniel. (1994), *A Radical Jew: Paul and the Politics of Identity*, Berkeley, CA: University of California Press.

Brown, Ernest Faulkner. (1917), *The Pastoral Epistles*, London: Methuen.

Brown, Rupert. (2000), *Group Processes: Dynamics Within and Between Groups*, 2nd edn, Oxford: Blackwell.

Bruce, Frederick Fyvie. (1985), *Romans*, 2nd edn, Nottingham: Inter-Varsity Press.

Bruce, Frederick Fyvie. (2015), *1 and 2 Thessalonians*, 2nd edn, Grand Rapids: Zondervan.

Büchsel, F. (1964), 'εἰδωλόθυτον', in Gerhard Kittel and Gerhard Friedrich (eds), trans. Geoffrey W. Bromiley, *Theological Dictionary of the New Testament*, vol. 2, 378–9, Grand Rapids, MI: Eerdmans.
Bultmann, Rudolf. (1924), 'Das Problem der Ethik bei Paulus', *Zeitschrift für die neutestamentliche Wissenschaft*, 23 (1): 123–40.
Campbell, William S. (2006), *Paul and the Creation of Christian Identity*, London: T&T Clark.
Capozza, Dora and Rupert Brown. (2000), 'Introduction: Social Identity Theory in Retrospect and Prospect', in Dora Capozza and Rupert Brown (eds), *Social Identity Processes: Trends in Theory and Research*, vii–xv, London: SAGE.
Cheung, Alex T. (1999), *Idol Food in Corinth: Jewish Background and Pauline Legacy*, Sheffield: Sheffield Academic Press.
Cole, R. Alan. (1989), *Galatians: An Introduction and Commentary*, 2nd edn, Nottingham: Inter-Varsity Press.
Collins, Raymond F. (1999), *First Corinthians*, Collegeville, MN: Liturgical Press.
Collins, Raymond F. (2002), *1 & 2 Timothy and Titus: A Commentary*, Louisville: Westminster John Knox.
Constantineanu, Corneliu. (2010), *The Social Significance of Reconciliation in Paul's Theology: Narrative Readings in Romans*, London: T&T Clark.
Conzelmann, Hans. (1975), *1 Corinthians*, Philadelphia, PA: Fortress.
Cranfield, C.E.B. (1975), *A Critical and Exegetical Commentary on The Epistle to the Romans*, vol. 1, Edinburgh: T&T Clark.
Cranfield, C.E.B. (1979), *A Critical and Exegetical Commentary on The Epistle to the Romans*, vol. 2, Edinburgh: T&T Clark.
Crisp, R.J., and M. Hewstone. (2000), 'Multiple Categorization and Social Identity', in Dora Capozza and Rupert Brown (eds), *Social Identity Processes: Trends in Theory and Research*, 149–66, London: SAGE.
Cullmann, Oscar. (1951), *Christ and Time: The Primitive Christian Conception of Time and History*, trans. F.V. Filson, London: SCM.
Cullmann, Oscar. (1957), *The State in the New Testament*, London: SCM.
Davies, Margaret. (1996), *The Pastoral Epistles*, Sheffield: Sheffield Academic Press.
Deming, Will. (2004), *Paul on Marriage and Celibacy: The Hellenistic Background of 1 Corinthians 7*, Grand Rapids, MI: Eerdmans.
Deschamps, J.C., and W. Doise. (1978), 'Crossed Category Memberships in Intergroup Relations', in Henri Tajfel (ed.), *Differentiation between Social Groups: Studies in the Social Psychology of Intergroup Relations*, 141–58, London: Academic Press.
Dibelius, Martin. (1909), *Die Geisterwelt im Glauben des Paulus*, Göttingen: Vandenhoeck & Ruprecht.
Dibelius, Martin. (1925), *An die Thessalonicher I II an die Philipper*, Tübingen: Mohr Siebeck.
Dibelius, Martin and Hans Conzelmann. (1972), *The Pastoral Epistles*, trans. P. Buttolph and A. Yarbro, Philadelphia, PA: Fortress.
Dobschütz, Ernst von. (1974), *Die Thessalonicher-Briefe*, 7th edn, Göttingen: Vandenhoeck & Ruprecht.
Dovidio, J.F., A. Validzic and S.L. Gaertner. (1998), 'Intergroup Bias: Status, Differentiation, and a Common In-Group Identity', *Journal of Personality and Social Psychology* 75 (1): 109–20.
Dunn, James D.G. (1988a), *Romans 1-8*, Nashville: Nelson.
Dunn, James D.G. (1988b), *Romans 9-16*, Dallas: Word Books.

Dunn, James D.G. (1993), *A Commentary on the Epistle to the Galatians*, London: Black.
Elliott, N. (1997), 'Romans 13:1-7 in the Context of Imperial Propaganda', in Richard A. Horsley (ed.), *Paul and Empire*, 184–204, Harrisburg: Trinity Press International.
Engberg-Pedersen, Troels. (2000), *Paul and the Stoics*, Edinburgh: T&T Clark.
Esler, Philip F. (1998), *Galatians*, London: Routledge.
Esler, Philip F. (2003), *Conflict and Identity in Romans: The Social Setting of Paul's Letter*, Minneapolis, MN: Fortress.
Eubank, Nathan. (2017), 'Damned Disciples: The Permeability of the Boundary between Insiders and Outsiders in Matthew and Paul', in Michal Bar-Asher Siegal, Wolfgang Grünstäudl and Matthew Thiessen (eds), *Perceiving the Other in Ancient Judaism and Early Christianity*, 33–48, Tübingen: Mohr Siebeck.
Fee, Gordon D. (1987), *The First Epistle to the Corinthians*, Grand Rapids, MI: Eerdmans.
Fee, Gordon D. (1988), *1 and 2 Timothy, Titus*, 2nd edn, Peabody: Hendrickson.
Fee, Gordon D. (2009), *The First and Second Letters to the Thessalonians*, Cambridge: Eerdmans.
Finney, Mark T. (2013), *Honour and Conflict in the Ancient World: 1 Corinthians in its Greco-Roman Social Setting*, London: T&T Clark.
Fitzmyer, Joseph A. (1993), *Romans*, New York: Doubleday.
Fitzmyer, Joseph A. (2008), *First Corinthians*, New Haven, CT: Yale University Press.
Flemming, Dean. (2002), 'Contextualizing the Gospel in Athens: Paul's Areopagus Address as a Paradigm for Missionary Communication', *Missiology*, 30 (2): 199–214.
Foerster, Werner. (1959), 'εὐσεβής, εὐσέβεια, εὐσεβέω', in Gerhard Kittel and Gerhard Friedrich (eds), trans. Geoffrey W. Bromiley, *Theological Dictionary of the New Testament*, vol. 7, 175–85, Grand Rapids, MI: Eerdmans.
Furnish, Victor Paul. (1984), *II Corinthians*, New York: Doubleday.
Furnish, Victor Paul. (2002), 'Inside Looking Out: Some Pauline Views of the Unbelieving Public', in Janice Capel Anderson, Philip Sellew and Claudia Setzer (eds), *Pauline Conversations in Context: Essays in Honor of Calvin J. Roetzel*, 104–24, London: Sheffield Academic Press.
Furnish, Victor Paul. (2009), *The Moral Teaching of Paul*, 3rd edn, Nashville, TN: Abingdon Press.
Gaertner, S.L., J.F. Dovidio, J.A. Nier, B.S. Banker, C.M. Ward, M. Houlette and S. Loux. (2000), 'The Common Ingroup Identity Model for Reducing Intergroup Bias: Progress and Challenges', in Dora Capozza and Rupert Brown (eds), *Social Identity Processes: Trends in Theory and Research*, 133–48, London: SAGE.
Garland, David E. (2003), *1 Corinthians*, Grand Rapids, MI: Baker Academic.
Gaventa, Beverly Roberts. (2016), *When in Rome: An Invitation to Linger with the Gospel according to Paul*, Grand Rapids, MI: Baker Academic.
Gladstone, R.J. (1999), 'Sign Language in the Assembly: How are Tongues a Sign to the Unbeliever in 1 Cor 14:20-25?', *Asian Journal of Pentecostal Studies* 2 (2): 177–93.
Gooch, Peter David. (1993), *Dangerous Food: 1 Corinthians 8-10 in Its Context*, Waterloo, ON: Wilfrid Laurier University Press.
Greeven, Heinrich. (1964), 'εὐσχήμων', in Gerhard Kittel and Gerhard Friedrich (eds), trans. Geoffrey W. Bromiley, *Theological Dictionary of the New Testament*, vol. 2, 770–2, Grand Rapids, MI: Eerdmans.
Grosheide, Frederik Willem. (1953), *Commentary on the First Epistle to the Corinthians*, Grand Rapids, MI: Eerdmans.
Halbwachs, Maurice. (1992), *On Collective Memory*, trans. Lewis A. Coser, Chicago, IL: University of Chicago Press.

Harris, Murray J. (2005), *The Second Epistle to the Corinthians: A Commentary on the Greek Text*, Milton Keynes: Paternoster Press.
Hauck, Friedrich. (1965), 'ἀκάθαρτος, ἀκαθαρσία', in Gerhard Kittel and Gerhard Friedrich (eds), trans. Geoffrey W. Bromiley, *Theological Dictionary of the New Testament*, vol. 3, 427–9, Grand Rapids, MI: Eerdmans.
Hays, Richard B. (1997), *First Corinthians*, Louisville, KY: John Knox.
Héring, Jean. (1949), *La Première Épitre de Saint Paul aux Corinthiens*, Paris: Delachaux & Niestlé.
Hinkle, Steve, Laurie A. Taylor, Lee Fox-Cardamone, and Pamela G. Ely. (1998), 'Social Identity and Aspects of Social Creativity: Shifting to New Dimensions of Intergroup Comparison', in Stephen Worchel, J. Francisco Morales, Darío Páez and Jean-Claude Deschamps (eds), *Social Identity: International Perspectives*, 166–79, London: SAGE.
Ho, Chiao Ek. (2000), 'Do the Work of an Evangelist: The Missionary Outlook of the Pastoral Epistles', PhD thesis, University of Aberdeen.
Hock, Ronald F. (1980), *The Social Context of Paul's Ministry: Tentmaking and Apostleship*, Philadelphia, PA: Fortress.
Hogg, Michael A. and Dominic Abrams. (1988), *Social Identifications: A Social Psychology of Intergroup Relations and Group Processes*, London: Routledge.
Hoklotubbe, T. Christopher. (2017), *Civilized Piety: The Rhetoric of Pietas in the Pastoral Epistles and the Roman Empire*, Waco, TX: Baylor University Press.
Holtz, Traugott. (1986), *Der erste Brief an die Thessalonicher*, Zürich: Benziger.
Horrell, David G. (1996), *The Social Ethos of the Corinthian Correspondence: Interests and Ideology from 1 Corinthians to 1 Clement*, Edinburgh: T&T Clark.
Horrell, David G. (2005), *Solidarity and Difference: A Contemporary Reading of Paul's Ethics*, London: T&T Clark.
Horrell, David G. (2016), *Solidarity and Difference: A Contemporary Reading of Paul's Ethics*, 2nd edn, London: T&T Clark.
Hurd, John Coolidge. (1965), *The Origins of 1 Corinthians*, London: SPCK.
Jenkins, Richard. (2008), *Social Identity*, 3rd edn, London: Routledge.
Jeremias, Joachim. (1954), 'Die missionarische Aufgabe in der Mischehe', in Walther Eltester (ed.), *Neutestamentliche Studien Für Rudolf Bultmann*, 255–60, Berlin: Töpelmann.
Jewett, Robert. (1986), *The Thessalonian Correspondence: Pauline Rhetoric and Millenarian Piety*, Philadelphia, PA: Fortress.
Jewett, Robert. (2000), 'Response: Exegetical Support from Romans and Other Letters', in Richard A. Horsley (ed.), *Paul and Politics: Ekklesia, Israel, Imperium, Interpretation. Essays in Honor of Krister Stendahl*, 58–71, Harrisburg, PA: Trinity Press International.
Jewett, Robert. (2007), *Romans: A Commentary*, Philadelphia, PA: Fortress.
Jobes, Karen H. (2005), *1 Peter*, Grand Rapids, MI: Baker Academic.
Johnson, Luke Timothy. (2001), *The First and Second Letters to Timothy*, New York: Doubleday.
Käsemann, Ernst. (1980), *Commentary on Romans*, London: SCM.
Keck, Leander E. (2005), *Romans*, Nashville, TN: Abingdon.
Keener, Craig S. (2018), *Galatians*, Cambridge: Cambridge University Press.
Kelly, John Norman Davidson. (1963), *A Commentary on the Pastoral Epistles. 1 Timothy, 2 Timothy, Titus*, London: Black.
Kiecolt, K. Jill. (1994), 'Stress and the Decision to Change Oneself: A Theoretical Model', *Social Psychology Quarterly*, 57 (1): 49–63.

Kim, Seyoon. (2008), *Christ and Caesar: The Gospel and the Roman Empire in the Writings of Paul and Luke*, Cambridge: Eerdmans.
Klassen, William. (1963), 'Coals of Fire: Sign of Repentance or Revenge?', *New Testament Studies*, 9 (4): 337–50.
Klassen, William. (1984), *Love of Enemies: The Way to Peace*, Philadelphia, PA: Fortress.
Knight, George William. (1992), *The Pastoral Epistles: A Commentary on the Greek Text*, Carlisle: Paternoster.
Kok, Jacobus, Tobias Nicklas, Dieter T. Roth, and Christopher M. Hays, eds (2014), *Sensitivity towards Outsiders: Exploring the Dynamic Relationship between Mission and Ethics in the New Testament and Early Christianity*, Tübingen: Mohr Siebeck.
Kok, Jacobus and Dieter T. Roth. (2014), 'Sensitivity towards Outsiders and the Dynamic Relationship between Mission and Ethics/Ethos', in Jacobus Kok, Tobias Nicklas, Dieter T. Roth, and Christopher M. Hays (eds), *Sensitivity towards Outsiders: Exploring the Dynamic Relationship between Mission and Ethics in the New Testament and Early Christianity*, 1–23, Tübingen: Mohr Siebeck.
Köstenberger, Andreas J. (2019), 'An Investigation of the Mission Motif in the Letters to Timothy and Titus with Implications for the Pauline Authorship of the Pastoral Epistles', *Bulletin for Biblical Research*, 29 (1): 49–64.
Lane Fox, Robin. (1986), *Pagans and Christians*, London: Penguin.
Lang, T.J. (2018), 'Trouble with Insiders: The Social Profile of the ἄπιστοι in Paul's Corinthian Correspondence', *Journal of Biblical Literature*, 137 (4): 981–1001.
Lawler, Steph. (2008), *Identity: Sociological Perspectives*, London: Polity.
Leenhardt, Franz J. (1961), *The Epistle to the Romans: A Commentary*, trans. H. Knight, London: Lutterworth.
Lefkowitz, Mary R., and Maureen B. Fant. (2005), *Women's Life in Greece and Rome*, 3rd edn, London: Bloomsbury Academic.
Lietzmann, Hans. (1949), *An Die Korinther 1-11*, Tübingen: Mohr Siebeck.
Lieu, Judith M. (2004), *Christian Identity in the Jewish and Graeco-Roman World*, Oxford: Oxford University Press.
Lockwood, Gregory J. (2000), *1 Corinthians*, St. Louis: Concordia.
Longenecker, Bruce W. (1995), *2 Esdras*, Sheffield: Sheffield Academic Press.
MacDonald, Margaret Y. (1988), *The Pauline Churches: A Socio-Historical Study of Institutionalization in the Pauline and Deutero-Pauline Writings*, Cambridge: Cambridge University Press.
MacDonald, Margaret Y. (1996), *Early Christian Women and Pagan Opinion: The Power of the Hysterical Woman*, Cambridge: Cambridge University Press.
Malherbe, Abraham J. (2000), *The Letters to the Thessalonians: A New Translation with Introduction and Commentary*, New Haven, CT: Yale University Press.
Marshall, Howard. (1991), *The Epistle to the Philippians*, London: Epworth.
Marshall, Howard. (1999), *The Pastoral Epistles*, Edinburgh: T&T Clark.
Martin, Ralph P. (1986), *2 Corinthians*, Waco, TX: Word.
Martyn, J. Louis. (1997), *Galatians*, London: Yale University Press.
Matera, Frank J. (1992), *Galatians*, Collegeville, MN: Liturgical Press.
May, Alistair Scott. (2004), *'The Body for the Lord': Sex and Identity in 1 Corinthians 5-7*, London: T&T Clark International.
Meeks, Wayne A. (1983), *The First Urban Christians: The Social World of the Apostle Paul*, London: Yale University Press.
Meiser, Martin. (2007), *Galater*, Göttingen: Vandenhoeck & Ruprecht.

Moffatt, James. (1938), *The First Epistle of Paul to the Corinthians*, London: Hodder & Stoughton.
Moo, Douglas J. (1996), *The Epistle to the Romans*, Cambridge: Eerdmans.
Moo, Douglas J. (2018), *The Letter to the Romans*, 2nd edn, Grand Rapids, MI: Eerdmans.
Morris, Leon. (1988), *The Epistle to the Romans*, Leicester: Inter-Varsity Press.
Morris, Leon. (1991), *The First and Second Epistles to the Thessalonians*, Grand Rapids, MI: Eerdmans.
Mounce, William D. (2000), *Pastoral Epistles*, Nashville, TN: Nelson.
Muir, Steven. (2014), 'Social Identity in the Epistle to the Hebrews', in J. Brian Tucker and Coleman A. Baker (eds), *T&T Clark Handbook to Social Identity in the New Testament*, 425–40, London: Bloomsbury.
Murphy-O'Connor, Jerome. (1991), *The Theology of the Second Letter to the Corinthians*, Cambridge: Cambridge University Press.
Murphy-O'Connor, Jerome. (2009), *Keys to First Corinthians: Revisiting the Major Issues*, Oxford: Oxford University Press.
Nanos, Mark D. (1996), *The Mystery of Romans: The Jewish Context of Paul's Letter*, Philadelphia, PA: Fortress.
Neil, William. (1950), *The Epistle of Paul to the Thessalonians*, London: Hodder & Stoughton.
Ngewa, Samuel M. (2010), *Galatians*, Grand Rapids, MI: Zondervan.
Osiek, Carolyn. (1992), *What Are They Saying about the Social Setting of the New Testament?*, New York: Paulist.
Osiek, Carolyn. (2000), *Philippians, Philemon*, Nashville, TN: Abingdon.
Páez, Darío, Christina Martinez-Taboada, Juan José Arróspide, Patricia Insúa and Sabino Ayestarán. (1998), 'Constructing Social Identity: The Role of Status, Collective Values, Collective Self-Esteem, Perception and Social Behaviour', in Stephen Worchel, J. Francisco Morales, Darío Páez and Jean-Claude Deschamps (eds), *Social Identity: International Perspectives*, 211–29, London: SAGE.
Parker, Holt. (1998), 'Loyal Slaves and Loyal Wives: The Crisis of the Outsider-Within and Roman Exemplum Literature', in Sandra R. Joshel and Sheila Murnaghan (eds), *Women and Slaves in Greco-Roman Culture: Differential Equations*, 152–73, London: Routledge.
Patterson, Orlando. (1982), *Slavery and Social Death: A Comparative Study*, Cambridge, MA: Harvard University Press.
Peerbolte, B.L. (2014), 'Morality and Boundaries in Paul', in Jacobus Kok, Tobias Nicklas, Dieter Roth and Christopher M. Hays (eds), *Sensitivity towards Outsiders: Exploring the Dynamic Relationship between Mission and Ethics in the New Testament and Early Christianity*, 209–24, Tübingen: Mohr Siebeck.
Peng, Kuo-Wei. (2006), *Hate the Evil, Hold Fast to the Good: Structuring Romans 12.1-15.13*, London: T&T Clark.
Portefaix, Lilian. (2003), '"Good Citizenship" in the Household of God: Women's Position in the Pastorals Reconsidered in the Light of Roman Rule', in Amy-Jill Levine (ed.), *A Feminist Companion to the Deutero-Pauline Epistles*, 147–58, London: T & T Clark.
Preisker, Herbert. (1964), 'ἔπαινος', 586–8 in Gerhard Kittel and Gerhard Friedrich (eds), trans. Geoffrey W. Bromiley, *Theological Dictionary of the New Testament*, vol. 2, 586–8, Grand Rapids, MI: Eerdmans.
Procksch, Otto. (1964), 'ἁγιάζω', in Gerhard Kittel and Gerhard Friedrich (eds), trans. Geoffrey W. Bromiley, *Theological Dictionary of the New Testament*, vol. 1, 111–12, Grand Rapids. MI: Eerdmans.

Punt, J. (2014), 'Mission, Ethics, and Outsiders/Insiders in Galatians', in Jacobus Kok, Tobias Nicklas, Dieter T. Roth, and Christopher M. Hays (eds), *Sensitivity towards Outsiders: Exploring the Dynamic Relationship between Mission and Ethics in the New Testament and Early Christianity*, 225–45, Tübingen: Mohr Siebeck.

Quinn, Jerome D., and William C. Wacker. (2000), *The First and Second Letters to Timothy: A New Translation with Notes and Commentary*, Grand Rapids, MI: Eerdmans.

Rabens, V. (2014), 'Inclusion of and Demarcation from "Outsiders": Mission and Ethics in Paul's Second Letter to the Corinthians', in Jacobus Kok, Tobias Nicklas, Dieter T. Roth, and Christopher M. Hays (eds), *Sensitivity towards Outsiders: Exploring the Dynamic Relationship between Mission and Ethics in the New Testament and Early Christianity*, 290–323, Tübingen: Mohr Siebeck.

Richard, Earl J. (1995), *First and Second Thessalonians*, Collegeville, MN: Liturgical Press.

Robertson, Archibald and Alfred Plummer. (1911), *A Critical and Exegetical Commentary on the First Epistle of St Paul to the Corinthians*, Edinburgh: T&T Clark.

Roloff, Jürgen. (1988), *Der erste Brief an Timotheus*, Zürich: Benziger Verlag.

Saller, Richard P. (1994), *Patriarchy, Property and Death in the Roman Family*, Cambridge: Cambridge University Press.

Sanday, William and Arthur Cayley Headlam. (1902), *A Critical and Exegetical Commentary on the Epistle to the Romans*, Edinburgh: T&T Clark.

Schellenberg, Ryan S. (2018), 'Subsistence, Swapping, and Paul's Rhetoric of Generosity', *Journal of Biblical Literature*, 137 (1): 215–34.

Schlatter, Adolf. (1958), *Die Kirche der Griechen im Urteil des Paulus: Eine Auslegung seiner Briefe an Timotheus und Titus*, 2nd edn, Stuttgart: Calwer Verlag.

Schlier, Heinrich. (1965), 'ἰδιώτης', in Gerhard Kittel and Gerhard Friedrich (eds), trans. Geoffrey W. Bromiley, *Theological Dictionary of the New Testament*, 215–17, vol. 3, Grand Rapids, MI: Eerdmans.

Schmithals, Walter. (1988), *Der Römerbrief: Ein Kommentar*, Gütersloh: Mohn.

Schnelle, U. (1990), 'Die Ethik des 1. Thessalonicherbriefes', in R.F. Collins (ed.), *The Thessalonian Correspondence*, 295–305, Leuven: Leuven University Press.

Schrage, Wolfgang. (1995), *Der erste Brief an die Korinther*, vol. 2, Düsseldorf: Benziger.

Schrage, Wolfgang. (2012), *Der erste Brief an die Korinther*, vol. 3, 2nd edn, Neukirchen-Vluyn: Neukirchener Theologie.

Schreiner, Thomas R. (1998), *Romans*, Grand Rapids, MI: Baker Academic.

Schrenk, Gottlob. (1965), 'ἱερόθυτος', in Gerhard Kittel and Gerhard Friedrich (eds), trans. Geoffrey W. Bromiley, *Theological Dictionary of the New Testament*, 252–3, vol. 3, Grand Rapids, MI: Eerdmans.

Schweitzer, Albert. (1931), *The Mysticism of Paul the Apostle*, trans. W. Montgomery, London: Black.

Seifrid, Mark A. (2014), *The Second Letter to the Corinthians*, Cambridge: Eerdmans.

Silva, Moisés. (2005), *Philippians*, 2nd edn, Grand Rapids, MI: Baker Academic.

Smit, Joop. (2000), *'About the Idol Offerings': Rhetoric, Social Context and Theology of Paul's Discourse in First Corinthians 8:1-11:1*, Leuven: Peeters.

Soden, H.F. von. (1964), 'Sakrament und Ethik bei Paulus. Zur Frage der literarischen und theologischen Einheitlichkeit von 1. Kor. 8 – 10' in Ulrich Luck and Karl Heinrich Rengstorf (eds), *Das Paulusbild in der Neueren Deutschen Forschung*, 338–79, Darmstadt: Wissenschaftliche Buchgesellschaft.

Stets, Jan E., and Michael J. Carter. (2006), 'The Moral Identity: A Principle Level Identity', in Kent A. McClelland and Thomas J. Fararo (eds), *Purpose, Meaning, and Action: Control Systems Theories in Sociology*, 293–313, New York: Palgrave-Macmillan.

Still, Todd D. (1999), *Conflict at Thessalonica: A Pauline Church and its Neighbours*, Sheffield: Sheffield Academic Press.
Still, Todd D. and Natalie R. Webb. (2014), '"Aliens" among "Pagans", "Exiles" among "Gentiles": Authorial Strategy and (Social) Identity in 1 Peter', in J. Brian Tucker and Coleman A. Baker (eds), *T&T Clark Handbook to Social Identity in the New Testament*, 455–72, London: Bloomsbury.
Strobel, A. (1956), 'Zum Verständnis von Rm 13', *Zeitschrift für die neutestamentliche Wissenschaft*, 47 (1): 67–93.
Stryker, Sheldon and Peter J. Burke. (2000), 'The Past, Present, and Future of an Identity Theory', *Social Psychology Quarterly*, 63 (4): 284–97.
Stuhlmacher, Peter. (1994), *Paul's Letter to the Romans: A Commentary*, Edinburgh: T&T Clark.
Tajfel, Henri. (1970), 'Experiments in Intergroup Discrimination', *Scientific American*, 223 (5): 96–102.
Tajfel, Henri., ed. (1978), *Differentiation between Social Groups: Studies in the Social Psychology of Intergroup Relations*, London: Academic.
Tajfel, Henri. (1981), *Human Groups and Social Categories: Studies in Social Psychology*, Cambridge: Cambridge University Press.
Tajfel, Henri., M.G. Billig, R.P. Bundy and C. Flament. (1971), 'Social Categorization and Intergroup Behaviour', *European Journal of Social Psychology*, 1 (2): 149–78.
Tajfel, Henri and J. Turner. (1979), 'An Integrative Theory of Intergroup Conflict', in William G. Austin and Stephen Worchel (eds), *The Social Psychology of Intergroup Relations*, 33–47, California: Brooks/Cole.
Theissen, Gerd and Petra von Gemünden. (2016), *Der Römerbrief: Rechenschaft eines Reformators*, Göttingen: Vandenhoeck & Ruprecht.
Thiselton, Anthony C. (2000), *The First Epistle to the Corinthians: A Commentary on the Greek Text*, Grand Rapids, MI: Eerdmans.
Thorsteinsson, Runar M. (2010), *Roman Christianity and Roman Stoicism: A Comparative Study of Ancient Morality*, Oxford: Oxford University Press.
Towner, Philip H. (1989), *The Goal of our Instruction: The Structure of Theology and Ethics in the Pastoral Epistles*, Sheffield: Sheffield Academic Press.
Towner, Philip H. (2006), *The Letters to Timothy and Titus*, Cambridge: Eerdmans.
Trebilco, Paul. (2004), *The Early Christians in Ephesus from Paul to Ignatius*, Grand Rapids, MI: Eerdmans.
Trebilco, Paul. (2014), 'Creativity at the Boundary: Features of the Linguistic and Conceptual Construction of Outsiders in the Pauline Corpus', *New Testament Studies*, 60 (2): 85–201.
Trebilco, Paul. (2017), *Outsider Designations and Boundary Construction in the New Testament: Early Christian Communities and the Formation of Group Identity*, Cambridge: Cambridge University Press.
Tucker, J. Brian. (2010), *You Belong to Christ: Paul and the Formation of Social Identity in 1 Corinthians 1—4*, Eugene, OR: Pickwick.
Tucker, J. Brian. (2014), 'Paul's Particular problem—The Continuation of Existing Identities in Philemon', in J. Brian Tucker and Coleman A. Baker (eds), *T&T Clark Handbook to Social Identity in the New Testament*, 407–24, London: Bloomsbury.
Tucker, J. Brian. (2017), *Reading 1 Corinthians*, Eugene, OR: Cascade.
Tucker, J. Brian and Coleman A. Baker, eds, (2014), *T&T Clark Handbook to Social Identity in the New Testament*, London: Bloomsbury.

Turner, John. (1978), 'Social Categorization and Social Discrimination in the Minimal Group Paradigm', in Henri Tajfel (ed), *Differentiation between Social Groups: Studies in the Social Psychology of Intergroup Relations*, 101–33, London: Academic.
Turner, John. (1987), *Rediscovering the Social Group: A Self-Categorization Theory*, Oxford: Basil Blackwell.
Unnik, Willem Cornelis van. (1980), 'Die Rücksicht auf die Reaktion der Nicht-Christen als Motiv in der altchristlichen Paränese' in *Sparsa Collecta, Part Two: The Collected Essays of W.C. Van Unnik*, 307–22, Leiden: Brill.
Verner, David C. (1983), *The Household of God: The Social World of the Pastoral Epistles*, Atlanta, GA: Scholars Press.
Wagener, Ulrike. (1994), *Die Ordnung des 'Hauses Gottes': Der Ort von Frauen in der Ekklesiologie und Ethik der Pastoralbriefe*, Tübingen: Mohr Siebeck.
Walters, James Christopher. (1993), *Ethnic Issues in Paul's Letter to the Romans: Changing Self-Definitions in Earliest Roman Christianity*, Philadelphia, PA: Trinity Press International.
Wanamaker, Charles A. (1990), *The Epistles to the Thessalonians: A Commentary on the Greek Text*, Grand Rapids, MI: Eerdmans.
Watson, Duane F. (1989), '1 Corinthians 10:23-11:1 in the Light of Greco-Roman Rhetoric: The Role of Rhetorical Questions', *Journal of Biblical Literature*, 108 (2): 301–18.
Weima, Jeffrey A.D. (2014), *1–2 Thessalonians*, Grand Rapids, MI: Baker Academic.
Wendland, Heinz Dietrich. (1980), *Die Briefe an die Korinther*, Göttingen: Vandenhoeck & Ruprecht.
Wiedemann, Thomas E.J. (1987), *Slavery*, Oxford: Clarendon.
Wilckens, Ulrich. (1978), *Der Brief an die Römer (Röm 1–5)*, Zürich: Benziger.
Wilckens, Ulrich. (1982), *Der Brief an die Römer (Röm 12–16)*, Zürich: Benziger.
Williams, Thomas. (1962), 'The Curses of Bouzyges: New Evidence', *Mnemosyne*, 15 (4): 396–8.
Williams, Travis B. (2014), *Good Works in 1 Peter: Negotiating Social Conflict and Christian Identity in the Greco-Roman World*, Tübingen: Mohr Siebeck.
Willis, Wendell Lee. (1985), *Idol Meat in Corinth: The Pauline Argument in 1 Corinthians 8 and 10*, Chico, CA: Scholars Press.
Wilson, Walter T. (1990), *Love without Pretense: Romans 12.9–21 and Hellenistic-Jewish Wisdom Literature*, Tübingen: Mohr Siebeck.
Winter, Bruce W. (1994), *Seek the Welfare of the City: Christians as Benefactors and Citizens*, Grand Rapids, MI: Eerdmans.
Winter, Bruce W. (2003), *Roman Wives, Roman Widows. The Appearance of New Women and the Pauline Communities*, Cambridge: Eerdmans.
Witherington, Ben. (1993), 'Not So Idle Thoughts about Eidolothuton', *Tyndale Bulletin*, 44 (2): 237–54.
Witherington, Ben. (1995), *Conflict and Community in Corinth: A Socio-Rhetorical Commentary on 1 and 2 Corinthians*, Grand Rapids, MI: Eerdmans.
Witherington, Ben. (2004), *Paul's Letter to the Romans: A Socio-Rhetorical Commentary*, Cambridge: Eerdmans.
Witherington, Ben. (2006a), *1 and 2 Thessalonians: A Socio-Rhetorical Commentary*, Cambridge: Eerdmans.
Witherington, Ben. (2006b), *Letters and Homilies for Hellenized Christians, Vol 1: A Socio-Rhetorical Commentary on Titus, 1–2 Timothy and 1–3 John*, Leicester: Apollos.
Wolter, Michael. (2009), *Theologie und Ethos im frühen Christentum*, Tübingen: Mohr Siebeck.

Wright, Nicholas Thomas. (2005), *Paul: Fresh Perspectives*, London: SPCK.
Yinger, Kent L. (1998), 'Romans 12:14–21 and Nonretaliation in Second Temple Judaism: Addressing Persecution within the Community', *Catholic Biblical Quarterly*, 60 (1): 74–96.
Zerbe, Gordon M. (1993), *Non-Retaliation in Early Jewish and New Testament Texts: Ethical Themes in Social Contexts*, Sheffield: JSOT Press.
Ziesler, John. (1989), *Paul's Letter to the Romans*, London: SCM.

Index of Biblical References

OLD TESTAMENT

Genesis
1.28	65
12.2	65
13.16	65
17.3	119
27	64
48.15	64
49.25-26	64, 65

Exodus
14.13-31	147
15.2	147

Deuteronomy
28.1-13	65
32.35	65

Joshua
15.19 LXX	64

2 Samuel
12.22 LXX	103
13.19	71
22.9, 13	70

1 Kings
19.3-9	147

2 Kings
5.15 LXX	65

1 Chronicles
16.35	147

Esther
4.14 LXX	103

Job
1.7-10	64
1.9	63
4.7-9	64
8.3-6, 13, 20	64
11.1-6	64
18.5-21	64

Psalms
17.9, 13 LXX	70
21.26 LXX	79
24.1	106
24.4-5	63
25.5	147
27.9	147
68.19	147
79.9	147
116.8	147
139.9 LXX	70

Isaiah
12.2	147
28.11-12	119, 120
43.3, 11	147

Ezekiel
1.13, 28 LXX	70
36.29	147

Daniel
2.21, 37-38	75
4.17, 25, 32 LXX	75
5.18	75
5.21	75
6.19-22	147
6.26-27	147

Hosea
13.4	147

Joel
2.14 LXX	103

Jonah
3.9 LXX	103

Index of Biblical References

Micah
7.7	147

Habakkuk
3.18	147

Zephaniah
3.17	147

APOCRYPHA

Wisdom of Solomon
6.1, 3, 5	75

Sirach
8.10	70

2 Esdras
15–16	71

NEW TESTAMENT

Matthew
1.21	147
5.13-16	68
5.31-32	99
5.44	63
8.9	74
12.17	81
19.3-12	99
28.18	75

Mark
10.2-12	99
15.43	41

Luke
1.46-55	147
1.47	147
6.27-28	63
7.8	74
11.48	99
12.11	74
16.18	99
19.17	74
20.20	74
23.7	74, 75

John
19.10, 11	74

Acts
4.13	117
5.29, 32	151
8.1	99
13.48	76
13.50	41
15.2	76
17.6-7	45
17.12	41
17.16-34	125 n.12
18.2	76
22.10	76
22.20	99
24.16	112
27.21	151
28.23	76

Romans
1–2	6
1.3	57
1.5-6	58, 93
1.6	57
1.7	1, 58, 93
1.8	58, 93, 141
1.8-15	132
1.10-11	58
1.12	58, 82
1.13	57, 58
1.16	13
1.18–3.20	13, 58
1.20	57
1.32	99
2.14-16	59
2.15	80, 108, 155
2.16	118
2.29	80
3.10-14, 18	57
3.15-17	57
3.21-25	59
3.22-23	58–9
3.24	59
4.6-8	57
4.11-12	13
5.2	57
5.3	60
5.14	57
6.1-14	17
6.3-11	2
6.4	39
6.17-22	3

6.19-22	101	12.18	60, 61, 63, 68, 103, 168
7.1	58		
7.5-6	3	12.19	57, 61, 63, 65, 66, 69, 152
8.1, 2	59		
8.4	39	12.19-20	36, 70
8.5-8	59	12.19-21	40
8.8	61, 114	12.20	60, 61, 63, 67, 69–72, 168
8.20	78		
8.26	141	12.21	79
8.29-30	58	13	12
8.31-39	60	13.1-2	14, 73, 75, 76
8.34	141	13.1-7	6, 57, 73–84, 151, 152, 172
9–11	57, 58		
9.1	81, 108	13.1-10	22
9.10	57	13.3	4, 40, 135, 168
9.21	74	13.3-4	60, 64, 82
9.30	34, 101	13.5	108
9.31	34	13.6	14
10.1	141	13.8-10	40, 73, 81–83, 105
10.3	78		
11.2-4	57	13.11-14	73
11.13	57, 58	13.12	59
11.25	62	13.13	39, 40, 59, 73
11.30	3	14–15	57
12–13	14, 84	14.1-6	58
12.1	61	14.10-12	57, 58
12.2	61	14.13	62, 113
12.3	62	14.15	39, 58, 114
12.3-8	61	14.16	79
12.5, 10, 16	82	14.19	34, 58, 62, 103
12.9	79	14.20-21	58, 113, 114
12.9-13	61	15.1-2	114
12.9-16	62	15.1-13	62
12.9-21	14, 34	15.2	58
12.10	62, 82	15.5	62
12.12	59, 141	15.7	58, 62, 111
12.13	34, 62	15.8	74
12.14	57, 59, 61, 62, 63–66, 67, 108, 154, 168	15.14	62
		15.15-19	57
		15.15-21	58
12.14-21	22, 60, 61, 70	15.16	74, 101
12.15	59, 61, 62	15.20	43
12.15-16	61, 62	15.22-29	58
12.16	62	15.25, 31	93
12.17	4, 36, 40, 59, 61, 65, 66–69, 79, 154, 168	15.30	141
		16.1	74
		16.3-16	58
12.17-21	61, 63, 65, 108	16.16	62

Index of Biblical References

16.17	58	7.5	62, 98, 141
16.17-20	57	7.8	100
		7.10	98, 99
1 Corinthians		7.12	98
1–4	15, 19–20	7.12-15	1, 4
1.2	1, 93, 101	7.12-16	22, 98–104, 108, 117, 123
1.4	93, 141		
1.4-9	132	7.15	126 n.20
1.5-7	93	7.17	39, 98
1.9	93	7.20, 24	98
1.10	1	7.26	98, 100
1.10-17	28, 93	7.32	114
1.23	103	7.32-35	98, 100
1.26	1, 93	7.40	98
2.1	1	8.1	105
2.6-8	76	8.4	11
3.1-23	93	8.4-6	106, 109
3.3-9	93–94	8.4-13	94
3.16	1, 94, 96	8.7	108
4.5	80, 118	8.9	112
4.6-7	93	8.9-13	93, 109
4.8	80	8.10	105
4.9-13	76	8.11-12	109, 113
4.12	63	8.13	113
4.14	93, 96	9.19-23	4, 12, 97, 101, 123
4.15	1, 93	10.1	107
4.21	96, 155	10.1-27	117
5–7	14, 15, 17	10.16-17	17
5.1	15, 25 n.31, 94, 96	10.23-33	4, 6, 22, 104
5.1-5, 7	96	10.23–11.1	104–115, 123
5.1-13	18, 94	10.24	82
5.9-10	15, 94	10.26	106
5.9-13	97	10.27	1, 104
5.10	98	10.27-33	117
5.12-13	1	10.32-33	12, 106
6.1	1, 76, 82, 94	10.32-11.1	98, 101, 123
6.1-8	93, 104	11.4-5, 13	115
6.4	94	11.17-34	17, 93, 94
6.6	1, 94	11.33	62
6.9-10	1	12.2	2, 96
6.9-11	2, 15, 96, 101	12.3	96
6.12-18	104	12.10	115
6.15-17	101	12.12-13	17
6.19	94, 96	12.25	17
6.20	111	12.26	62
7	16, 169	12.28	115
7.1, 2	98	13.1-3	115
7.1-11	117	14.1	34, 115

14.3	115	9.14	141
14.4	105, 115	10.1	155
14.5	94, 115	10.2	39
14.6-12	115	10.3	39
14.12	94, 115	11.16	117
14.13-25	22, 115–122, 123	11.23, 25	76
14.16	141	12.18	39
14.17	82	13.13	93
14.20-25	4, 6		
14.22-24	1	**Galatians**	
14.23	12, 104	1.1	12
14.23-25	41, 101	1.2	1
14.26	94	1.3	1
14.31	116, 119	1.4	147
14.32, 34	78	1.6	12
14.34-35	78	1.6-7	12
14.39	115	1.6-9	28
14.40	41	1.10	114
15.12	93, 94	1.11-12	12
15.24-25	76	2.15	1
15.27-28	78	3.2, 5	12
16.15	76	3.15	1
16.16	78	3.26-29	17
16.20	62	3.27	2
		3.28	3
2 Corinthians		3.28-29	16
1.1	1, 93	4.8	1, 5
1.8	1	4.19	1
1.8-10	76	5.2-6	13
1.11	141	5.15	62
1.12	81, 108	5.16	39
3.3	39	5.16-25	12
4.2	39, 80, 108, 118	5.23	155
4.4	1, 112	5.26	62
4.6	112	6.1	155
4.15	141	6.8	35
5.9	43	6.10	3, 35, 36, 131
5.10	1		
5.11	80, 108	**Ephesians**	
5.17	21	1.16	141
6.5	76	2.2	39
6.14-15	1	2.7	155
6.14-18	3, 23 n.12	2.10	39, 152
6.16	95	4.1	39
8.21	67, 68	4.2	155
8.24	155	4.17	39
9.5	65	4.28	45
9.11-12	141	5.2	39

Index of Biblical References

5.8	39	1.5	1, 27, 31, 32
5.15	39	1.6	28, 32, 48
5.21, 24	78	1.7	29, 48, 93
5.21–6.9	12	1.7-8	29
5.23	147	1.8	48, 93
		1.9	2, 27, 29, 48
Philippians		1.10	29
1.1	1, 93	2.1	1, 27
1.3-4	141	2.1-12	48
1.4	141	2.2	28, 76
1.6	152	2.4	114
1.10	112	2.5	30
1.11	111	2.7	1, 11, 27, 28, 93
1.12	1	2.8	31, 32
1.14	1	2.9	27
1.19	141	2.10	27
2.11	111, 112	2.11	1, 27, 28, 39, 93
2.15	1, 2	2.12	27, 28, 31, 39
3.1	1	2.13	27, 48, 141
3.17	39	2.13-14	48
3.18	39	2.14	27, 28, 32
3.20	1, 147	2.15	114
4.5	4, 36, 131	2.17	27
4.6	141	2.17-18	28, 31, 58
4.8	67, 80, 131, 145	2.18	76
4.22	93	2.19	27, 29, 52
		2.19-20	48
Colossians		3.1-3	31, 58
1.3	141	3.1-5	32
1.10	40	3.2	28
1.13	147	3.3	28
1.21-23	2	3.4	28
2.6	39, 40	3.5	28, 31
2.8-15	74	3.6	30, 31, 32, 48
3.7	39	3.6-9	48
3.12	155	3.7	27
3.18	78	3.9	141
3.18–4.1	12	3.10	28, 31, 48, 58
4.3	40	3.11	31
4.5	1, 40	3.12	22, 30, 31, 32, 34, 35, 36, 37, 39, 46, 51, 62, 82, 167
4.5-6	131		
4.6	40		
4.12	141	3.13	31, 32, 51, 53–54 n.11
1 Thessalonians		3.19	29
1.2	31, 141	4.1	27, 37, 38, 39, 40, 48, 49, 114
1.2-10	48, 132		
1.3	31, 32, 48	4.1-7	31, 101

Index of Biblical References

4.1-12	41	**2 Thessalonians**	
4.2	38, 49	1.3	141
4.2-8	37	2.13	141
4.2-12	37	3.6-12	42
4.4	38		
4.5	1, 3, 5, 28, 29, 38	**1 Timothy**	
		1.1	146
4.6	27, 30, 38, 48, 49	1.2	132
4.7	38, 41	1.3	132
4.9	31, 32, 37, 38	1.10-11	133
4.9-10	46	1.12-16	133
4.9-12	37	1.13	154
4.10	27, 30, 31, 32, 37, 48, 49	1.15	146
		1.16	147, 155
4.11	3, 37, 38, 42, 43, 44, 46, 47, 48, 49, 52, 68, 142	1.17	148
		1.20	154
		2.1-2	140–146, 172
4.11-12	6, 12, 22, 30, 45, 47, 48, 49, 50, 51, 167	2.1-3	5, 75
		2.1-7	22, 135, 140–149, 159, 170
4.12	1, 3, 28, 34, 38, 39, 40, 42, 44, 46, 47, 48, 50, 52, 62, 73, 81, 172	2.2	139
		2.3	134, 146
		2.3-4	146–148
		2.8	133
4.13	27, 28, 29	2.9-15	133, 137, 144, 153
4.13-18	29	2.10	138, 143, 144, 153, 154
4.18	28		
5.1	27	2.15	138
5.2-10	29	3.1-7	133, 135
5.4	27, 28	3.3, 7	155
5.5	2, 28	3.4	145
5.6	2, 28	3.7	5, 22, 135, 161 n.6
5.7	2, 28	3.8-10	133, 145
5.8	32	3.9	81, 108
5.9	2, 28	3.11	133, 145
5.11	3, 28, 105	3.12-13	133
5.12	22, 27	3.14-15	133
5.12-13	30, 48	3.16	147
5.12-14	33	4.3	144
5.13	30, 32	4.3-5	101, 106
5.14	27, 28, 30, 42, 45	4.4	149
5.15	28, 30, 31, 33, 34, 35, 36, 37, 39, 46, 48, 51, 61, 62, 67, 82, 108, 167	4.4-5	142, 144
		4.5	141
		4.6	132
		4.8	157
5.16-22	33	4.10	146, 147, 157
5.23	29, 31, 101	4.11, 12, 13	132
5.25-27	27	4.16	132, 146

5.1-2	133	1.3	146
5.3-8	45, 144	1.4	146
5.3-16	133, 139	1.4, 5	132
5.4	133, 134, 138, 143, 144, 160	1.5-6	133
		1.7-9	133
5.7	139	1.13	132
5.8	67, 133, 134, 139, 144, 160	1.16	153
		2.1	132
5.9-10	138, 139, 153	2.2	145
5.11	139	2.2, 6	133
5.13	139	2.3-5	133, 137
5.14	137, 138, 139	2.4-5	138
5.16	138	2.5	5, 22, 78, 137, 154
5.17-22	133	2.7-8	133, 145, 153, 154
5.23	132	2.8	132, 135, 145
5.24-25	153	2.9-10	78, 133, 136
6.1	5, 22, 136, 154	2.10	146, 155
6.1-2	133, 139	2.11	133, 146, 156
6.2	132	2.11-12	143
6.3	143	2.12-14	156
6.4	154, 155	2.13	146
6.15-16	148	2.14	152
6.17-19	133, 153	2.15	132
6.18	153	3.1	74, 75, 78, 172
		3.1-2	5, 133
2 Timothy		3.1-8	22, 135, 140, 149–158, 159, 170
1.2	132		
1.3	108		
1.5	147	3.3-5	133
1.10	146	3.4, 6	146
1.13	81	3.8	5, 75
2.1	132	3.9	153, 155
2.4	114	3.10	132
2.14	132	3.12-13	132
2.25	132, 155	3.13-14	153
2.21	152		
2.23-24	155	**Philemon**	
3.2-4	133, 154	1.4	141
3.5-9	133	4	141
3.16-17	157–158		
3.17	152	**Hebrews**	
4.2	132	1.14	74
4.5	132		
4.9-15, 21	132	**James**	
4.18	148	3.13	155
Titus		**1 Peter**	
1.1	143	2.12, 15	68

2.13-17	75, 151	4.12ff	68
2.14	80		
3.1-2	104	**Jude**	
3.9-12	54 n.16	25	147
3.13ff	68		
3.15-16	155	**Revelation**	
3.16	81, 108	7.11	119
4.4	28	11.16	119

www.ingramcontent.com/pod-product-compliance
Lightning Source LLC
Chambersburg PA
CBHW051524230426
43668CB00012B/1726